INTERNATIONAL RELATIONS
OF SOCIAL CHANGE

INTERNATIONAL RELATIONS
OF SOCIAL CHANGE

Jan Aart Scholte

Open University Press
Buckingham · Philadelphia

Open University Press
Celtic Court
22 Ballmoor
Buckingham
MK18 1XW

and

1900 Frost Road, Suite 101
Bristol, PA 19007, USA

First Published 1993

A catalogue record of this book is available from the British Library

ISBN 0 335 09329 9 (pb)   0 335 09330 2 (hb)

Library of Congress Cataloging Publication Data is available

Typeset by Type Study, Scarborough
Printed in Great Britain by Biddles Ltd, Guildford and Kings Lynn

In memory of
Hence van Praag-Brommer

CONTENTS

PREFACE

International Relations of Social Change is the sort of book that might be expected from a child of the 1960s who was twice an immigrant before turning twenty-five. My academic education further encouraged me in the direction of this subject. After following an alternative curriculum in a multicultural inner-city school, I completed interdisciplinary university programmes in International Relations in several countries. Now my own teaching at the University of Sussex is undertaken in a multidisciplinary 'school of studies' rather than a conventional subject-based 'department'. Hence my formal training has from early days encouraged scepticism, if not a subversive streak, in respect of academic orthodoxy. Over the years this critical disposition has been turned increasingly on the traditions that have tended, on the one hand, to keep issues of social change off the research agenda of International Relations and, on the other hand, to relegate questions of the international to the margins of other fields of enquiry.

An interest in social change was apparent in many of my undergraduate essays, but it became more focused during my doctoral research concerning the effects of international relations on the course of the Indonesian Revolution. The present book builds on the conceptual chapters of that dissertation (Scholte 1990), as well as a paper given to the British International History Group in 1991, and an article which has recently been published in the *Review of International Studies* (Scholte 1993).

This text therefore forms part of a long-running and quite unfinished project. In the present writing I map out some general starting points for a study of social change in world perspective. I have not as yet consolidated a more detailed theoretical position, although it will be apparent from the book that I am in one way or another dissatisfied with modernization theory, Marxism, world-system theory, postmodernism, and the international historical sociology of authors such as Skocpol and Mann. Clearly there is a need in my future work to extend and further to specify the argument developed in the current volume.

A host of academic colleagues, undergraduate and postgraduate students and friends have helped me to reach the present way-station. I hope that those whom I do not cite here by name will understand that I have chosen to devote more of the publisher's word limit to the text itself. However, I must acknowledge my foremost intellectual debt to the late Christopher Thorne, whose goading encouragement is a principal reason why this book is appearing at all. In addition, Tom Bottomore, Richard Little, John Maclean, William Outhwaite, Julia Stapleton and anonymous reviewers offered helpful comments on earlier drafts of material relating to the argument presented here. I am also particularly grateful to other former and present Sussex colleagues Rosemary Foot, Zdenek Kavan, Julian Saurin and Marc Williams for thoughtful criticisms of my work over the past decade. During my undergraduate studies I was fortunate to have, in David Elliott and Hans Palmer, dedicated teachers who nurtured my early interest in international and general social theory. Outside the university my special thanks go to my father, my mother and Julia Stapleton for showing, in personal relations during the period when this book was being written, that continuity and change can unfold in constructive combinations.

However, it is appropriate to dedicate this book to Hence van Praag-Brommer, who first inspired me to think about social change, and through her acts gave a child an example of how progressive transformations can be achieved with quiet determination. Years later, and in spite of debilitation at the hands of a terminal illness, she encouraged me in the early design of this book. I am glad now to keep my promise to her to finish it.

LIST OF ABBREVIATIONS

AIDS	acquired immunodeficiency syndrome
ANC	African National Congress
BBC	British Broadcasting Corporation
BIS	Bank for International Settlements
BISA	British International Studies Association
CERN	Centre Européen de Recherches Nucléaires
CIA	Central Intelligence Agency (of the United States Government)
EC	European Community
ESPRIT	European Programme for Research in Information Technology
FAO	Food and Agriculture Organization
FBI	Federal Bureau of Investigation (of the United States Government)
FDI	foreign direct investment
FLN	Front de la Libération Nationale (of Algeria)
Frelimo	Frente de Libertaçao de Mozambique
GATT	General Agreement on Tariffs and Trade
IGO	intergovernmental organization
IMF	International Monetary Fund
INGO	international non-governmental organization
Interpol	International Criminal Police Organization
IPCC	Intergovernmental Panel on Climate Change
IR	International Relations (the academic discipline)
ISA	(North American) International Studies Association
ISBN	International Standard Book Number
ITT	International Telephone and Telegraph Corporation
NICs	newly industrializing countries

OAU	Organization of African Unity
OECD	Organization for Economic Co-operation and Development
OEEC	Organization for European Economic Co-operation
OPEC	Organization of Petroleum Exporting Countries
SHAFR	Society for Historians of American Foreign Relations
TNC	transnational corporation
UNDP	United Nations Development Programme
UNEP	United Nations Environment Programme
UNESCO	United Nations Educational, Scientific and Cultural Organization
UPU	Universal Postal Union
WHO	World Health Organization
WIPO	World Intellectual Property Organization

INTRODUCTION

We are currently living through the dawn of a 'new world order', so runs the prevailing common wisdom. The Cold War, apartheid, the working class and authoritarian government are each allegedly in retreat, and the resulting fluid situation creates space, so commentators variously claim, for a 'post-secular' worldwide spiritual resurgence, the advent of a 'post-industrial society', the realization of women's emancipation and the 'new man', a shift from states to markets in the operation of the economy, moves towards demilitarization and new designs for security in international life, and other radical rearrangements of the way that society is ordered. The early 1990s are thus widely depicted as a time of social change on a global scale.

It is by no means the first time in history that fundamental reorganizations of social life have exhibited an obvious international quality. For example, the French Revolution, two hundred years ago, had immediate pan-European and eventual global repercussions. The American Revolution in the long run was, as Ralph Waldo Emerson lyrically put it, a 'shot heard round the world'. The Russian Revolution of 1917 became a beacon for socialist strivings on every inhabited continent; indeed, Trotsky declared that the Bolshevik programme could only be successful as a *world* revolution. A global movement of decolonization involved dozens of countries in a score of years in the middle of the twentieth century. In 1989, as 140 years before, steps towards social transformation unfolded largely simultaneously throughout Central Europe. Repeatedly over the past several centuries, and with increasing frequency and intensity in recent times, a wide spectrum of social movements, from fascists to lesbian and gay activists, have striven through international campaigns to create a new social order. In short, international relations of social change have been a recurrent if not constant feature of the present epoch.

One of the most striking transformations in contemporary social history has been the process of globalization itself. 'Society', the life of persons in a collectivity, has in many respects acquired planetary proportions. Interactions and interdependencies between people have obtained a deeply international character alongside the more commonly recognized national and local contexts of society. Moreover, a number of the key organizing principles of social relations today – for example, nationality, capitalism, industrialism, bureaucracy – have become entrenched in one form or another across the various continents. Pursuing this line of observation a step further, we may also ask whether the process of social transformation in fact involves international causes as well as international effects. In other words, can we explain the incidence, the direction, the speed and the degree of social change in terms of international relations?

This book explores possibilities of understanding social change in world perspective. As such, it advances an alternative research agenda for the field of International Relations (IR), where the issue of social transformation has to date been largely ignored. At the same time the text seeks to stimulate those academics who have traditionally made it their business to study social change – in particular historical sociologists and social historians – to give greater attention to the international quality of social relations than they have so far tended to do in their work. Indeed, these three normally separated groups of researchers could perhaps best abandon their disciplinary boundaries and engage in a common endeavour of what might be dubbed 'world-historical-sociological' studies of social change.

Like all academic enquiry, such a project involves basic ontological, epistemological and methodological issues. What are the characteristics and consequences of social life, and its international aspect in particular? How is social action constituted? What does it mean to 'understand' (international) social relations, and how do we go about acquiring that knowledge? These in many respects overlapping and interrelated metatheoretical issues confront all students, whether their more specific theoretical inclination is towards liberalism, Marxism, postmodernism, or whatever. Hence this (as far as I am aware first-ever) general textbook on international relations of social change concentrates on establishing some 'pre-theoretical' ground rules for research on this subject. The chapters review contrasting positions on some of the core problems of the enquiry, while at the same time advancing what I at this point in my thinking regard as the most satisfactory conceptualization of the given issue.

The opening chapter begins by considering more precisely what is meant by 'social change' and then elaborates on the assertion made above that processes of transformation can have a significant international character. Thereafter a compact intellectual history of the social sciences, and the field of International Relations in particular, reviews the ways in which researchers have in the past generally neglected to examine the international aspects of social development. Chapter 1 then closes with a survey of existing studies that do address this issue, for these writings provide us with a cross-disciplinary starting bibliography for world-historical-sociological investigations.

Chapter 2 assesses the relationship between international relations and the domestic (i.e., internal) circumstances of countries in triggering and moulding social change. The central question here is the respective causal significance of local, national and international spheres of social life in the process of change. Do transformations originate in the domestic arena, as 'internalist' arguments would have it, and then perhaps reverberate outwards to affect international relations? Or, following the converse 'externalist' premise, do international relations instigate and shape rearrangements of the social order? My own position, detailed in the second half of Chapter 2, is to reject both endogenism and exogenism in favour of a particular 'world-systemic' conception of causation.

Chapters 3 to 5 examine more closely what is meant by the words 'international relations' in the phrase 'international relations of social change'. To begin with, I argue that we should reject the view that limits international affairs to interstate and political matters: the concept should be extended to cover cross-border relations of all kinds. Adopting this perspective, these chapters discuss in turn three interconnected ways that international relations can figure in the process of social change: (i) cross-border exchanges may convey transformations that have occurred in one country to other lands; (ii) international transactions may help to stimulate and determine the shape of transformations in the first place; and (iii) pillars of international order may contribute to provoking and moulding changes in social relations.

Chapter 6 considers the issue of what, borrowing a Marxian term, might be called the 'base' of world-systemic dynamics of social change. In other words, what is the relationship between politics, economics, culture, psychology and ecology in effecting social transformations in a world context? This chapter reviews materialist arguments that explain social change in terms of political, economic and/or ecological forces, as well as idealist positions that reduce the process of transformation to cultural and/or psychological engines. Both of these conceptions are rejected, however, and indeed the very idea of a causal 'base' is repudiated. Instead, I suggest, the study of social change in world perspective is best served by a postulate of interpenetration and concurrent mutual determination of politics, economics, culture, psychology and ecology within social relations.

Chapter 7 discusses the relationship between agency and order in the process of social change: in a sense the connections between (ii) and (iii) above. An evaluation is made of both the individualist position and the structuralist position. The former holds that social transformation can be explained in terms of the initiatives, conscious choices and deliberate plans of decision-making units, while the latter maintains that reconstructions of social life result from structures and historical trends over which persons and groups have no effective control. My own stance in this debate is to take distance from both voluntarism and determinism and instead to conceive of social transformation in what Anthony Giddens has dubbed 'structurationist' terms, where units and social patterns are simultaneously cause and effect of each other.

Chapter 8 addresses the matter of connections between theory and practice in international relations of social change. The discussion here begins with a critique of the positivist notion that knowledge can be precise, definitive and value-free, so that the academic can aspire to be a detached final authority on the problem of social transformation. However, the abandonment of positivism does not imply that a theory of social history is invariably so incomplete, relative, changeable and subjective that it can offer no secure basis whatsoever for knowledge and political action. The basic problem with both the objectivist and the subjectivist positions, I go on to suggest, is that each in its own way separates consciousness and reality. In contrast, if we hold that theory and practice are essentially intertwined, then our conceptualization of social relations – whatever form it takes – will contribute in some way to a reproduction and/or transformation of the prevailing social order. Thus students of social change in world perspective unavoidably face problematic value judgements and the need to assess the political implications of their work.

In sum, then, this text draws together work from various fields of social inquiry for readers who, like myself, find that prevailing academic conventions are not equal to the challenge of understanding social change, and who are therefore searching for an alternative knowledge and politics that can better equip us to participate with awareness and vision in a volatile world situation. As I said at the outset, this book is very much an exploratory text. I do not claim to offer a final resolution of core issues such as the relationship between the international and the domestic, between the ideal and the material, between structure and agent, and between practice and theory. Nor do I formulate a fully-fledged theory of social change in world perspective. However, the following chapters do discuss in a systematic and detailed manner some of the starting postulates around which such a theory could be constructed, and I hope in this modest way to advance our still inchoate understanding of social change in an era of globalization.

≡1≡

INTERNATIONAL RELATIONS
AND THE STUDY
OF SOCIAL CHANGE

Compactly stated, this book is concerned with *the study of world-systemic dynamics of change over time in social relations*. Before proceeding any further we need to consider the very notion of social change itself and to elaborate a case for fundamentally reconceptualizing the process of transformation so that theory will adequately incorporate the international dimension of social history.

SOCIAL CHANGE

We can start with the most obvious of truisms: people are social beings; human life is social life. There is no such thing as the individual, in the sense of an isolated, wholly self-determining person. Human experience is an experience of constant and intense interaction and mutual dependence between persons within groups and larger collectivities; relations with the other are constitutive of the self. Even behaviour in moments of solitude is socially constructed.

Social interchanges and interdependencies tend to fall into patterns. That is, social activity transpires in accordance with both explicitly proclaimed rules (e.g., immigration laws) and tacitly reproduced customs (e.g., the norm of woman-the-homemaker in much of contemporary society). Specific guidelines of this kind in turn often correspond to more general organizing principles of social life, such as race, gender, class, nationality, citizenship, bureaucracy, secularism, individualism, capitalism, militarism and the like. Social order therefore constitutes an integral part of social behaviour.

Although social life may be ordered, its frameworks are not fixed. For one thing, the organization of social relations may show variation across space and between specific contexts. The patterns often differ from one country to the next, with, for example, single-party government defining one land's politics and multiparty competition prevailing across the border. Contrasts may also exist within a single country (e.g., the predominance of manufacturing in one area and the prevalence of subsistence agriculture in another), or at a more micro-level between individual households (e.g., the nuclear family in one residence versus communal living in another). In short, then, to say that social relations are organized is not to say that they are everywhere the same.

Nor – and this point is of more particular concern to us here – is the organization of social life fixed over time. However deeply entrenched and immutable a given ordering principle of social activity may seem at one juncture, it normally gives way to a different pattern at some later moment. Social life thus has an inherent historical quality: it undergoes change over time. In certain cases these shifts take the form of radical and perhaps also unanticipated discontinuities. For example, who in tenth-century Europe would have predicted that the Universal Church would subsequently yield to the primacy of the national state? Who in fifteenth-century Africa would have foretold a world steeped in racial discrimination several hundred years later? Who in eighteenth-century matrilineal Minangkabau villages on Sumatra would have envisioned the future move to a male-dominated society? Who amongst the peaceful Eskimos in an earlier epoch would have imagined the present century of total war? Who in an isolated locality anywhere in the world five hundred years ago could have imagined the process of globalization that now, to one degree or another, links together settlements across the planet in a world society? By the same token, who today expects that future social relations could well lack the currently prevalent features of the national state, racialism, patriarchy, militarism and globality?

Whether it is anticipated and intended or not, change appears to be integral to social life. It will be clear from the preceding paragraph that we are not particularly concerned here with superficial shifts, or what one text calls 'ubiquitous' changes in social relations (Buzan and Jones 1981: Ch 1). Day-to-day alterations of prices, of legislation, of news stories, of weather conditions and so on do not in themselves entail a profound reorganization of social activity. Nor do elections, recessions, fads, the succession of seasons and other such recurring cycles constitute actual transformations of social life. Even seeming major upheavals may disguise more basic continuities, as Kenneth Boulding suggests when he describes many so-called 'revolutions' as:

> storms on the surface of history . . . which raise a great deal of dust and cause a lot of trouble, but which generally end up with the same old things called by a new set of names.
>
> (1968: xxvii)

Short-term adjustments and medium-term movements like those just mentioned generally take place in the context of more fundamental constancy.

They entail what could be called 'continuous changes' or 'persistence through change', where the underlying continuity is more significant than the surface shift. In this light Fernand Braudel makes a helpful distinction between *l'histoire événementielle* (changes at the level of events), *conjonctures* (historical movements in accordance with medium-term regular trends), and the *longue durée* (long-term structural properties) (Braudel 1958; Hexter 1972).

Our prime concern here is to study change in basic and deeply rooted social facts, to trace and explain transformations in the character of the *longue durée*. We are seeking to understand major ruptures in the course of social history: changes *of* the social framework rather than changes *within* an existing framework. In instances of fundamental change one social order is undone and, through the recombination of persons in new forms of interaction and interdependence, an alternative organization of collective human life emerges. Social change in this sense entails 'significant rearrangements and modifications' of social relations (Smith 1976: 6). These profound discontinuities may occur suddenly, quickly and obviously, in the form of a social revolution. Or they may unfold gradually and subtly, as Raymond Williams suggested with his concept of 'long revolution' (1961: x).

This is not to say that social transformations mark complete historical breaks. Only in the original change which produced the fact of time itself has change been absolute. In every social development the past, the present and the future are linked together by continuity as well as distinguished by change. For instance, the shift from the absolutist to the constitutional state at the same time entailed a continuity of the more general fact of government. The close of the Second World War simultaneously involved lasting militarization. In the end continuity and change are only separable analytically; in concrete social history persistence and transformation are interwoven and mutually defining. Nevertheless, there are developments in regard to which, in making this analytical distinction, change is the more striking and significant characteristic, and continuity by comparison seems negligible and superficial. On these occasions we affirm that a major reconstruction of social life has transpired.

The general definition of social change just outlined presents us with a problem for extensive research and discussion. The debates begin around the issue of identifying the key transformations that have occurred in social history. Commentators often cannot agree that a major reorganization of social relations has actually taken place. For example, while some observers today proclaim that the demise of communist regimes has brought the dawn of a new world order, sceptics are more struck by the persistence of structures such as nationality and militarism across this purported historical watershed. In this and countless other cases, one observer's change is another's continuity. When is a shift significant; which rearrangements of social life are fundamental?

Even when analysts concur that a major discontinuity has transpired in the organization of a human collectivity, they as often as not characterize it differently. For instance, liberal evolutionists highlight a change from 'traditional' to 'modern' society, whereas Marxists describe, in relation to roughly the same historical contexts, a transition from 'feudalism' to 'capitalism'. Meanwhile some authors hold that transformations unfold in a progressive sequence, whereas others see a regressive or a cyclical pattern, and still others discount the notion of such historical laws altogether. However, arguments of this kind need not distract us at this stage: our main concern for the moment is to establish the basic point that social change involves a fundamental reconstruction of the way that transactions and interdependencies between people are ordered.

THE INTERNATIONAL QUALITY OF SOCIAL CHANGE

In pursuing explanations of social transformation, the present volume concentrates in particular on the role of international relations in the dynamics of change. The next four chapters will assess more specifically the ways that international forces might be significant. At this stage we consider the basic proposition that international relations can play an important part in the process of social change and note that this insight has generally been overlooked in conventional studies of the subject. Numerous textbooks on theories of social change are available, but none focus on, and many do not even mention, international relations (see, for example, Eisenstadt 1970; Nisbet 1972; Strasser and Rundall 1981; Boudon 1984). Instead, transformations have traditionally been defined and explained in relation to national or other more localized collectivities.

In currently prevailing usage, most people treat the word 'society' as being roughly synonymous with the terms 'country' and 'nation': that is, society is conceptualized as a discrete territorially bounded administrative and cultural unit which is clearly separated from other similarly unitary societies in its 'environment'. Thus we speak of 'Brazilian society', 'Thai society', 'Italian society' and the like. Moreover, we generally describe social change in relation to such national units. Hence we say that 'Korea industrialized', that 'South Africa imposed apartheid', that 'Czechoslovakia abandoned communism', and so on. As a matter of habit we characterize moments of major disruption and fluidity in social history as the English, American, French, Russian, Chinese, Algerian, Vietnamese, Angolan and Nicaraguan Revolutions. In all of these cases, social change is viewed in the context of a national entity.

Conventional investigations of social transformations treat this nation-bound notion of society as a key explanatory concept, too. In such so-called 'endogenous' explanations of change, individual countries constitute the focal unit of analysis, and geographical boundaries are reified as borderlines of social forces. As a consequence, the causes of a reorganization of society are presumed to reside within the country-unit in question. For example, an endogenous argument might explain the course of the Iranian Revolution in terms of the strains of the country's modernization process and internal competition between secularists and Islamic fundamentalists. Decolonization would be understood as a result of clashes inside the territory concerned between an imperial administration and the local population. Adopting the premise of endogenism, most social historians and historical sociologists have in the past conducted their investigations with only passing, if any, reference to international circumstances. On the same grounds, academics in the field of International Relations have generally assumed that social change is a process internal to individual countries, and therefore not a direct concern for their research.

Here we challenge this ruling supposition about social change, as well as the academic division of labour that both reflects and sustains it. For one thing, it seems plain that society does not fall into neatly distinguishable self-contained national compartments, into 'simple totalities' that are clearly marked off from an external environment (Mann 1986: 13–17; Wallerstein 1986a). Indeed, the habit of associating the term 'society' with territorial frontiers and the nation-state arose only some two hundred years ago (Luhmann 1982: 131). It was at this time, too, that J.G. von Herder (1784–91) introduced the notion of 'cultures' in the plural and that Jeremy Bentham coined a new word 'international' to denote relations between separate national entities (1789: 296).[1] Thus forerunners of modern social scientists did not presume that lines of social interaction and interdependence have a one-to-one correspondence with boundaries of state jurisdictions. In practice, social activities have throughout recorded history very often crossed borders in long-distance relations of trade, migration, warfare, communications and so on. At the same time, many other social conditions have been restricted to a limited part rather than the whole of a country, e.g., a strike in a particular town or the folklore of a particular region. Indeed, with respect to some transnational and local circumstances the national context has only minor relevance. For example, national boundaries may have little causal significance in relation to certain by-election results or cross-border ecological problems such as acid rain. Anthony Smith is therefore quite right to criticize what he terms a ruling 'methodological nationalism' in the various fields of social enquiry (1979: 191). John Hall concludes in a similar vein that 'the sense of "society" that we received from classical sociological theory is of no use to us when we seek to understand our own social condition' (1986a: 151).

In regard to the present discussion, the most significant objection to the conventional notion of society is that it fails to take account of world contexts: that is, the fact that social life extends beyond local and national confines. Social relations have for centuries, if not millennia, transcended narrow territoriality (cf. Braudel 1967: 30–1). Contemporary history has moreover witnessed 'globalization', a process of increasing and deepening social interrelatedness on a planetary scale. Some authors date this trend from the sixteenth century, with the early interlinkage of the eastern and western hemispheres (Thompson 1983). For his part, William McNeill asserts that what he calls a 'global ecumene' had consolidated by the end of the eighteenth century (1985: 42). Other researchers focus their attention on the past 150 years, agreeing with Roland Robertson that the latter part of the nineteenth century constituted 'the crucial take-off period of globalization' (1990: 19; also Robertson 1992). Meanwhile writers such as Silviu Brucan (1978b) and Anthony Giddens (1985: 5, 33) see the onset of genuinely global social life as a development of the twentieth century. Yet wherever in time they begin their analysis, social theorists have come increasingly to agree that contemporary society in many respects has global proportions.

In this age of planetary social relations, a number of social transformations, too, have spread across various countries and several continents to acquire a global character. Indeed, the world religions reshaped social life over far-flung spaces long before the modern era (Hall 1985; Mann 1986). The cross-border repercussions of certain social revolutions between the eighteenth and twentieth centuries were mentioned in the introduction to the present book. More recently the Iranian Revolution has inspired Islamic revivalism from Trinidad in the west to Indonesia in the east (Esposito 1990; Ehteshami and Varasteh 1991). In addition, anarchists, feminists, black-consciousness campaigners, communists, pacifists, environmentalists and others have over the years conducted transnational campaigns for a reorganization of society (e.g., respectively, Woodcock 1963; Bulbeck 1988; Esedebe 1982; Deakin et al. 1975; Day 1986; McCormick 1989). Surveying contemporary history, we can concur with Daniel Chirot's conclusion that 'no major social change occurs outside of the world context' (1986: 6).

Can we also take the further step and establish that the *causes* of social change lie, at least in part, in international relations? In the light of globalization and the transnational spread of many social transformations, a number of researchers across the spectrum of academic disciplines have in recent decades rejected endogenous models of history and have sought instead to explain social change in world perspective. For example, Michael Mann has stressed that 'the sources of change are geographically and socially "promiscuous" – they do not all emanate from within the social and territorial space of the given "society"' (1986: 503). A number of other historical sociologists have likewise endorsed the call, here articulated by Theda Skocpol, for a study of 'the interrelations of societies within world-historically developing international structures' (1979: 18). Extending this proposition further, Immanuel Wallerstein has challenged his colleagues to reconstruct the analysis of social change in the modern era around the premise that world-scale processes *predated* and *created* the various national 'societies'. In his eyes the world system has produced the nations rather than vice versa (1986a: 11–12). Meanwhile, in a cognate discipline, various anthropologists have taken the line, with Eric Wolf, that 'the inhabitants of the world are increasingly caught up in continent-wide and global change' (1982: 18; Ekholm and Friedman 1980; Appadurai 1990). In Psychology, Edward Sampson has argued that currently unfolding social change requires 'a dramatic transformation' of his discipline, with the development of 'theories and methods oriented toward a more global type of entity' (1989: 914, 916). Geographers such as Peter Taylor (1989) and Richard Peet (1991) have also turned the focus of their research to theories of global history, while others in their field have of late directed attention to the global context of urban and regional development (King 1990a,b) and to the currently much-publicized issue of global environmental change (Kemp 1990). Meanwhile a number of political scientists have assailed the internalist premise that has traditionally guided the study of political development (Almond 1989). Amongst social historians, Braudel (1979b) has taken a lead in promoting 'world time' rather than national or local contexts as the primary framework of explanation. In the field of International History, too, Thomas McCormick and others have been 'asking diplomatic historians to be also social historians' (1970: 139; Lilley and Hunt 1987; Thorne 1987). Finally, on the fringes of IR, Robert Cox has maintained that social transformations must be understood with reference to world-order structures (1987: 105–9), and Fred Halliday has posited that revolutions are 'international events in their causes and effects' (1990: 213). Silviu Brucan for his part has affirmed that 'the international dimension of change has become decisive' (1978a: xi).

Yet, in spite of these conversions to world-systemic approaches in many academic quarters, research on social change that incorporates international relations into the analysis has for the most part remained on the periphery of the various disciplines. The rest of this chapter will examine some of the reasons for this marginalization. At the same time, though, existing literature – particularly from the fields of IR, History and Sociology – will be surveyed to show that considerable material is available around which to construct a more fully developed study of social change in a world context.

THE UNDERDEVELOPMENT OF INTERNATIONAL
STUDIES OF SOCIAL CHANGE

Change has long ranked as one of the focal concerns of social enquiry. Nineteenth-century pioneers of social science were largely spurred by a desire to make sense of transformations unfolding in their midst such as industrialization, democratization, secularization and so on. Auguste Comte, originator of the term 'sociology', propounded a concept of three stages of human progress, and his Religion of Humanity was intended to be a movement to transform society to its third and highest level (Comte 1830–42). Several decades later Karl Marx explored the origins, maturation and future fate of capitalism as part of a project to advance emancipatory social change. Herbert Spencer (1862: Ch 15) and Emile Durkheim (1893) in their respective ways studied social reorganization in regard to a process of differentiation. For their part, Edward Tylor (1871) and Lewis Morgan (1877) traced social evolution through successive phases of what they characterized as 'savagery', 'barbarism' and 'civilization'.

Several nineteenth-century theorists included some reference to international circumstances in their explanations of social change. For example, Claude Henri de Saint-Simon argued that 'the full establishment of the industrial order would be impossible to achieve in each nation in isolation' (1821: 23n). Marx spoke in *Das Kapital* of 'the international character of the capitalist regime' of his day and highlighted the creation of the world market as one of 'three cardinal facts of capitalist production' (1867: 763; 1894: 266). At Cambridge, meanwhile, John Seeley was castigating his peers for 'assuming that whatever has happened in England can be explained by English causes' (1885: 133). However, in these early days of globalization no theorist fully consolidated a concept of the international as a distinct realm of social life, and the likes of Marx and Weber mainly conceived of 'society' as a national entity (Turner 1981: Ch 8). From the dawn of modern social science, then, endogenism prevailed in the study of social change (Smith 1973).

The nineteenth century also witnessed an increasing compartmentalization of social enquiry along the lines of separately institutionalized academic disciplines. The field of History was the first to undergo a process of professionalization in universities; yet it was pursued there mainly as a study of political and diplomatic history, not social history in a wider sense that would explore issues of change in the social order as a whole (Marwick 1989: Ch 2). By the turn of the century, new specialisms called 'Economics', 'Political Science' (with a much narrower scope than had traditionally been covered by the study of Politics), 'Psychology' and 'Social Geography' were also consolidating, but few practitioners in these fields focused on questions of social transformation (cf. Collini *et al.* 1983). This concern was allocated in the deepening academic division of labour mainly to the newly emerging disciplines of Social Anthropology and Sociology (Abrams 1968; Eggan 1968; Besnard 1983; Bulmer 1984).

These two fields proceeded to perpetuate the tradition of endogenous explanations of social transformation that had been established in the nineteenth century. Anthropologists for their part normally took the local community as the unit of analysis, with a methodology that prescribed 'living amongst the natives' in their immediate environment as the chief means to gain knowledge of social structure and social change. The nearest approximation to an international perspective to emerge at this time was perhaps the theory of dualism, which characterized certain 'backward' countries as being divided into a 'Western', 'modern' capitalist sector that operated next to, but separately from, an 'Eastern', 'traditional' subsistence sphere (Sadli 1971). Endogenism also reigned in sociological 'modernization theory', which saw its heyday during the 1950s and 1960s. Principally formulated by Talcott Parsons and his students, variants of modernization theory subsequently also inspired a number of political scientists and economic historians (Bernstein 1971; O'Brien 1979; Harrison 1988). These writers did describe moderniz-ation as a 'worldwide revolution', insofar as this social change was said to be occurring sooner or later all over the planet; however, they explained the process in terms of the domestic circumstances of each individual country (Halpern 1966: 194, 210; Parsons 1971: 137). As Aidan Foster-Carter notes in relation to one of the best-known works of modernization theory, *The Stages of Economic Growth* by W.W. Rostow (1960), the author:

> firmly takes the given society as his unit of analysis and assumes that all the crucial dimensions of change are internally generated within each society.
>
> (1985: 105)

Much Marxist writing of the decades prior to 1970 also relied on an endogenous conception of society and social change. Although Marxists opposed modernization theory in many other respects, they generally shared with liberals a blind spot when it came to international relations (cf. Dobb 1963; Althusser and Balibar 1968; Rey 1973).

For many decades, then, disciplinary specialization, coupled with the tradition of endogenism, greatly restricted the development of international studies of social change. When a distinct subject of International Relations began to take shape from around 1910 onwards, it drew its initial concepts, literature and researchers principally from the existing fields of Politics, International Law and Diplomatic History (Mathisen 1959; Krippendorff 1975a: Ch 2). Only an occasional economist such as Arthur Greenwood and an incidental social philosopher like C.D. Burns joined the fledgling departments of international studies, while professional sociologists and anthropologists were completely absent. The first professorship in IR, the Wilson Chair in International Politics at the University College of Wales, Aberystwyth, was endowed in 1919 specifically for the study of 'Political Science in its application to International Relations' (Webster 1923: 5). True, a few prominent pioneers of IR did describe the new discipline as 'the study of Sociology in its widest extent' (Zimmern 1935: 7) and as 'a special type of sociology' (Bailey 1938: 266–7). However, this insight generally remained no more than a vague slogan, as international relationists of the day in practice engaged in little cross-disciplinary dialogue with sociologists. Not surprisingly, then, the question of social change did not figure significantly on the new field's research agenda. Instead, early students of International Relations concentrated on the issues of war and peace, international law and institutions, and – albeit to a much lesser extent – cross-border trade and communications (cf. Moon 1925; Russell 1936).

In investigating these prime concerns, IR researchers relied for the most part on a framework of analysis that had by the 1940s consolidated under the label of 'realism', or 'power politics' (Carr 1939; Schwarzenberger 1941; Wight 1946; Morgenthau 1948). (NB: 'political realism' in international theory should not be confused with the similarly named 'realist' theory of social science (Bhaskar 1975). The same label designates two very different outlooks on social life.) Realist notions were prominent in the new field from its beginnings and then held a near monopoly over international studies from the 1940s through the 1960s.[2] Realist international theory has remained quite resilient over the past twenty years, too, as challenges to this orthodoxy from liberalism, Marxism, feminism and other alternative perspectives have been countered with so-called 'neo-realist' renovations of the dominant approach (Vasquez 1983; Keohane 1986; Dougherty and Pfaltzgraff 1990: Ch 3). Thus, although IR has recently enjoyed greater theoretical pluralism, on the whole realism has remained a clear first among equals. Proponents of the power politics conception can still claim to expound the 'commonsense' view of international relations (Morgenthau 1967; Garnett 1984).

Like many designations of academic traditions, the term 'realism' is used in a variety of ways and often quite loosely in discussions of IR theory. However, as it is understood here the realist conceptualization of international affairs is marked by statism; by politicism; by a separation of the domestic and the international; frequently, though not always, by reductionism; and by the assumption that there is an underlying continuity in international history (cf. Taylor 1978; Vasquez 1983). As the following paragraphs indicate, each of these five basic premises has in some way severely discouraged the development of international studies of social transformation. The mainstream of International Relations research has therefore consistently overlooked the question of social change during the three-quarters of a century that IR has existed as a distinct academic discipline.

In regard to the first of these postulates, realism has inhibited the analysis of social change in world perspective by defining international relations essentially as interstate relations.[3] Since IR's beginnings, by far the greater bulk of investigations in the field have sought to explain state behaviour, rather than the international activities of the full range of social entities. The state is usually considered to be the main if not sole international actor (James 1989); and international society (when such a thing is acknowledged to exist at all) is generally conceived of as a society of states (Manning 1962; Bull 1977). Proponents of what is often called a 'transnationalist' approach in IR have, especially since the 1970s, attempted to replace the statist premise with a multiactor conception of international relations (Keohane and Nye 1971; Mansbach et al. 1976). These authors have maintained that not only national states, but in addition companies, religious bodies, ethnic associations, political parties, social movements, entertainment groups, academic institutions and intergovernmental organizations are potential agents in international affairs. In this view informal groups and individuals in their personal capacity can also be important in shaping international life: for example, as refugees, mercenaries, authors and so on. Yet the transnationalist critique has met with strong resistance from realists (Northedge 1976b; Miller 1981), and it has on the whole only tempered rather than dislodged state-centrism in IR. Studies of the past twenty years have generally given increased attention to non-governmental units, but non-official bodies are still usually placed in a secondary position. In other words, the involvement of non-state actors in international affairs is held to be essentially governed by official decisions and/or the dynamics of the states-system, and thus not to have a significant autonomous influence on the course of international events.

This is not to deny the potential significance of the state in international relations of social change. Indeed, historical sociologists have undertaken a number of important investigations into the impact of the states-system on social transformations (e.g., Shaw 1984; Evans *et al.* 1985; Hall 1986b; Tilly 1990). However, social life is not a question of the state alone. To borrow a line from Michel Foucault, 'the State, for all the omnipotence of its apparatuses, is far from being able to occupy the whole field of power relations' (1977a: 122). Hence a conception that restricts international relations to interstate relations ignores the (possibly crucial) role of non-governmental activities in the process of social change.

A second major shortcoming of realism in respect of the study of social change is this theory's concentration on international *politics* rather than international *social* life in a broader sense. IR's focus has traditionally been in the first place on the acquisition, maintenance and exercise of power (in particular state power) on the world stage. The prevailing view has thus held that, in the classic formulation of Morgenthau and Thompson:

> the core of international relations is international politics, and . . . the subject matter of international politics is the struggle for power among sovereign nations [*sic*].
>
> (1950: Preface)

With a politics-centric orientation of this kind, students of IR have tended to neglect economic, ecological, psychological and cultural dimensions of social relations, except insofar as they might affect interstate conflict and cooperation (cf. Knorr 1973; Connelly and Perlman 1975; Hermann 1980; Sampson 1987). From a realist perspective, these other facets of social life are not principal objects of IR inquiry in themselves. On the same premise, realists examine social revolutions only in terms of their implications for the states-system (cf. Kim 1970), and not as products of and forces shaping world social relations.

For most students of International Relations, then, 'change', if it is addressed at all, has meant *international political change* rather than *social change in a global context* (Holsti *et al.* 1980; Buzan and Jones 1981; Hughes 1991). Some research in IR has examined subjects such as shifting foreign policy orientations, the impact of new technology on interstate relations, movements within the balance of power, and so on. But few IR investigations have focused on transformations of the overall organization of social life and the role not only of politics, but also of culture, psychology, ecology and economics in effecting those changes.

In combination with statism and politicism, a third feature of realism that hampers studies of social change in world perspective is the separation between domestic affairs and international affairs which this theory postulates. In conventional usage, the term 'international' is taken to refer to 'external' relations and 'foreign' policies of states. Meanwhile, what are variously called 'internal', 'domestic' and 'national' conditions are held to belong to a different sphere of social life which is of only secondary, if any, interest to students of IR. According to the tenets of classical realism, the *inter*-national and *intra*-national realms are kept separate from one another by the state, which by virtue of its sovereignty mediates and controls any flows between the 'inside' and the 'outside' of a country (James 1986).

In recent decades many in IR have questioned the notion of a complete division between national and international life. A number of studies have explored matters such as 'domestic sources of foreign policy' (Rosenau 1967) and 'external influences on the internal behaviour of states' (Deutsch 1966; Gourevitch 1978). However, even when IR researchers have recognized the effects that 'internal' and 'external' affairs can have on each other, the writers in question have continued to maintain a dichotomy between the domestic and the international, and to treat countries as units of analysis which are somehow separate from the international. Thus, for example, Brucan in spite of his many criticisms of orthodox approaches still operates 'at two levels of analysis – the national and the world level' (1980: 756).

Since the prevailing assumption in the human sciences has maintained that social change is something which transpires inside a country, realism by removing the domestic from the international has effectively excluded the issue of social transformation from IR's range of concerns. If reorganizations of society are held to occur only at the 'national level', and if, as realism postulates, state sovereignty insulates internal conditions from international circumstances, then international relations will have no significant involvement in the dynamics of social change. Even today, when many in IR acknowledge that there is considerable interplay between internal and international affairs, international relations are rarely considered to be more than a background context for what are posited to be essentially endogenous causes of social change. Yet, as will be argued at length in Chapter 2, the legalistic distinction between domestic jurisdictions and international relations does not correspond to an actual separation of internal and external affairs in social reality; and this interlinkage of the 'outside' and the 'inside' has become all the more apparent in the current era of globalization.

As an extension of this point, reductionism is a fourth characteristic of conventional approaches to IR which has limited work on international studies of social change. In other words, most researchers in the discipline have taken the concept 'international relations' to refer to interactions between units, rather than to designate as well certain irreducible conditions of the international sphere itself (Waltz 1979). Thus on the question of the relationship between units and the international order (discussed more fully in Chapters 5 and 7), attention within IR has traditionally been directed at the former. Realists and others in the field have usually conceived of causation in terms of state-actors or country units; they have not regarded the international arena as a distinct and to some extent autonomous sphere of social life with features and forces of its own. As a result, research on orthodox lines has neglected the particular insight that IR could bring to the study of social change: namely, the involvement in the transformation process of international structures and international trends.

That said, reductionism is not inherent in the realist conception of international relations. For example, theorists in the so-called 'English School' of IR have for some forty years highlighted the impact that the norms of 'international society' can have on state behaviour (Jones 1981; Wilson 1989). In addition, systemic approaches, regime theory and structuralist neo-realism have over the past three decades weakened the hold of reductionism on international studies (Knorr and Verba 1961; Krasner 1983; Little 1985). However, these holistic perspectives have usually limited their notions of the international 'whole' to configurations and rules of interstate relations, i.e., excluding cross-border transactions between other kinds of actors. The studies in question have therefore not looked beyond purported structures of polarity and hegemony to develop broader notions of an international social order which might include organizing principles of, say, nation, race, gender and class. Moreover, holistic variants of realism suffer from the same politicism that afflicts reductionist versions of the theory. For example, structuralist realism highlights the effects that, say, balance-of-power mechanisms, procedures in intergovernmental organizations and so on can have on conflict and cooperation between states. However, such an analysis does not consider the repercussions that structures and trends in the states-system can have on social change.

Finally, realism in its various forms has inhibited the development of studies of social change in world perspective because it underplays or even denies the notion that basic discontinuities can and do occur in international life (Vincent 1983; Katzenstein 1989). Instead, the state and interstate competition for power are generally treated as essentially immutable facts of international relations (cf. Morgenthau 1948: Ch 1; Frankel 1988: 12–19). In this vein Robert Gilpin's *War and Change in World Politics* rests, in seeming contradiction to its title, on the premise that:

> the fundamental nature of international relations has not changed over the millennia. International relations continue to be a recurring struggle for wealth and power among independent actors in a state of anarchy.
>
> (1981: 7, also 230)

Some realists have even ascribed the struggle for power among states to unchangeable 'human nature', which is supposedly aggressive, self-aggrandizing and sinful (Niebuhr 1940). Harry Hinsley in like fashion has described the balance of power amongst states as 'an idea which has probably been pursued instinctively throughout history' (1986: 199). Writers in the English School have postulated that the history of international society involves evolution within an essentially transhistorical framework of the states-system (Purnell 1973: 23–32). Similarly, recent IR research on purported 'long cycles of world leadership' and hegemonic stability mechanisms has examined regular movements within the international states-system; yet changes of that system are not contemplated (Modelski 1987; Thompson 1988; Webb and Krasner 1989). On the basis of this assumption of underlying continuity, many international theorists have claimed that texts by Sun Tzu and Mo Ti in ancient China, Kautilya in ancient India and Thucydides in ancient Greece – in addition to centuries-old writings by Machiavelli, Grotius, Hobbes, de Vattel and others – contain timeless truths about international politics which make them directly relevant to contemporary problems (cf. Ramaswamy 1962; Fliess 1966). From a realist perspective, then, the basic facts of international order have not changed in the past and in all likelihood will not do so in the future either.

The preceding discussion makes it clear that to examine social change in global perspective means to take distance from IR's realist orthodoxy. Investigations of international relations of social change would be based not on statism, but on a wider conception of international actors. Such research would rest not on politicism, but on a multifaceted notion of social relations. It would posit not a separation of the national and the international, but their fusion in world-systemic conditions. An understanding of transformation in global perspective would be premised not on reductionism, but on a keen appreciation of social structures and historical trends. And this project would be founded not on a supposition of underlying continuity, but on a concern with actual and potential fundamental change.

WANTED: A WORLD-HISTORICAL-SOCIOLOGICAL SYNTHESIS

To achieve this reconceptualization of 'international relations' we would do well to start by breaking down the disciplinary boundaries that have effectively removed the issue of social change from the field of IR since its beginnings early in this century. In the study of social transformation in world perspective, as with so many other research problems, the academic division of labour can be more of a hindrance than a help (Wallerstein 1991b). In particular we can look for inspiration to that discipline which has over the years laid first claim to the study of social order, Sociology, as well as to that field which has traditionally 'owned' investigations of continuity and change through time, History. The resulting historical-sociological understanding of international relations would, to take a phrase from Peter Burke (1980: 30), combine 'the sociologist's acute sense of structure with the historian's equally sharp sense of change'. In addition, forays into Anthropology, Psychology, Economics and Geography may serve to clarify respectively cultural, psychological, economic and ecological aspects of international relations of social change.

A number of students of International Relations have already crossed these academic boundaries during the past two decades. For one thing, there has been a significant revival of the interest in sociological enquiry which Alfred Zimmern, Sidney Bailey and others first vaguely articulated in the 1930s. The 1970s saw the publication of several 'sociologies' of international affairs in IR (Brucan 1971; Merle 1974; Luard 1976; Pettman 1979), as well as the further development of 'world society' (as distinct from 'world politics' and 'international society') conceptions of IR's subject-matter (Landheer et al. 1971; Burton 1972; Bornschier and Lengyel 1990). Meanwhile a new subfield of 'world order studies' incorporated an explicit commitment to changing the prevailing patterns of social organization on a global scale (Falk and Kim 1983). However, these initiatives have on the whole remained minority enterprises within the discipline, so that Fred Halliday has with good reason continued to urge that 'it is time for [International Relations] to engage in greater dialogue with sociology' (1985: 412; 1987a).

Also during recent years, some in International Relations have questioned the traditional division between their field and History. As Chris Hill has noted with regret, the relationship between international studies and historical investigations has over the years generally been 'one of quite separate paths of development' (1985: 143). Thus, for example, no formal link has so far been established in the USA between the International Studies Association and the Society for Historians of American Foreign Relations (SHAFR); and the British International Studies Association did not sponsor an International History section until 1988. Traditionalist international historians like Donald Watt and Alan Sked have resisted any substantial rapprochement between the two groups of researchers, insisting that there is, and must remain, a clear and marked distinction between historical and social-scientific approaches to the study of world affairs (Watt 1983; Sked 1987). Yet others have rejected this argument and have sought to incorporate more of the historian's sensitivity to time, context and change into IR

(Halliday 1987b; Thorne 1988: Ch 1). Certainly a tighter interweaving of an historical orientation and international relations theory could promote increased understanding of social change in world perspective.

However, although students of International Relations have made various approaches to History or to Sociology, relatively few IR writings have to date synthesized investigations of structure, change and the international in order to explore social transformation in a global context. Nevertheless, the 1980s did see greater borrowing from Historical Sociology in IR, particularly in regard to studies of the formation and global spread of the modern states-system (Rosecrance 1986; Jarvis 1989; Rasler and Thompson 1989; Banks and Shaw 1991). Meanwhile, Ekkehart Krippendorff (1975b,c), John Maclean (1981; 1988) and Robert Cox (1987) have on broadly Marxist lines interlinked questions of international relations, social structure and a concern with change. Others in IR have dabbled in dependency theory and the world-system approach to social history (Caporaso 1978; Hollist and Rosenau 1981). More recently, further challenges to realist orthodoxy from feminism, Critical Theory and postmodernism have attracted growing minority followings amongst students of international relations (respectively, Grant and Newland 1991; Linklater 1990; P. Rosenau 1990). As each of these alternative perspectives in one way or another addresses questions concerning the reorganization of social relations, there would seem to be a good prospect that increasing numbers of academics will in the generation to come treat International Relations as a study of social change.

In the field of History, too, a number of researchers have over the years explored social development in a world context. Yet to date they have remained a minority, as most social historians, including leading figures such as Edward Thompson and Emmanuel Le Roy Ladurie, have focused their academic studies on national and local settings rather than the international arena. On the other hand, several pioneering professional historians of the nineteenth century sought to understand so-called 'Universal History', which was seen, in the words of Acton, as being 'distinct from the combined history of all countries . . . [moving] in a succession to which the nations are subsidiary' (1898: 317). One of Acton's contemporaries, Erich Marcks, remarked in 1903 that 'the world is . . . more than ever before, one great unit in which everything interacts and affects everything else' (Barraclough 1964: 53). In subsequent decades the world point of view on 'civilizational' history also engaged the likes of Oswald Spengler (1918; 1922), James Bryce (1919), H.G. Wells (1920), Arnold Toynbee (1934–61), Jacques Pirenne (1943–56) and Kavalam Panikkar (1953). More recently, social change in world perspective has been the concern of William McNeill's various studies of the rise of the West (1963; 1964; 1974), Geoffrey Barraclough's analysis of contemporary history (1964), histories of the world by Kenneth Cameron (1973) and John Roberts (1976), Fernand Braudel's examination of capitalist development (1979a,b), Leften Stavrianos' long-term history of relations

between 'First', 'Second' and 'Third' worlds (1981), Philip Curtin's investigation of cross-cultural trade as a stimulus to social change (1984), and
Theodore von Laue's account of modernization as a global revolution
(1987).

Regrettably, however, this literature has made little impact on the subfield
of International History, which, heavily steeped in realism, has made
comparatively little contribution to the study of social change. Indeed, many
present-day practitioners continue to describe their enterprise as *Diplomatic
History* (Watt *et al*. 1985). Most international historians therefore focus on
'relations between states, particularly on the causes and results of conflict
between them', with 'an overriding concern with crises in the politics of
power and the officials who wield such power' (DeConde 1988: 286–7).
'Change' for the mainstream international historian therefore means not
social transformation, but matters such as shifting alliances or, as in one
recent bestseller, the cyclical rise and fall of great powers (Kennedy 1987).

On the other hand, some developments at the margins of International
History look more promising for studies of social change in an age of
globalization. For example, lively debates within SHAFR since 1980 have
brought gender issues, world-system theory, cultural analysis and other
alternative concerns onto the research agenda of International History
(McMahon 1990; Paterson *et al*. 1990). Several writings have explored the
effects of United States foreign policy in reshaping the social order in a target
country (e.g., Hogan 1987). In addition, certain other historians have studied
the world wars as catalysts for social transformation (e.g., Marwick 1988).
On the whole, though, little literature has so far emerged in International
History to advance our understanding of, as Christopher Thorne expressed
the point in his study of social change resulting from the Pacific War of
1941–5, 'the interrelationships involved in the development of "the social
system of the modern world" and of all societies within it' (1985: 55).

Considerably more literature on social change in world perspective has
emanated from Sociology, where students of IR and History will discover,
perhaps to their surprise, a long-standing concern with the international.
Several early sociologists were among the first to become alert to the process
of globalization. For example, Leonard Hobhouse bore witness at the turn of
the century to the fact that, in his words, 'Humanity is rapidly becoming,
physically speaking, a single society' (1906: 316). At roughly the same time
Emile Durkheim and Marcel Mauss described what they called an emerging
'international life' beyond the national territory: an 'interdependent system'
of 'supranational facts' with 'their own unity and form of existence' which
'sociology needs to know' (1913: 810–12; also Durkheim 1915: 445). By the
1920s and 1930s sociologists were according sufficient attention to world
affairs that one of their number felt able to assert that 'Sociology . . . could
legitimately compete with political science in studying international relations' (Landecker 1938: 175; Bernard and Bernard 1934).

Something of a lull occurred in sociological investigations of the international during the 1940s and 1950s, when only an occasional general article appeared on this subject (e.g., Behrendt 1955); but such research resumed on a significant scale in the early 1960s, with work on international politics by Talcott Parsons (1961), Raymond Aron (1962), Amitai Etzioni (1963) and others. Interest on the part of sociologists in international social relations (i.e., in a sense that extended beyond interstate politics) increased from the mid-1960s. For example, in 1966 the World Congress of Sociology for the first time included 'the sociology of international relations' amongst its themes (ISA 1966). In the same year Wilbert Moore anticipated what is today a widely accepted insight when he questioned Sociology's predominant notion of 'society as coterminous with national states' and advocated 'freeing the concept of [social] system from automatic limits at the "boundaries" of societies or cultures' (1966: 481). The ensuing years saw the publication of sociological studies concerning transnationalism (e.g., Angell 1969), the internationalization of capital (e.g., Berberoglu 1987), underdevelopment in a world context (Brewer 1990: Ch 8), global militarization (e.g., Wallensteen *et al.* 1985), internationalized patriarchy (e.g., Mies 1986), and state formation in an international setting (e.g., Hall 1986b).

Thus by the 1980s a number of sociologists were arguing that globalization was *the* issue of concern for their discipline as it approached its centenary (Outhwaite 1989: 166). For instance, Edward Tiryakian (1986) argued in the second issue of the newly founded journal, *International Sociology*, that undergraduate Sociology curricula should be reconstructed with a focus on internationalization and global issues. Mike Featherstone in a recent book concerning globalization agrees that, in the 1990s:

> the challenge for sociology . . . is to both theorize and work out modes of systematic investigation which can clarify these globalizing processes and distinctive [global] forms of social life.
>
> (1990: 2)

True, not every sociologist has become preoccupied with the question of globally generated social structures and trends. Indeed, such major social theorists of the late twentieth century as Peter Berger, Pierre Bourdieu, Ralf Dahrendorf, Michel Foucault, Ernest Gellner, Jürgen Habermas, Jean-François Lyotard, Barrington Moore and Alain Touraine have at most made only passing and loosely conceptualized references to the international (cf. Habermas 1973: 44, 120; 1976: 196–7; Berger 1974; Lyotard 1979: 5–6). Still, International Relations students of the 1990s will find much of interest if they drift from their usual home in the Politics section of a university library and explore the Sociology shelves.

Some of this sociological work has tended to replicate realist arguments which already dominate the field of IR. For example, Randall Collins, who indeed explicitly calls himself a 'realist', has elaborated a geopolitical analysis in which he argues that the underlying principles of interstate competition have remained essentially the same over the centuries, in spite of the advent of modern technologies and a capitalist world economy (1981: 18–23; 1985: 109; 1986: 184). In a similar vein, Michael Mann and John Hall have devoted a recent volume to the quintessentially realist question of how hegemonic states rise and decline in world politics (Mann 1990). For the reasons discussed earlier in this chapter, this literature takes Sociology into a cul-de-sac as far as studies of social change are concerned.

However, in a number of other instances sociologists have coupled their discovery of the international with a sensitivity to time and change, thereby producing something of a world-historical-sociological conception of the global scene. Indeed, such a synthesis was pioneered earlier in this century in work by Max Weber (1922b) on the world religions and the rise of the West; by Otto Hintze (1929) on interconnections between the states-system and capitalist development; by Harry Elmer Barnes (1930) on the effects of nationalism, capitalism and militarism on a world scale; by Werner Sombart (1913) and Piritim Sorokin (1942) on the relation of warfare to social transformations; by Norbert Elias (1939) on state formation in an international context; and by Karl Polanyi (1944) on the worldwide spread of commercialization and the system of national states.

This attention to international relations of social change receded during the middle decades of this century when, as mentioned above, sociologists generally lost sight of the international; however, it has resurfaced again over the past twenty years as part of a general revival of Historical Sociology (Skocpol 1984). A study by Peter Nettl and Roland Robertson (1968) foreshadowed an upsurge of investigations during the 1980s into international aspects of the modernization process (Featherstone 1990). In addition, much Marxist research in the 1970s and 1980s returned to questions of international capitalism which had been raised early in the century by the likes of Rudolf Hilferding (1910) and Nikolai Bukharin (1915). Meanwhile, as a means to promote their particular brand of world-system theory (with a hyphen), Immanuel Wallerstein and his colleagues in 1976 set up the Fernand Braudel Center for the Study of Economies, Historical Systems, and Civilizations at the State University of New York at Binghamton (Shannon 1989). At the same time a few anthropologists such as Eric Wolf (1982) and Peter Worsley (1984) began to examine social development in the 'Third World' in the context of long-term global history. Also during the 1970s and 1980s, historical sociologists including Charles Tilly (1975), Theda Skocpol (1979), Aristide Zolberg (1986), John Hall (1986b), Michael Mann (1988) and Martin Shaw (1989) adopted an international perspective on questions of state formation and associated social changes. A few researchers have of late drawn on the Critical Theory tradition in order to explore current prospects for emancipatory social transformation in world-historical terms (Giddens 1990), while others have linked the process of globalization to a transition from a modern to a postmodern social order (Featherstone 1991). Thus some important groundwork for international studies of social change has been laid within Sociology, albeit that the research just noted has often been conducted in ignorance of relevant concurrent developments in the fields of IR and History.

The preceding discussion indicates that the notion of a theoretical reconstruction that would bring insights from IR, History and Sociology together into one inquiry into social change is by no means entirely new. A number of practitioners within each of these disciplines have in the past shown interest in such an enterprise, even though communication, cross-fertilization and coordination between the three fields has so far remained limited on the whole. What is advocated here, then, is a fully integrated world-historical-sociological enterprise that fundamentally reformulates, and thereby in fact transcends, the different disciplinary traditions out of which it develops.

$\equiv 2 \equiv$

WORLD SOCIETY AND WORLD-SYSTEMIC DYNAMICS OF CHANGE

The previous chapter put forward a general case for studying the role of international relations in producing major reorganizations of social life. The argument at that stage consisted mainly of a refutation of traditional, nation-bound conceptions of society and, in connection with this point, of prevailing endogenous explanations of social change. Yet the question of how, in an alternative perspective, one might incorporate notions of international forces of transformation into the analysis has thus far not been elaborated. The present chapter now moves on to address the question of international causation of rearrangements of social life and, in particular, the relationship between international aspects of the dynamics of change on the one hand and the role of national conditions and local circumstances in the process on the other.

The following pages develop the suggestion made earlier, in the course of the critique of realism, that social relations should not be conceived, in the conventional fashion, in terms of ontologically separate domestic and international realms. Instead, we might better explore the problem of social change in terms of what may be called 'world society' and 'world-systemic' relations within that society.[1] In this conception of the transformation process the timing, location, character and speed of change are held to result from the coexistence, interconnection and mutual determination of local, national and international conditions. In other words, reconstructions of social life are explained not as a consequence of micro-level causes and/or of macro-level causes, but as an outcome of 'world' relations, which encompass locality, country and the international in combination. Following this principle, the task of research would not be to seek out separately generated sub-national, national and supra-national promptings of social change, since causality is not conceived of as being apportioned between discrete territorial spheres. Instead, studies would examine how world-systemic dynamics produce transformations in local settings, in national contexts and/or in cross-border situations through the continuous interplay of these arenas, where each simultaneously shapes and is shaped by the others. A re-arrangement of the social order therefore is not caused by one or several 'levels', but by 'world' relations that envelop parochial, country and international circumstances in a systemic whole.

The first part of this chapter notes and illustrates how social change is usually explained in terms of distinctions between local, national and international causes. This convention is then rejected in favour of a holistic concept of world-systemic relations. According to the latter approach, international relations do not constitute a distinct *cause* of social transform-ation, but are an important *dimension* of the process: one which is cause-and-effect of the local and national aspects in the dynamics of change. A number of qualifications and disclaimers are elaborated in the third section of the chapter in order to establish more exactly what is entailed by the notions of world society and world-systemic dynamics of social change. Finally, as a prelude to Chapters 3 to 5, the discussion at the end of the present chapter specifies several general ways in which international relations are formative of world social life.

'LEVELS' OF SOCIAL CAUSATION

Social interaction takes place in settings ranging from narrowly circum-scribed spaces to very widely spread horizons. At one end of this spectrum, people can live collectively at close quarters, such as within a household or a neighbourhood. On a somewhat larger scale, the social context may be a town, a city-state or a province. Expanding beyond localities, social relations may stretch across a country or over a region made up of several countries. In other respects social contact and interdependence may extend to a full continent, the entire surface of the planet, or even – given recent technological developments – into outer space. By 1986 some 3500 operational satellites were facilitating global communications from outside the earth's atmosphere (Wilhelm 1990: Ch 3).

A development in social history, too, may have anything from a very localized to a planetary scope. For example, the rise of illicit drugs traffic has taken place in an intercontinental realm, whereas the advent of Hindu revivalism has featured mainly in a regional setting, viz. the Indian Subcontinent. Other shifts in social relations have transpired on a national scale: Thatcherism in Britain and democratization in Chile, for instance. In the case of urbanization, change has occurred in a quite localized space, e.g., within the city limits of Brasilia or Nairobi, but not in the surrounding countryside. Sometimes social life may be reorganized across all of these spheres at once; for example, bureaucratization has altered the way that administration is conducted in local, national and international contexts.

While we can clearly describe social change in relation to a variety of territorial settings, how do distinctions between locality, country, region and globality figure in *explanations* of transformation? From where do the forces of social reconstruction emanate? Do changes taking place in a local sphere have local causes; do reorganizations on a national scale have national causes; and do shifts in international relations have international causes? If so, then society would exist and develop on separate and independent local, national and international planes. This division may be analytically tidy, but it quickly breaks down in practice: even our personal lives are blends of local, national and international experiences, as, among other things, we simultaneously reside in a particular locale, live under a national government and trade largely in an international economy.

If local, national and international spheres are in constant contact with one another, then an explanation of social change must address the causal relationship between them. One general approach to this problem is to conceive of causation in terms of 'levels'. We would then trace processes of transformation in whichever arena back to local origins, or back to national sources, or back to international causes. In other words, one of these levels would be purported to hold the key to explaining social change. For reasons indicated in the following paragraphs, these forms of reductionism are fundamentally flawed. Nor is it satisfactory to adopt a more complex variant of reductionism that accounts for change in terms of an aggregation of discrete local, national and international 'factors'. There are no separate local, national and international societies; there is only a world society with local, national and international dimensions.

One reductionist approach, local determinism, posits that social change proceeds 'from the bottom up'. In this conception, the impetus for a fundamental reconstruction of social life comes in the first place from small-scale situations where people maintain regular face-to-face contact with one another. The transformation then may or may not spread outwards to embrace a wider community, perhaps on occasion affecting a whole country or even extending to foreign lands as well. From this perspective, change originates at the grassroots, so that persons who seek to reorganize world society should indeed 'begin at home' (Ekins 1992). On this premise, for example, local measures such as the declaration of nuclear-free zones, which had been established in over 3500 towns in twenty-four countries by 1987, could, in aggregation, yield world disarmament (Boulding 1988: 45). Similarly, local self-help initiatives such as *ujamaa* villages in Tanzania and *shramadana* community projects in Sri Lanka might offer a road from underdevelopment to development in those countries (Nyerere 1968: Ch 7; Tehranian 1990: 228–35).[2] In these and other instances social change on a national or international scale is said to originate in the local sphere.

Yet localist explanations of social transformation are not viable, much as they may appeal to our desires to have full control of our lives close at hand. In the case of strivings for disarmament, for example, local initiatives confront the countervailing power of national military–industrial complexes and international forces of militarization through the arms trade and the like. Similarly, village cooperatives in poor areas of the world face constraints on their development efforts from national policies, international debt problems and so on. Even a highly localized change such as urbanization of a particular town is likely to be affected as much by, say, international capital and national migration patterns as by planning decisions of the municipal authorities concerned (cf. Timberlake 1985). These and countless other examples make it clear that a unidirectional bottom-up model of social change is not sustainable and that, to be effective, local social movements need to take heed of the prevailing global situation (Feather 1980).

Meanwhile other students of social change – indeed, the majority – have sought to explain the process of transformation primarily in national terms. This approach sees the world as a collection of discrete national societies, links causation to the country-unit, and posits that social history is essentially driven by national forces.[3] On this assumption it might be argued, for instance, that legislation by a national government could bring about an end to age discrimination, or that a national campaign could secure democratic institutions in the place of previous authoritarian rule, or that the dialectic of a country's internal class structure could produce a transition from capitalism to socialism. On the same principle, social revolutions are held to be intrinsically national phenomena: their causes can allegedly be isolated in the national arena in question. National promptings of change might 'trickle down' to reorganize social life at the local level, and they might also 'filter up' to transform conditions at the international level, but the impulse for change is held to emanate in the first place from the national entity. According to the premise of national causation, when a similar reorganization of social life occurs in a number of countries, this is because certain requisite conditions have come to prevail in each country separately. Thus a transformation that has been replicated in many lands and perhaps has even acquired global proportions would still be explained in terms of national circumstances.

However, the hypothesis of national determinism, too, does not stand up to scrutiny. Although national 'societies' have in recent centuries become quite sharply delineated, the causes of social change cannot be fixed on country units. On the one hand, local spheres often maintain a substantial degree of autonomy from national power centres. For example, many Kachin, Karen, Shan and other minority peoples in the peripheral areas of Myanmar (formerly known as Burma) remain well outside the mainstream of national life in that country. Likewise, within Canada there are differential dynamics of development in the western provinces, Québec, the eastern seaboard and the arctic territories. Nor does social change in a national arena unfold in isolation from the wider international context (Almond 1989).

National sovereignty may be a widely endorsed formal principle of international relations, but it has never been a fully operative condition, even at the time of absolute monarchy and mercantilism in seventeenth-century Europe. True, national states do impose many legal impediments on cross-border activity, including trade barriers, immigration restrictions, jamming of broadcasts, censorship, non-convertible currencies and so on; yet significant external involvement in national life has persisted all the same (Mendershausen 1969). Thus, for example, communist-ruled countries were in their day singularly unable to draw an 'iron curtain' around the Soviet bloc. As a one-time Rumanian ambassador to the United Nations acknowledged:

> we live in a world in which the socialist nations must adapt themselves
> to the patterns of behavior prevailing in the international system.
> (Brucan 1978a: viii)

Similarly, it has not proved possible, as some radical proposals of the 1970s advocated, to 'delink' newly decolonized countries from the international political economy in order that they might pursue independent national courses of development (Amin 1984). In the 1990s national control of social change is as elusive as ever, given the recent emergence of large-scale minimally regulated transnational financial movements, huge unmonitored data flows through transborder computer networks, and detailed extraterrestrial surveillance by satellite remote sensing. Hence, although the frontiers of national states can sometimes severely hamper transnational contacts, they do not create self-contained national units of social life which produce distinct national causes of transformation.

If change is not initiated at the local or national level, then perhaps it is instigated at the international level. The premise of international determinism holds that reorganizations of social life result from the way that countries are related to one another. In this 'top-down' conception of the dynamics of transformation, cross-border interactions and the collective international circumstances of countries generate forces of change which do not 'rise up' out of domestic settings, but arise out of international relations in the first place and then impinge on national and local situations. Expressing this notion that the international is primary, Emile Durkheim argued some eighty years ago that 'there is no national life which is not dominated by a collective life of an international nature' (1915: 426). In a similar vein, Leon Trotsky described the international economy as 'a mighty and independent reality which . . . imperiously dominates the national markets' (1930: 146). Likewise, Randall Collins has recently asserted that 'politics works from the outside in'; for him, 'the international arena writes the plot' (1986: 145, 147). As an example of specifically international causation of social change, it could be maintained that interstate competition has instigated and sustained the process of militarization over the centuries, so that, were it not for international relations, we would not today be facing a world of large armies and weapons of mass destruction (Duffy 1980; McNeill 1982). Another 'top-down' explanation might hold that international market conditions provided the initial stimulus for the emergence of modern capitalist society (Wallerstein 1974b: 18–19). Such theses affirm that social change originates in a distinct international realm of social life with its own overriding dynamics of transformation.

Yet the notion of international determinism is no more sustainable than postulates of fundamental local or national causation. While the preceding remarks suggest that international relations certainly can affect the course of social development, it is quite another thing to treat internal circumstances merely as outcomes of international forces. In regard to the first illustration above, for instance, militarization has often been encouraged not only by relations between countries, but also by locationally domestic affairs such as civil wars, opportunities for employment and profit through armament factories, and so on. As for the second example given, capitalism seems to have arisen as much out of conditions in the countryside of Europe as out of international commerce (Hilton 1978). Turning to other situations, how could we maintain that characteristics specific to the Sicilian and Italian-national contexts had no bearing on the rise of Mafia organizations in that particular part of the world rather than other places (cf. Blok 1975)? And surely the various *adat* formations, which for centuries shaped village life in insular South East Asia, arose at least in part from the respective local settings within that region (cf. Haar 1939)? In short, to reject endogenism is one thing, but it is no less mistaken to suppose that local and national conditions are purely products of the international and lack any significance of their own in the process of transformation. Hence a concern to understand international relations of social change must not lapse into what certain critics have termed 'the tyranny of globalism' and 'macro-batics' (respectively, Petras and Brill 1985; Mintz 1977: 266). John Hall in this light rightly distinguishes between 'international *constraint* and full-blooded international *control*' (1985: 15).

It seems, then, that none of the three positions discussed so far offers an adequate basis for understanding social transformation. Local impulses to change are responses to national and international circumstances as well as products of the local situation itself. National stimuli to change are at the same time also outcomes of local pressures on the one hand and international conditions on the other. And international promptings of social change are in many respects themselves shaped by local and national situations. In sum, then, the endogenism-versus-exogenism debate is a chicken-or-egg argument that does not get us very far.

WORLD-SYSTEMIC CAUSATION

The preceding discussion makes it clear that although the *manifestations* of change appear in local, national and/or international settings, *causality* is not specifically located in any of these realms, since they overlap so much as to be inseparable from one another. So perhaps we need to formulate the question of causation differently. Indeed, postulates of local, national and inter-national determination all rely upon an analytic methodology which compartmentalizes social life into discrete spheres and then distributes causality amongst them. In each case the issue of explanation is conceptual-ized in terms of the so-called 'level-of-analysis problem' (Waltz 1959; Singer 1961). Alternatively, however, we could turn away from this prevailing approach and instead construct our understanding in line with the holistic notion of a 'system'. At its most elementary, the systems principle holds that the various parts of a given situation are connected to one another as both cause and effect at the same time. Hence the interlinkages of the parts are as important as those components themselves, and the system as a whole – not one, or several, or even all of its constituent parts – produces the outcome in question (Bertalanffy 1968). In the present context the relevant 'outcome' is change and continuity in social life; the 'parts' are localities, countries and international relations; and the 'whole' is the world society. Thus the world-societal whole is more than its local, national and international parts.

What is being suggested here, then, is a shift of conceptual focus from the parts to the whole in the study of social change. On this premise, forces of transformation lie in a world situation in its totality, where that 'world' encompasses local contexts, national settings, international circumstances and, with equal significance, the interpenetration and mutual constitution of those spheres within a systemic whole (cf. Boulding 1985: 8, 75–6). Robertson and Lechner in this vein advocate the adoption of 'a "multidimen-sional" world-system theory [which] ranges across levels of analysis' (1985: 103). In short, the micro–macro division is bridged (Alger 1984–5), and the world society as a whole becomes the primordial unit of analysis (Bergesen 1980). We can then cast aside the merry-go-round question of domestic-versus-international primacy as a red herring.

It is no small matter to make this move to a non-territorial, non-national conception of society. Through our daily experience we are constantly encouraged to partition the social world into separate territorial realms. For instance, most journals and news broadcasts present local, national and international stories in successive sections. Governments operate through distinct local, national and international tiers of agencies. Cartographers draw separate district, country and global maps. Educational curricula place local, national and international history under different course headings. And so the division of social relations into discrete 'societies' becomes a 'commonsense' premise in our understanding of the world.

However, social forces cannot in fact be compartmentalized in this manner, as they flow across and between the 'levels' with such abandon that causes of transformation cannot be pinned to any one sphere. Indeed, those 'levels' do not exist except as an analytical construct, and this simplification readily becomes an obstruction rather than an aid to understanding social change. The notion of 'world-systemic dynamics' offers the less territorial conception of social life that we need. 'World' forces of social change are international/national/local forces. They are not reducible to the local, the national or the international. Nor are world-systemic dynamics a matter of summation, so that we could explain a given transformation as a result of, say, 40 per cent international factors, 35 per cent national factors and 25 per cent local factors. As local, national and international circumstances are simultaneously cause and effect of one another, causality can never be isolated and measured at one or several of these 'levels'. A world-systemic process encompasses domestic and international conditions in one causal dynamic.

A number of students of social change have endorsed a world system notion of this kind. For instance, Theda Skocpol has suggested that industrialization is best conceived as both an 'intrasocietal' process and an 'intersocietal' phenomenon (1976: 179). Rosemary Galli and her colleagues have explored rural development in terms of an interplay between peasant activity in the village setting, state policy in the national sphere and the dynamics of international capital (Galli 1981). Carol Smith's research on 'local history in global context' in relation to Western Guatemala rejects 'global functionalism' and concentrates instead on 'the articulation of different layers in a multilayered system' (1984: 194). On similar lines, we might hypothesize that the recent termination of communist rule in Eastern Europe resulted from local mobilization in combination with national reforms and international pressures.

A WORLD PERSPECTIVE: SOME CLARIFICATIONS

The terms 'world society' and 'world system' can be used in multiple ways and are prone to breed confusion and misinterpretation if they are not carefully specified. The following pages therefore elaborate more than a dozen qualifications and disclaimers relating to these notions, including in particular several points relating to the place of international relations in world-systemic dynamics of social transformation.

First of all, we need to distinguish between the generic world system concept and the specific (usually hyphenated) world-system theory associated with the Braudel Center, the journal *Review*, and the *Political Economy of the World-System Annuals* published since 1978 (Shannon 1989). As the repeated references to Wallerstein and his colleagues in Chapter 1 indicated, world-system theory has done much to bring endogenous models into disrepute and to advance a world perspective on social history. However, these authors present only one possible conception of world-systemic dynamics, and indeed their accounts are open to a number of powerful criticisms (cf. Brenner 1977; Skocpol 1977; Aronowitz 1981; Chirot and

Hall 1982; Nelson 1983; Pieterse 1988). In short, to promote the concepts of world society and world system as a general orientation to explanations of social change is not to endorse world-system theory's particular notions of actors, structures and trends in a capitalist world-economy.

Second, as already noted, a world-systemic conception of the process of transformation does not entail a premise of international determinism. As they are used here, the terms 'international' and 'world' are not interchangeable. To maintain that social relations have an important international dimension is not to hold that the international constitutes the motor of social change. Circumstances in world society have distinctive local and national qualities alongside their international features, and these 'internal' arrangements have a measure of autonomy from international relations (though not complete independence). Indeed, certain domestic conditions in world society may have implications that deviate sharply from prevailing international circumstances, creating a particularly volatile mix of social forces. For example, the Khmer Rouge in a national setting in the 1970s and the women's peace camp at Greenham Common in a local context in the 1980s advanced projects of social reconstruction which ran squarely against, respectively, dominant liberal principles and militaristic tendencies of the international order of the day. Moreover, situations in local and national spheres have repercussions for international relations as well as vice versa: world society is a complex of interrelated international and domestic conditions. Hence, for example, effects of the Chinese Revolution reverberated outwards into the wider international arena at the same time that China's external contacts affected the course of the country's internal development. According to the conception adopted here, the world economy encompasses both the international economy and the various national economies. World politics involves international politics and domestic politics in combination (cf. Modelski 1972). World culture incorporates both cross-border and internal communications of meaning. World ecology braids together international, national and local environmental issues, where none is reducible to the others. In a word, then, a world-systemic explanation of social change treats the international as one dimension of the process of transformation, not its source.

Third, as intimated in the previous chapter, the general premise of micro–macro interrelations within a world society can be relevant not only in regard to contemporary history, but also in respect of social changes that unfolded in earlier centuries and in some cases even millennia ago. For example, Martin Bernal (1987) argues persuasively that ancient Greek civilization developed not as a distinctively 'western' product, but out of intermingling in the second millennium BC between preexisting local peoples of the Aegean, Indo-European infiltrators from the north, Egyptian colonizers from the south and Phoenician arrivals from the Levant. On a larger geographical scale, William McNeill emphasizes that more or less continuous contact and exchange took place across what he calls the 'Eurasian ecumene', stretching from Spain to the China Sea, from the second century AD onwards, thus more than a thousand years before the voyage of Vasco da Gama (1963: Ch 7). Indeed, McNeill argues that the stimulus of alien contact provided perhaps the major impulse for social change in early Middle Eastern, Chinese, Indian, and Hellenic–Roman civilizations (1963: 253). Janet Abu-Lughod (1989) has analysed a thirteenth-century world society which extended from Flanders to China and had the Middle East as its heartland. Jane Schneider (1977), too, suggests that the world system notion can help us to understand pre-capitalist developments. Michael Mann affirms that the 'rise of the West' was due in part to Europe's relations with regions such as the Near East and Central Asia, together with the blending within Europe of Germanic, late-Roman, Scandinavian and Hellenic social formations (1986: 503–8). Immanuel Wallerstein (1974a) studies the development of capitalism in world-systemic terms from what he calls the 'long sixteenth century' (circa 1450–1640), while George Modelski (1987) takes his research into cycles of world leadership back to 1494. Hence, in addition to shedding light on twentieth-century events such as the rise and decline of communism and the decolonization process, the principle of world-systemic relations might help as well to explain continuity and change in social life of earlier times.

Fourth, as implied in several of the examples just cited, world social relations do not necessarily extend to every location and every person on planet earth. The term 'world' is used here to refer to significant and sustained social interrelatedness across a large geographical expanse, but those wide horizons do not have to reach a global scale (cf. Braudel 1979b: 21–2; Luhmann 1982: 132–3). For example, the thirteenth-century world society described by Abu-Lughod mainly involved a long-distance Eurasian trading network centred on a limited number of coastal ports and market towns. Fernand Braudel focused much of his historical-sociological study on the Mediterranean 'world' (1949). Wallerstein for his part conceives of the 'modern world-system' as being initially limited geographically to Europe (1974a: 10). True, long-range contacts and interdependence were considerably less prominent in world-systemic dynamics of those earlier eras than they are in the present day. Moreover, in spite of large-scale Islamic expansion into Africa and Asia from the seventh century onwards and sustained European incursions into many overseas areas after the fifteenth century, a country such as Japan managed to retain a large measure of isolation from international movements from 1642 until the middle of the nineteenth century.

Only in recent history, then, has something approximating 'planetary' social relations emerged. Today, in contrast to earlier times, we confront a 'global-human circumstance' (Robertson and Lechner 1985). In the current era of global relations, those who have endeavoured to avoid involvement with the wider world have with time been drawn seemingly inexorably back into international networks and world-systemic dynamics of continuity and change. Such has been the fate of, amongst others, American isolationists in the 1930s, proponents of the inward-looking 'Burmese Road to Socialism' during the 1960s, and maverick Stalinists of Albania in the 1980s. Nevertheless, even world social relations of the present do not entail a planetary totality which incorporates all of humanity into a single society. Certain populations – for example, forest dwellers deep in the interior of South America – continue for the most part to slip through world-systemic nets.

A fifth rider that needs to be attached to the world system concept is that this notion does not imply that geography is irrelevant to explanations of social change. Issues such as physical proximity, spatial differentiation, territorial boundaries and other matters relating to locational situation continue to be important even in an age of advanced globalization. True, as will be elaborated in the next chapter, electronic communications have today substantially weakened the relationship between physical place and social 'place' (Meyrowitz 1985: ix). Indeed, Richard O'Brien's catchphrase, 'the end of geography' (1992), carries considerable weight in regard to the present-day worldwide integration of financial markets. On the other hand, though, climatic differences and problems of long-distance transport remain significant in the current age of global agriculture, and topography obviously continues to inhibit trans-Himalayan commerce relative to trade on the flat between Belgium and the Netherlands. In addition, on a more general point, face-to-face dealings by their very nature have a different sort of social dynamic than situations where interpersonal contact is sustained through technical media such as fax machines and telephones (Meyrowitz 1985; Thompson 1990). In short, then, to formulate an understanding of social change in terms of world-systemic forces is not to ignore time–space considerations.

Sixth, the concept of world-systemic dynamics of transformation does not imply that the same degree of integration prevails between all parts of the world. Due to geographical, technological, historical, cultural, political and other circumstances the intensity of interactions and the immediacy of interdependence is in fact often quite uneven. For example, in contemporary world social relations the largest concentrations of external investment, cross-border transport, transfrontier data flows, diplomatic contacts and other transnational interchanges exist between the so-called 'trilateral' countries, i.e., Western Europe, North America and Japan. By comparison, Africa, Asia and Latin America have substantially less infrastructure for long-distance interaction. For example, there were only ten television sets per thousand people in Sub-Saharan Africa in 1981, as compared with 618 per thousand head of population in North America (Varis 1985: 18). Myanmar's thirty-eight million inhabitants made a mere 149,000 international telephone calls in 1988, while sixty-one million West Germans dialled abroad over three thousand times more often in that year (ITU 1990: 38, 254). Moreover, on all continents internationalization of social relations has been most intense in urban areas, especially in the so-called 'world cities', i.e., central nodes of global networks such as London, Tokyo, New York and Singapore (Friedmann 1986; Knight and Gappert 1989). Meanwhile, provincial districts in whatever country are in general involved in direct long-distance exchanges on a far smaller scale. Of course it does not follow that the significance of those transactions will be less simply because they are fewer in number; the indirect effects of internationalization – e.g., as mediated through 'world cities' – can run deep in even the most remote settlements. In sum, then, while every place in a world society is in some way connected to all the others, the distribution of interactions and the depth of interdependence is irregular. Some locations and some people may to that extent be more immediately and more intensely involved in international relations of social change than others.

Seventh, to speak of a world society is not to imply uniformity, i.e., that social conditions are the same throughout the world. In some respects it may be so that, as Cees Hamelink has declared in regard to contemporary history, 'the impressive variety of the world's cultural systems is waning due to a process of "cultural synchronization" that is without historical precedent' (1983: 3). Blue jeans and Barbie dolls have come to span the globe, while various local art forms have been disappearing at a stunningly rapid rate. For instance, the epic 'long songs' of the Dayaks in Sarawak, passed on orally for an untold number of generations in the past, have now suddenly been largely erased from memory in less than twenty years (Rubenstein 1991). Yet it is important not to exaggerate the degree of homogenization. By one calculation, there are still some 3500 verbal and 500 written languages in the world today (MacBride *et al.* 1980: 49). As no nation-state has ever wholly achieved its ostensible mission of securing cultural uniformity within its borders, we can hardly expect identical conditions to prevail across boundaries on a world scale. Not only are cultural objects often visibly different from one part of the world to the next, but in addition a globalized object may be interpreted in sharply contrasting ways in the light of the local context (cf. Tomlinson 1991). Thus, for example, the television serial *Dallas* may be viewed in a significantly different manner in a village in Turkey than on Main Street USA. An early student of social change in world perspective, Wilbert Moore, initially equated globalism with universalism (1966), but after a decade of further research he came instead to emphasize 'the limits of convergence' (1979). Arjun Appadurai (1990) takes this observation further and views the global condition in terms of a contest between sameness and difference, with concurrent pulls towards homogenization and heterogenization. Viewed from this perspective, the notions of globality and plurality are anything but mutually exclusive. The fact of world society does not preclude variety, disjunctions and contradictory patterns of social life within that world; and, conversely, the fact that there is diversity of social conditions across the globe does not negate the fact of international/national/local interlinkages and world-systemic causation of social change. As Ulf Hannerz sees it, world social relations are 'marked by an organization of diversity rather than by a replication of uniformity' (1990: 237; also King 1991). In other words, the concept of world society is not antithetical to, but incorporates, the premise of particularity. World-systemic dynamics can sustain and even create heterogeneity. Indeed, the interplay of differences might well constitute a key world-systemic engine of transformation. McNeill suggests as much with his assertion that:

> the main drive wheel of historical change [has been] contacts among strangers, causing both sides of such encounters to reconsider and in some cases to alter their familiar ways of behaving.
>
> (1974: 42)

Eighth, and as an extension of the preceding point, the premise of world-systemic causation of social change need not entail a supposition that history takes the same course everywhere in the world. Thus although the process of transformation unfolds in a world-societal context and involves international circumstances, social change does not as a result take identical forms in each region, country and locality. For example, if we were to conceive of contemporary social history in terms of a capitalist world system, we would not thereby necessarily be affirming that capitalist relations have been or will in future become equally entrenched at every point in the world, nor that capitalism has taken, or will eventually take, the same course of development in every part of the world, nor that capitalism has had or will in due course have the same consequences for each location in the world. Unity within a world-systemic whole does not imply singularity of history in all of its parts. Indeed, world-systemic interrelations may cause different changes to occur in different areas. In this vein dependency theory posits that development in the core (or metropolitan countries) and underdevelopment in the periphery (or satellite countries) have been mutually constitutive (Amin 1973; Frank 1978). In this respect too, then, globality does not negate domain-specificity.

Ninth, the notion of world society does not as a matter of logical necessity assume a high degree of institutional centralization and power concentration in the world. True, as the next chapter will indicate, transnational corporations, intergovernmental organizations and international non-governmental agencies have proliferated in the context of the globalization process. Yet even today many sectors of world production are not oligopolistic; nor is a global government on the model of the sovereign nation-state in prospect; and much pressure-group activity proceeds in the absence of significant international coordination. Indeed, while the twentieth century has seen a high tide of globalization, it has also witnessed the worldwide dissolution of colonial empires, a host of secession movements and civil wars, and upsurges of ethnic sentiment on all continents. The shrinking world has in these senses also been a fragmenting world (Groom and Heraclides 1985; Camilleri and Falk 1992). We might even ask whether forces of indigenization have been as much a part of the process of globalization as impulses towards centralization. In other words, people have perhaps pursued devolution in an attempt to retain or regain a sense of place, identity, community and control of destiny, in reaction against experiences of rootlessness, depersonalization and alienation which may accompany the development of social interrelatedness on a planetary scale. It is perhaps no coincidence that the emergence and maturation of the nationality principle historically parallelled the geographical extension of world social relations and the intensification of transnational links (cf. McNeill 1985: 59). In short, the concept of world society involves no presumptions about the degree of fragmentation or unification within the world situation in question.

Tenth, as preceding points have already broadly implied, the postulate of world-systemic dynamics of transformation does not assume that circumstances of social equality prevail amongst the various parts in the system. Such an eventuality is not ruled out in principle, but equality certainly does not characterize contemporary world society. Asymmetries of opportunity and reward currently abound both between and within countries: *inter alia* between women and men; between children and adults; between blacks and whites; between homosexuals and heterosexuals; between disabled and able-bodied persons; between rural and urban dwellers; between wage-earners and employers; between professionals and their clients; and so on. Some in the present-day world society have greater decision-taking capacities than others, receive privileged access to resources, secure claims to superior knowledge and values, and/or enjoy better health and longer lifespans. Indeed, the globalization process characteristic of contemporary history appears in a number of respects to have increased rather than diminished social inequalities.

That said, we need at the same time to guard against an eleventh possible misunderstanding of the world perspective on history: namely, the reductionist notion that the dominant parts in the system determine the course of social change. Thus, for example, although men on the whole have disproportionate power relative to women in the world society of today, the key to understanding social change lies in gender relations between the sexes as well as in characteristics of men per se. Similarly, in a class analysis of world society it is the relationship between classes, not the dominant class by itself, which shapes the course of contemporary history. Likewise, the primacy of the USA in the twentieth-century global society has not entailed American control of contemporary social history the world over; nor did the *Pax Britannica* in the nineteenth century place London in the role of global puppeteer. Even at their respective moments of hegemony, Britain and the United States have been fundamentally shaped by world-systemic dynamics which interlink the domestic circumstances of the respective countries and their contacts with external areas. It is the relationship between hegemon and clients, as much as the leading state itself, which might provide a world-systemic motor of continuity and change. In sum, then, no matter how dominant certain of the parts of world society may be, it is ultimately systemic relations rather than locations of concentrated power that determine the incidence and nature of social transformation.

Twelfth, as should be clear from the tone of discussion so far, the notions of world society and world-systemic dynamics do not assume a condition of world community. World social relations are marked by opposition as well as consensus, competition as well as collaboration, discord as well as harmony, shared as well as divergent interests, war as well as peace. Contrary to many hopeful forecasts, globalization has not produced a cosmopolis of communitarian 'world citizens' within a 'global village' (McLuhan and Fiore 1968). The process has brought us world wars as well as Band Aid concerts. Yet we do not need to subscribe to liberal utopianism in order to acknowledge the realities of world interrelatedness. In short, when analysing transformation in terms of world social relations, we do well to follow an early student of International Relations, Nicholas Spykman, in his observation that 'the word "social" . . . gives no indication . . . as to peace or struggle' (1933: 60).

Likewise, to analyse social change from the perspective of world relations is not in itself either to endorse or to condemn the fact that history unfolds through world-systemic dynamics. Preceding remarks have made it plain that world interdependence is not by definition a good thing. World social relations do not guarantee us equality or community, although these eventualities are not logical impossibilities either. On the other hand, worldwide interdependence can be positively detrimental to one, or several, or even all of the parties involved. In this vein Theodore von Laue (1969) characterizes the 'global city' as a pretty unhappy place. In another pessimistic scenario, many environmentalists warn that global industrialism could prove ecologically disastrous for the entire human population of the earth, not to mention the planet's other species. For good or ill, then, world-systemic dynamics on a global scale are a central fact of contemporary history, and the study of social change needs to take account of that circumstance.

Finally in this long string of qualifications and disclaimers, to affirm that we have reached a state of globality does not entail saying that we have arrived at history's final resting place. Globalization has not been a linear process in the past; and it possibly could go into reverse in the future. For example, Abu-Lughod (1989) argues that the world system which had consolidated by 1250 AD was in retreat by the middle of the fourteenth century. In more recent history, an unprecedented degree of internationalization emerged in the world economy of the late nineteenth century, but the

1930s in particular saw significant declines in cross-border trade and finance (Deutsch and Eckstein 1961; Sterling 1974: 624). By the same token the current high profile of international relations in the world-systemic dynamics of social change may not be sustained indefinitely. Nevertheless, even if globalization were to lessen in the future, international relations would have to be greatly dissipated before that dimension of the transformation process became insignificant.

Clearly, then, notions of world society and world system can easily be misconstrued. Students of social change might wrongly suppose that this general orientation implies an endorsement of Wallersteinian world-system theory; that it entails a premise of international determinism; that a world social whole is unique to contemporary history; that a world society by definition encompasses the whole of humanity; that geography is irrelevant in world-systemic analysis; that all parts of a world system are evenly interconnected; that the notion of a world society assumes worldwide uniformity; that social history has followed a single course at every point in a given world-societal whole; that internationalization *ipso facto* involves centralization on a world scale; that globality has egalitarian consequences; that a world-systemic situation is reducible to its dominant parts; that world-systemic relations have communitarian implications; that globaliz-ation is intrinsically desirable; and that globalization in contemporary world society is a linear and irreversible process.

However, if we avoid these false corollaries and employ a world perspective with precision and care, then this conceptual frame of reference is useful – indeed, indispensable – for an understanding of social change. It is no small matter to reorientate our explanations of transformations away from endogenism or international determinism towards an altogether different epistemological basis in world-systemic holism. A radical break of this kind implies a wholesale revision of the way that we view society and history and suggests as well the need for a fundamental reappraisal of the strategies that we might employ in pursuit of social change.

THE INTERNATIONAL WITHIN WORLD SOCIETY

The preceding discussion has stressed that attention to international relations of social change need not and should not imply an assumption of international determinism and a disregard of local and national aspects of the transformation process. International relations can best be seen as one of several co-determining dimensions of world-systemic dynamics of continuity and change. Having so strongly asserted that international relations of social change can only be understood in terms of their interconnections with domestic circumstances, it may seem contradictory to shift the discussion in the next three chapters from world society as a whole to the international in particular. However, two justifications can be advanced for this bias.

First there is a question of compensation. As indicated in Chapter 1, studies of social change have for the most part sooner suffered from endogenism than from an 'internationalist' extreme. Local and national aspects of the transformation process are well-nigh universally recognized and require no emphasis beyond the overemphasis that they have generally been given in past investigations. In contrast, researchers have for the most part down-played the importance of the international dimension, and many have not attended to it at all. Hence there is a distinct need to establish, through more extended discussion and illustrations from the historical record, that international relations are indeed highly significant and should be duly integrated into world-systemic explanations of social change. The ultimate aim would be to dispense with even the analytical separation of the domestic and the international. This will be done in the final three chapters of this book, but at this stage an examination of the international in relative isolation can still serve the positive purpose of helping to make amends for past neglects.

A second and complementary reason for highlighting the international dimension of social transformations concerns clarification. The concept 'international relations' is often only vaguely understood in the various social sciences. Hence those social historians and historical sociologists who have sought to move beyond a national frame of reference in their accounts of social change have frequently relied on rather crude conceptions of what the international involves. Indeed, the notion 'international relations' is often used loosely even within the field of IR, where there is in addition considerable disagreement regarding the exact meaning of the term, as we saw in the first chapter. In regard to those debates we have already taken distance from statist, politicist and unit-based approaches in favour of a multiactor, multifaceted, holistic conception of international relations (recall Chapter 1, pp. 14–18). Now we need to consider more precisely the implications of that alternative conceptualization for studies of social change.

In terms of the general non-realist position outlined in Chapter 1, international relations can be seen to constitute part of world-systemic transformation processes in three broad ways. In one sense, international relations involve cross-border transfers, i.e., the movement of persons, materials and ideas across national frontiers. As such, international relations can serve as channels for the conveyance of a given social change from one country to others. Taken on its own, this notion of diffusion is largely an extension of endogenous arguments, insofar as it implies the prior unfolding of the given transformation inside a country before it is transmitted abroad. However, in two other senses international relations have other qualities which make them more than an offshoot of domestic conditions. World society includes distinctly *international* activities and distinctly *international* aspects of social order. These social events and circumstances are embedded in the international itself and are not wholly reducible to local and national circumstances (though they are not fully independent of domestic situations either). Such specifically international aspects of world-systemic dynamics can be involved in the process of rearranging patterns of social relations. For example, international forces may help to shape a locationally domestic transformation, which transnational movements in turn may spread further afield.

Needless to say, international relations in any of these three senses can tend to *impede* as well as encourage reorganizations of social life. Continuity and change coexist and interconnect in international relations as much as in any other aspect of society. (Recall the remarks in Chapter 1 concerning the interplay of persistence and transformation.) The following chapters will therefore cite instances of conservative as well as transformative impacts of cross-border movements and international forces.

The various international aspects of the transformation process are in practice intertwined. When examining actual historical scenarios we cannot neatly distinguish three different kinds of international influences, any more than we can separate distinct international, national and local causes of transformation. An event in social history usually involves transnational diffusion, international interaction and international order at the same time – and in combination with domestic circumstances as well. Nevertheless, for the purpose of demonstrating in detail the full scope of international involvement in processes of social change these three aspects are discussed below in artificially separated chapters.

$\equiv 3 \equiv$

CROSS-BORDER TRANSMISSION
OF SOCIAL CHANGE

One sense in which we can speak of 'international relations of social change' relates to the pervasiveness and significance in society of transfrontier movements. For centuries in the past, cross-boundary flows of people, goods, money, diseases, information and ideas have been sufficiently numerous, persistent, wide-ranging and important to make major impacts on national and local circumstances, as well as on the international situation itself (Burns 1924). In particular, though, the past hundred years have seen a marked intensification of transnational exchanges and an unprecedented compression of effective distance in social life across the planet. As Chadwick Alger notes, 'most people . . . now live their lives in a sea of worldwide transactions' (1988: 321).

Cross-border transfers have over the centuries provided continual opportunities for the diffusion of new patterns of social relations from one country to another. For instance, it might be argued that the emergence of modern nationalism was due, amongst other things, to the spread of that social movement from France to the rest of Europe through the wars of 1792–1815 and its extension from Europe to the wider world through colonialism and the like (Best 1988). On the other hand, transnational interventions can also stifle a potential reorganization of social relations, as Soviet policy in Eastern Europe during the period 1947–85 and one hundred years of US Government incursions into Central America have amply illustrated (Wolfe 1970; LaFeber 1983). The possibilities for the cross-boundary delivery to foreign parts of spurs and/or inhibitions to social change have become especially great in the globalized world society of the twentieth century, with the growth of a dense network of transnational institutions and the construction of a huge cross-border transport and communications infrastructure.

TRANSNATIONAL INSTITUTIONAL LINKS

A variety of institutional links across frontiers have long provided conduits for the cross-boundary transmission of social change. For example, national states have since their beginnings maintained contacts with one another through diplomatic channels, and multilateral conference diplomacy has been a regular feature of the world scene since the Congress of Vienna in 1814–15 (Langhorne 1981–2; 1992). More recent times have in addition seen a growth of so-called 'transgovernmental' interchange between traditionally 'domestic' ministries such as departments of justice, finance, health and the like (Nye 1975; Hopkins 1976). Provincial and municipal governments, too, have increasingly conducted their own 'foreign policies', separately from central national authorities (Duchacek 1988). Permanent intergovernmental organizations (IGOs) have added a further dimension to links between national states since the early nineteenth century, when international river commissions began operating in Europe (Chamberlain 1923). IGOs have since then proliferated at a generally accelerating rate, particularly after the creation of the United Nations and a host of other global bodies in the middle of the present century (Wallace and Singer 1970). Outside official circles, international non-governmental organizations (INGOs) have long fostered cross-border contact between non-official groups with shared concerns and objectives (White 1951). For instance, transfrontier collaboration in the anti-slavery campaign began amongst the Quakers in the eighteenth century (Bolt 1969: Ch 1); cross-national peace movements have flowered periodically since the middle of the nineteenth century (Beales 1931; Calvocoressi 1987); and the first international secretariats of trade unions date from 1889 (Lorwin 1953). One source calculates that the great majority of the nearly 3000 international gatherings held between 1840 and 1914 were of a non-governmental nature (Northedge 1986: 16). Meanwhile, transnationally organized firms have existed since at least the twelfth century, when banks and merchant houses of the Italian city-states operated branches across the European continent (Braudel 1979a: 390–5). Two hundred years later the English, Dutch, French and Danish East India Companies and other trading enterprises maintained networks of headquarters and overseas posts. International manufacturing concerns date back to 1852, when the US-based revolver producer, Colt, opened a factory in Britain (Stopford and Strange 1991: 13).

Today institutional frameworks for cross-border contact are phenomenal in number. By one fairly conservative count, there were as of the early 1980s close to 700 IGOs, which between them were convening almost 5000 meetings per year (Jacobson 1984: 4, 9). Over 17,000 INGOs were active in the mid-1980s, including cross-border associations in the professions, international federations of political parties, transnational academic bodies, cross-boundary pressure groups on a host of specific issues, international foundations and other service organizations, and so on (Skjelsbaek 1971; UIA 1987: Appendix 7). In addition, more than 35,000 transnational corporations (TNCs) with some 150,000 foreign subsidiaries between them were operating in 1990 (UNCTC 1992: 11; also Dunning and Cantwell 1987). That year saw a record annual outflow of new direct investment from 'home' to 'host' countries of US $222 billion (BIS 1992: 93). TNCs (often also called multinational corporations)[1] have become involved in every field of business enterprise from agriculture to retail trade, and from accountancy firms to advertising agencies. Moreover, these companies now originate not only from North America, Western Europe and Japan; around 4000 have their head offices in ex-colonial and former communist-ruled countries (respectively, UNCTC 1992: 12; Khan 1986; McMillan 1987).

Transnational institutions have often facilitated the transmission of social change from one country to others. For instance, a network of imperial administration encouraged the spread of Roman social innovations across Europe some 2000 years ago. More recently, colonial extensions of European, Japanese and American governments facilitated the diffusion of structures of modernity (nationality, capitalism, bureaucracy, etc.) to occupied areas in Asia, Africa, the Caribbean and the Pacific (Albertini 1982b). Likewise, overseas offices of the United States Government helped to effect an 'Americanization' of social life in Western Europe and Japan in the aftermath of the Second World War (Schonberger 1989; Willett 1989). To illustrate the conveyance of change through intergovernmental institutions, we may note that bodies such as the United Nations Development Programme (UNDP), the Food and Agriculture Organization (FAO) and the World Bank have, with a male bias in their development aid projects, promoted a transfer of patriarchal patterns to a number of recipient countries: for example, by fostering a shift from matrilineal or bilateral patterns of land tenure to a patrilineal principle of inheritance (Rogers 1980; Elson 1991). Cases of the cross-boundary spread of social change through INGOs include efforts of the Communist International (in existence from 1919 until 1943) to export the Bolshevik model of social revolution from Soviet Russia to many other countries (Drachkovitch 1966); and the role of organizations such as Amnesty International in bringing liberal notions of human rights to all corners of the globe. In respect of TNCs, a number of researchers have suggested that, for instance, transnational electronics and mass media companies have served to export dominant cultural forms from North America and Europe to parts of the world where these structures of meaning did not previously hold sway (e.g., Mattelart 1976; Hamelink 1983).

On the other hand, cross-border institutional links can also carry *checks* on moves for social change from one country to another. For example, the US Central Intelligence Agency (CIA) has, since its establishment in 1947, frustrated attempts to reorganize social relations in numerous foreign lands (e.g., Immerman 1982). In relation to IGOs, various critics have charged that the International Monetary Fund (IMF) has through its 'stabilization programmes' transmitted conservative policies from leading capitalist states to countries that might otherwise have been ripe for transformation (e.g., Brett 1983; Onimode 1989). INGOs, too, can transpose constraints on social change from one country to the next, as has arguably occurred through international churches on many (though by no means all) occasions in modern times. As for TNCs, there is well-established evidence of measures taken during the early 1970s by the International Telephone and Telegraph Corporation (ITT) to thwart the change-minded Allende government in Chile (Sampson 1973: Ch 11).

CROSS-BORDER TRAVEL

Transnational movements may spread social transformations through less formally organized channels as well, for example, through cross-frontier travel by people. The itinerant religious teachers, holy warriors and traders who centuries ago disseminated Christianity and Islam far from their points of origin constitute an early instance of this form of transmission. Transport difficulties inhibited long-distance travel in previous epochs, of course; but on the other hand an international regime of travel documents and passport controls was not instituted to check cross-border movements until the 1920s (Turack 1972). Moreover, the world knew no legislated immigration restrictions until the second half of the nineteenth century, when the governments of Australia, New Zealand, Canada and the US began to exclude poor and/or non-white would-be settlers (Tinker 1977: 18–20).

Even with tighter border controls, however, transboundary movements of people have continued to encourage the diffusion of social change in the current era of globalized world relations. For example, in the first half of the twentieth century, colonial troops who fought in the world wars, together with youth from the overseas empires who studied in the metropoles, often returned to Africa, Asia and the Caribbean with newly acquired 'Western' ideas that helped to fuel the decolonization process (Albertini 1982a: Ch 1). At the present time, large cross-border flows of labour constitute a major potential conduit for the transmission of new social patterns from a given local or national setting to external areas. Such migrations involved over thirty million new residents in Western Europe, the USA and South Africa alone as of the 1970s (Cohen 1987: 30). International refugees, of whom there were some sixteen million scattered throughout the world in the 1980s, further reduce the effectiveness of national-state boundaries as a check on the spread of social changes (Loescher and Monahan 1989: 54). In addition, over one million students were enrolled for higher education degrees outside their country of permanent residence at the end of the 1980s, up from a total of 600,000 fifteen years earlier (UNESCO 1982: 17; UNESCO 1991: Table 3.15). Short-term cross-border student exchanges and the plethora of international academic conferences further increase opportunities for the diffusion of new knowledge and the social changes which that learning might encourage. Many other people cross frontiers as tourists: an estimated 425 million travellers worldwide took vacations abroad in 1990 (WTO 1991: 11). In the same year some 275 million holidaymakers and other passengers crossed national borders on scheduled air services alone (i.e., exclusive of charter flights) (ICAO 1991: 19). Indeed, the late twentieth century is seeing the advent of the transoceanic commuter. Furthermore, given the widespread incidence of international warfare and the existence of foreign military bases in over half of the countries of the world, there is much occasion for soldiers deployed abroad to carry new social patterns from one part of the globe to another – as well as to counter moves for change abroad by their interventions (Sivard 1986: 10–11, 26–7). For example, the Japanese military had a considerable effect during the Second World War in remodelling social life in the direction of a Nipponese pattern in many of the areas of Asia that temporarily fell under their rule (Newell 1981).

CROSS-BORDER COMMUNICATIONS

In addition to, and often in conjunction with, transnational institutions and cross-border traffic of people, mechanized communications networks provide a further means of carrying social changes between countries. Information technologies permit the long-distance conveyance of social facts through signs and symbols. In this way new features of social life can spread to many countries even in the absence of human travel and face-to-face contact between persons from different corners of the globe.

The advent of print technology provided the first major stimulus to large-scale international dissemination of information. The invention of movable type in China as early as the ninth century, and in Europe 600 years later, encouraged the growth of cross-border flows of the written word through books, pamphlets and subsequently newspapers. In the absence of patent laws, printing presses were set up in 110 towns throughout Europe within twenty-five years after the appearance of the Gutenberg Bible in 1456. At least 150–200 million books were printed during the sixteenth century, contributing to the transnational spread of social movements including the Renaissance and the Reformation (Febvre and Martin 1958: 182, 262). Mass circulation of printed material developed after steam-driven and rotary presses became available in the first half of the nineteenth century, and the international book trade ensured that publications could be distributed far beyond domestic markets. Regular cross-border postal deliveries also multiplied during this period, and the completion of transoceanic cables from 1858 onwards dramatically increased the speed with which messages could be conveyed between continents. International news agencies appeared with the establishment of Associated Press in 1848, Reuters in 1851 and a dozen other such firms during the ensuing decades (Kurian 1982: 1134–7).

The twentieth century has brought major advances in audio and visual information technology which largely overcome the restrictions that illiteracy has placed on cross-border communication through the medium of print (Pool 1990; Tehranian 1990; Thompson 1990: 182–205). The telephone, invented in 1876, has now been installed at some 500 million connection points throughout the world (ATT 1982: 13), and the recent introduction of satellite links and international direct dialling have facilitated a growth of cross-border telephone calls to a worldwide total of well over three billion per annum (ITU 1990).[2] The first wireless transmissions between countries were made across the English Channel in 1899 and over the Atlantic Ocean in 1901. Scheduled intercontinental radio broadcasts were initiated in 1929, only nine years after station programming had begun inside national boundaries (Huth 1937). In the late 1980s more than 120 million people throughout the world (excluding China) were listening regularly to the BBC External Services (BBC 1987b), while the Voice of America claimed in the early 1980s to have a core audience of 104 million listeners (Mowlana 1986: 59). Transfrontier radio transmissions by thirty-one official broadcasting agencies (thus excluding commercial stations) totalled well over 15,000 programme hours per week in June 1986 (BBC 1987a: 180). Meanwhile, cross-border trade in film has expanded hand in hand with the growth of the motion picture industry since the early twentieth century, conveying images of social life in one part of the world to audiences at widely scattered foreign locations (K. Thompson 1985). The first transatlantic transmission of pictures by television was achieved in 1928, only three years after the invention of that device (Dizard 1966: 258). By the early 1970s over 200,000 hours of television programmes were annually being exported across national boundaries (Nordenstreng and Varis 1974: Ch 3). American and adapted versions of the show *Sesame Street* have been viewed in fourteen languages across 115 countries (Gettas 1990). Many countries receive more than half of their TV output from abroad, and as of 1983–4 the worldwide average import share was around one-third of total programme time (Lee 1979: Appendix A; Varis 1985: 53). Moreover, using direct broadcast satellites (DBS) televised information can today reach a global audience almost instantaneously around the clock. Television has thus come as close as any medium to uniting the whole of humankind; aerials today ascend even from such unlikely places as the underground sand dwellings of Malmata at the edge of the Sahara Desert. Other electronic media such as audiocassettes, video cassette recorders and compact discs have in recent years further facilitated the cross-border transmission of image and sound.

Finally, digital technologies have in recent decades greatly increased the possibilities for cross-border exchanges of information. Computers offer previously unimaginable potentials for data storage, and, with the introduction of optical fibres in place of copper cables, long-distance transmission has markedly improved, too. Now Integrated Services Digital Networks (ISDN) permit connections to be maintained between various types of communications equipment, including telephones, computers and fax machines. Although we must be careful not to overestimate their capacities, transnational computer networks today allow firms, governments, academics and others to conduct hundreds of millions of cross-border information transactions each year (Mowlana 1986: Ch 5; Sauvant 1986; Goodman 1991).

In this age of mass communications and advanced microelectronic technologies, information concerning social change can be transmitted across borders with unprecedented rapidity and intensity. For example, news of steps to dismantle state socialism spread quickly between the countries of Central and Eastern Europe in the late 1980s, helping to stimulate a 'domino effect' of a quite different kind than anti-communist cold warriors had once feared. Within months, moves towards multiparty elections were also in train in many countries of Africa. Similarly, mass media instantly internationalized news of Ayatollah Khomeini's *fatwa* on Salman Rushdie in 1988, feeding a rapid cross-border chain reaction of Muslim demonstrations against *The Satanic Verses*. Student protesters of 1968 in the USA, China, Western Europe and Czechoslovakia were also quickly aware of and inspired by one another's activity. Some thirty years earlier, reports of foreign examples helped to trigger fascist agitation across Europe, in some Latin American countries and in certain colonies (Laqueur 1976; Wal 1968). Present-day information technology has allowed news of a remote local campaign for social change, such as that pursued by Chico Mendes and the rubber tappers of the Brazilian interior, to spread worldwide and encourage environmentalist movements in many countries (Mendes 1989).

CROSS-BORDER COMMERCE

Cross-boundary transfers of goods and finance may serve to transmit social change abroad, too. According to one calculation, transnational trade in primary materials and manufactures was already flowing at a rate of US $2.31 per capita in the year 1800 (in terms of then-current dollar values) (Day 1922: 271). By 1980 the money value of international exports totalled US$ 1855.7 billion worldwide, equivalent to 21.2 per cent of global GNP (Ushiba *et al.* 1983: 83). Arrivals of new types of goods from other countries have in some instances brought with them an impulse for notable changes in social organization. For example, the shipment of a mechanical clock from Arabia to the Holy Roman Empire in the ninth century helped to create a revised conception and role of time in social life in Europe (Cipolla 1967: 7, 25). In another case, international arms transfers, which began in the fifteenth century and became especially prominent from the 1860s onwards, have facilitated the global spread of militarism (McNeill 1982: 241, 354–7).

As for financial transfers, cross-frontier loans were issued by banks in the Italian city-states as early as the fifteenth century (Braudel 1979a: 393; 1979b: Ch 2). Stock market slumps readily spread from one country to the next in the Great Depression of 1873–96. Today a multitude of transboundary grants and credits are meant to induce social change through the spread of a particular form of 'development' from rich to poor countries. More will be said about finance in the discussion of international interdependence in the next chapter.

In sum, then, cross-border movements have long figured in social relations and have become especially pervasive during the past century. In this sense, as well as others discussed in the following two chapters, international relations do, in the words of Stanley Hoffmann, constitute 'the very condition of our daily life' (1960: 4). Together, the various kinds of transnational flows discussed above have provided countless means by which social transformations can spread to widely dispersed locations in world society. Indeed, the intensity of cross-boundary transfers makes it unlikely that a given reconstruction of the social order will remain confined to a single country.

=4=

INTERNATIONAL ACTIVITY AND SOCIAL CHANGE

Significant as cross-border transmissions of social change may be, the involvement of international relations in the dynamics of transformation does not stop there. As noted earlier, we can conceive of international relations as entailing not only movements across national boundaries, but also forces that reside in transnational events and circumstances per se. Accordingly, international relations do more than transport rearrangements of social life from one country to another; the international also has a prior significance of its own, with relative autonomy from domestic contexts, which can help both to induce a discontinuity in history and to mould the character of the consequent social change.

Many circumstances of social life are quite evidently not entirely reducible to national or local conditions. Take, hypothetically, a radio set that is constructed with, say, minerals from Zaïre, electrical components from Japan, plastics technology developed in Germany, and assembly-line labour in Malaysia. Should we say that the resulting apparatus is 'made in Zaïre', 'made in Japan', 'made in Germany' or 'made in Malaysia'? The receiver is in effect a product of all of these countries – but it is also more than an aggregation of the various national inputs. Like countless other goods, this radio is in part an international commodity: although manufacture was undertaken in several countries, the connections and coordination between those countries were just as vital to the construction of the appliance as the different national contributions. Without international relations, this radio set would not have come into existence.

Extending this general point to the issue of social change, we may suggest that this 'production process', too, combines distinctly international forces with domestic inputs. The specifically international nature of the transformation process is examined in this book from two angles: namely, in terms of international actors and cross-boundary interactions on the one hand; and in terms of international order on the other hand. In the first of these two senses, which is discussed in the present chapter, international relations can be important insofar as transnational units and interchanges between actors in different countries can help to shape the course of social change. In the second sense, which is the subject of Chapter 5, forces connected with the organizing principles of international relations may influence the incidence and direction of social transformations. Again, it needs to be stressed that international activity and international order are being considered under separate chapter headings for analytical purposes only. As I will argue at greater length in Chapter 7, these two aspects of international social forces – action and order – are in practice interrelated and mutually determining. In the meantime, the involvement of international activity in the process of social change is examined in the current chapter with regard to, first, international actors (i.e., persons and groups who span across or move between different countries) and, second, the international interdependence that is established through transfrontier interactions.

INTERNATIONAL ACTORS

The large-scale transnationalization of institutions was noted at some length in Chapter 3, but at that juncture these organizations were considered only as intermediaries for the cross-border transmission of social change. Yet transnational corporations, international non-governmental organizations and intergovernmental agencies have a character and significance that amounts to more than just a reflection and extension of social forces emanating from the countries out of which participants in these bodies are drawn. Thus these institutions can be positively involved in the transform-ation process as actors in their own right.

For one thing, it certainly seems reasonable to posit that transnational corporations can count as international actors, i.e., as behavioural units in world society which have a degree of independence from forces in both their 'home' and their 'host' countries. The book value of foreign direct investment (FDI) increased little during the first sixty years of the twentieth century, but then expanded at twice the rate of GNP growth of the OECD countries in the 1960s and more than four times as fast as national incomes during the 1980s (Julius 1990: 6).[1] By 1988 the world total of accumulated stock of FDI was estimated to be US$ 1040 billion (Stopford and Strange 1991: 17). Already in the 1970s transnational corporations were accounting for over one-third of world industrial output (Vernon 1977: 15); and product sales by TNC affiliates, at an estimated US$ 4.4 trillion in 1989, now surpass the value of cross-border movements of goods between national firms, at some US$ 2.5 trillion (UNCTC 1992: 54). Indeed, the biggest individual TNCs have come to sustain levels of worldwide sales which well exceed the gross domestic products of many national economies, topped in 1984 by Exxon's total turnover of US$ 73.6 billion (Jenkins 1987: 9).[2] Smaller as well as larger international companies often have access to technological innovations, managerial expertise, financial resources and stores of data that are not available to local and national actors. Decisions by TNCs to invest or to relocate in another country can sustain or frustrate national economic development plans. Transfer-pricing accounting techniques allow these companies to reduce tax liabilities by 'exporting' their earnings from the country where the profit was made to the balance sheet in another jurisdiction where taxation rates are lower (Murray 1981). In addition, large-scale movements of money and goods by TNCs can deeply affect a country's balance of payments. By the 1980s transnational companies conducted some three-quarters of world trade outside the centrally planned economies (King 1990a: 15). These statistics are not a direct measure of influence, of course, insofar as resources do not maintain a one-to-one relationship with power. Moreover, TNCs remain subject to varying degrees of national regulation, and host governments in principle have the option to nationalize the local subsidiary of an international corporation. However, such expropriations have in practice occurred only rarely, and TNCs by no means fall under full national control.

Given their substantial capacities, transnational corporations have in many situations markedly influenced the course of social development. For instance, it is arguable that, to refer back to a previously cited example, ITT was acting in part as an *international* corporate entity when it opposed the Allende regime in Chile, i.e., not merely as a national company, in the form of the Chilean subsidiary or the US parent firm. Likewise, the international oil giants charted their own path between oil-exporting and oil-importing countries during struggles in the mid-1970s over the world petroleum market and the wider global economic order (Sampson 1975: Chs 12–13). In regard to another question of social change, pressure from international banks, coupled with large-scale disinvestment by manufacturing TNCs, has encouraged the current retreat from legalized racial segregation and discrimination in South Africa (Ovenden and Cole 1989). In the Indonesian Revolution nearly half a century ago, the activities of a number of TNCs – including several companies based in the Netherlands – lent strength to nationalist forces in their struggle to remove Dutch colonial rule from South East Asia (Scholte 1990: 375–8). Shifting our focus to recent events in China, we might ask whether international mass media companies not only reported, but through their actions also positively fuelled the student demonstrations at Tiananmen Square in 1989 (cf. Shapiro 1989). Each of these scenarios suggests that TNC participation in a process of social change can have a specifically international quality (cf. Villamil 1979).

INGOs, too, have in various instances figured as a distinctly international force of social transformation, i.e., with some degree of autonomy from national and local conditions. Many of these organizations attach only secondary importance to territoriality, operating on the principle of 'human association by "affinity" rather than "vicinity"' (Tehranian 1990: 13). Some INGOs are what Johan Galtung (1980) prefers to call TRANGOs (transnational non-governmental organizations), in that they coordinate the activities of individuals and groups without dividing the membership into national branches. Yet even when an INGO takes the form of a coalition of country-based bodies, it often derives its main impetus from an issue concern and an action network that transcend national boundaries.

Transnationalism of this kind has arisen in a host of social movements. For example, international campaigns to secure laws permitting abortion have put questions of a woman's right to choose and population control before concerns about nationality and locality (Francome 1984). The Organization of the Islamic Conference, too, has since its creation in 1969 drawn together an international constituency: in this case in order to promote traditionalist forms of the Muslim faith (Levtzion 1979). Indeed, orthodox Islamic doctrine recognizes no concept of nationality and places the significance of the *umma*, the worldwide community of Muslims, before any other group affiliation (cf. Piscatori 1986). Another INGO, Greenpeace, has deployed international teams which crusade against environmental degradation and inhumane slaughter of animals, irrespective of the geographical location of the offence or the nationality of the perpetrators. Nor has the International Commission of Jurists been identified with any particular country in its enquiries into human rights questions. Even a movement with a definite national and territorial orientation such as the Palestine Liberation Organization has in practice had a transnational character, insofar as the diaspora of Palestinians has in effect internationalized locality (cf. Appadurai 1990). Other instances of 'international nationalism' (Day 1967) include the activities of the World Zionist Congress since 1897, the South West Africa People's Organization (SWAPO) between 1959 and 1990, the Revolutionary Front for the Independence of East Timor (Fretilin) since 1974, and various other transnational associations. In these and countless other cases, INGO activities to promote or hinder social change cannot be described or accounted for wholly in national and local terms: they also have an irreducible international quality (cf. Willetts 1982).

This notion of a distinctly international character applies to intergovernmental organizations as well. Conventional realist wisdom holds that IGOs are no more than a policy instrument of national states, and as such they would have no significance of their own in questions of social change (cf. Claude 1971; James 1976). It is true that, by the letter of their charters, most of these institutions formally have no power beyond that which their member states are willing to accord to them. However, IGOs have their own staffs (in some cases running into thousands of international civil servants) who might take initiatives in pursuit of one or the other social transformation. Several of these bodies moreover have their own means of covering running costs, independently from contributions by national states. IGOs also have an autonomous significance insofar as they perform operations that their members on their own could accomplish only with difficulty, if at all. Thus, for example, the Universal Postal Union greatly facilitates cross-border postal flows, the World Meteorological Organization prepares global weather forecasts, the UN High Commissioner for Refugees coordinates the execution of a number of international relief operations, and so on. In addition, involvement in an IGO often leads member governments to take measures that they would not have initiated by themselves. In other words, the international agency as a framework for taking and implementing decisions has a certain life of its own: not only do the members shape the institution, but the IGO's procedural rules, organizational ethos and the like also affect the parties who interact in the international forum (Cox and Jacobson 1973).

Thus intergovernmental organizations can exert a distinct – albeit not wholly independent – influence on the course of social change. For example, organs of the United Nations have encouraged the decolonization process in a number of instances: namely by passing formal resolutions, by recognizing national liberation movements, by undertaking official investigations, by sponsoring plebescites, by despatching observers and peacekeeping contingents, by issuing judgements through the International Court of Justice, by imposing commercial sanctions, and so on (Luard 1989). Within a regional framework, rulings by the European Court of Human Rights have constrained *inter alia* the British Government to alter several national statutes that discriminate according to sex. Meanwhile, initiatives in the 1970s towards the creation of a New International Economic Order gained a high profile in large part due to pressure from the so-called 'Third World coalition' through intergovernmental institutions such as the United Nations Conference on Trade and Development (UNCTAD) (Mortimer 1984; Williams 1991). In all of these cases IGOs have themselves given an impetus towards change, even if the intended transformation has not always come to pass. We will return to these issues in the discussion of international regimes in Chapter 5.

Other international actors can contribute to the process of social change without being bureaucratically organized in the way of TNCs, INGOs and IGOs. For example, a cross-border movement of population may do more than extend a particular transformation from the country of origin to the country of resettlement: the migration itself may help to induce a fundamental rearrangement of social relations. Thus the decline of Amerindian social formations in the western hemisphere several hundred years ago was due in large part to the migration of settlers from Europe in combination with the slave trade which forcibly brought some 8–10.5 million people across the Atlantic from Africa (Curtin 1969: 87). Likewise, the course of world economic development in the second half of the nineteenth century was significantly shaped by the migration of about fifty million people from

Europe to the Americas, Australasia and South Africa; and by the movement of around the same number of labourers from India and China to various destinations in the tropics (Lewis 1978: 14).

In addition, instances arise when an individual who has no particular institutional affiliation may contribute through her or his international action to social change. For example, Mahatma Gandhi took his campaigns for transformations to South Africa, India and Britain, and his method of *satyagraha* gained adherents in a variety of other social movements at far-flung corners of the globe. Roving lone revolutionaries have occasionally gathered followings in a succession of countries: for example, Tan Malaka in Asia between the 1920s and 1940s; and Che Guevara on several continents during the 1950s and 1960s (Sinclair 1970; Mrázek 1972). Moreover, numerous authors have inspired strivings for social change through their publications and international speaking tours. For instance, black aspirations articulated in writings of the 1920s Harlem Renaissance gave heart to Africanist movements in the Caribbean, North America, Europe and Africa itself (Bontemps 1972). Amin al-Rihani, Sami Shawkat and other intellectuals encouraged the rise of Pan-Arabism in the 1930s and 1940s (Mansfield 1976: 263–7). Herbert Marcuse and other philosophers of the New Left spurred anti-establishment activism in the 1960s, and a host of internationally renowned feminist authors have in recent decades added impetus to the women's movement worldwide.

None of the preceding comments are meant to imply that international actors exercise an overriding power above all other persons and groups in the process of social change. Claims that, say, TNCs have attained full control of the world with their 'global reach' are exaggerated (Barnet and Müller 1974). Nor is it being suggested here that the strivings of international actors are always successful in effecting a reorganization of society. Clearly many INGO campaigns and IGO initiatives have ended in frustration. On the other hand, a student of social change would be equally mistaken to overlook – as many researchers have done to date – the frequently important role of international actors in world-systemic dynamics of transformation.

INTERNATIONAL INTERDEPENDENCE

The distinctly international aspect of the process of social change entails more than the influence of international actors, though; circumstances of international interdependence can also provide important stimuli to transformations. In a word, 'interdependence' denotes a relationship in which transactions between two or more parties affect the condition of each of the participants. In a condition of interdependence, it is not merely the characteristics of the interacting units individually, but also their mutual involvement with one another that shapes their respective situations. Already in the middle of the nineteenth century, Marx and Engels perceived a 'universal inter-dependence of nations' (1848: 64), a circumstance that has become all the more extensive and entrenched during the hundred and fifty years since they made that observation. Of particular interest to us here is the suggestion that this interdependence may help to instigate and shape a process of social reconstruction. In such instances domestic as well as international situations develop as they do to a substantial degree because of international connections that tie different countries together. For better or for worse, then, international interlinkages of various kinds – including ecological, commercial, industrial, monetary, financial, ideological, diplomatic, military and recreational interdependencies – often deeply mould the course of social history, as the following pages indicate.

Ecological interdependence is one obvious example of the international interconnectedness of national and local populaces. Harmful gases, hazardous solid wastes, radioactive fallout and marine pollution can, through transfrontier movements, produce ecological nightmares far from the point of original emission. Such scenarios have unfolded in recent years in relation to the depletion of stratospheric ozone, the *Karen B* affair, the Chernobyl accident and the Sandoz chemical spill into the Rhine. Indeed, these and other international mishaps have encouraged the rapid worldwide expansion of environmentalist movements ranging from global associations to very localized initiatives such as the *Chipko* ('hug the tree') peasant resistance to commercial forestry in the Himalaya (Guha 1989; McCormick 1989; Caldwell 1991). Whether these efforts will yield the intended reorganizations of social life remains to be seen. In any case, future shifts in the global climate, loss of biodiversity and massive growth of the planet's human population will, if they transpire as forecast, no doubt have significant repercussions, catastrophic or otherwise, for social development.

International circulation of infectious diseases is another aspect of ecological interdependence which has over the centuries affected processes of social change in a number of contexts. For example, when Mongol expansions from Central Asia brought bubonic plague to China, India, the Middle East and Europe in the fourteenth century, the resulting epidemics helped to induce, *inter alia*, a number of major migrations, various increases in social tensions, shifts in language patterns, and changes in religious practices (McNeill 1976: Ch 4). Two hundred years later, smallpox and other diseases taken from Europe to the western hemisphere contributed to the collapse of Aztec and Inca civilizations in the Americas (McNeill 1976: Ch 5). The currently unfolding global AIDS epidemic may well have social consequences including shifts in sexual behaviour, greater visibility of (and perhaps increased discrimination against) homosexuality, and so on.

Trade is another aspect of international interdependence that figured in the process of social transformation well before the twentieth century. For example, imports of bullion from the Americas, Africa and Siberia between the sixteenth and eighteenth centuries were important to the growth of the money economy in Europe (Braudel 1979b: Ch 5). Karl Marx on a number of occasions argued that long-distance commerce played a significant role in 'destroying the feudal fetters on production' and creating 'the dawn of the era of capitalist production' (1894: 332–3; 1867: 751; also Marx and Engels 1846: 74–5).[3] Concerning a related social change, Daniel Chirot (1986) notes that in the eighteenth and nineteenth centuries international trade helped to stimulate and carry forward the Industrial Revolution. In addition, strivings in Western Europe, the USA and Japan to secure export markets and overseas supplies of primary commodities contributed to an emergence of capitalism in some occupied countries during the era of colonialism (Alavi et al. 1982). Researchers have argued at length about whether international trade constituted a *necessary* precondition for the occurrence of the changes just described. However, we do not have to resolve those debates to note that, in the event, commercial interdependence has played a role in these and other transformations.

Mutual involvement of countries through trading activities remains highly significant in contemporary history, of course. Although, as noted in Chapter 3, only about one-fifth of total world production crosses national boundaries, much of the four-fifths that does not leave domestic confines is in some way directly dependent on transfrontier exchanges of raw materials, equipment, knowledge, labour and other indispensable factors of production. For example, as of 1973 international shipments by sea provided three-fifths of world supplies of oil, the fuel which at that time covered almost half of global energy demand (Ferrier and Fursenko 1989: xi–xii). Recognizing that restrictions on these deliveries would have critical reverberations for the whole of the economy, the Organization of Petroleum Exporting Countries (OPEC) and the wider Third World Coalition sought to exploit this dependence in order to change the international economic order. In the event, however, the ultimate effect of OPEC initiatives of the 1970s has perhaps been to deepen underdevelopment of the poorest countries through higher oil import bills and an increased burden of international debt brought on amongst other things by the glut of petrodollars (George 1989).

Recent decades have also seen the emergence of cross-border trade within the manufacturing process itself, giving rise to direct international industrial interdependence. This kind of production is generally organized by locating the more technologically advanced stages of the process in older industrialized countries, while assembly operations are conducted using low-cost labour in poor countries. So-called 'global factories' have emerged especially in the motor vehicle, clothing and electronics sectors (Grunwald and Flamm 1985; Jenkins 1985; Henderson 1989). The consequences of this new form of interdependence in regard to social change have included: an expansion of manufacturing activities in what are widely termed the newly industrializing countries (NICs); a decline in union bargaining power in the older industrial centres; and a growing body of non-unionized poorly paid women workers on assembly lines in both of these areas (Fröbel *et al.* 1977; Mitter 1986).

International interdependence has also been sealed over the centuries through money. Indeed, national monetary sovereignty, i.e., the monopoly of a single currency over commerce within a domestic jurisdiction, was unknown before the nineteenth century; until then foreign coins generally circulated without legal restriction alongside local pieces in a national economy (Cipolla 1956: 14). A succession of 'dollars of the Middle Ages' held the dominant position as international monies of the Mediterranean world: namely, the Byzantine *solidus* from the fifth to seventh centuries; the Muslim *dinar* in combination with the *solidus* from the eighth to the middle of the thirteenth century; the *fiorino* of Florence during the next hundred and fifty years; and the *ducato* of Venice in the fifteenth century (Cipolla 1956: Ch 2). Some cross-currency trade in coins took place in medieval Europe, but large-scale exchanges of national monies began mainly after the consolidation of a worldwide international gold standard in the latter decades of the nineteenth century (DeCecco 1974; Kenwood and Lougheed 1983). Yet by the end of 1913 official foreign exchange holdings throughout the world still had a total value of only around US$ 1 billion (Cohen 1977: 284). Exchange controls during the two world wars, unstable exchange rates in the 1920s, and widespread resort to autarkic policies in the 1930s limited international money transactions in the first half of the twentieth century. However, when the Bretton Woods framework, adopted at the United Nations Monetary and Financial Conference in 1944, was fully implemented in the late 1950s, it triggered large-scale international use of the main convertible currencies, especially the United States dollar (Tew 1985). The world total of foreign exchange reserves rose as a result to around US$ 100 billion by 1970 (Spero 1990: 41), and two decades later, in 1992, an estimated US$880 billion of foreign exchange transactions were being conducted globally *each day* (BIS 1993: 196; also Strange 1986). This expansion in international money dealings parallelled the growth of the so-called Eurocurrency markets: that is, banking and other financial dealings which use national currencies outside their country of origin (Johnston 1983). In addition, for the first time in history, distinct international monetary units, managed by international authorities rather than national central banks, appeared with the creation of the Special Drawing Right (SDR) through the IMF in 1968 and the inauguration of the European Currency Unit (ECU) through the European Community (EC) in 1978.

The significance of international monetary interdependence has frequently extended beyond effects on inflation rates and the like to influence shifts in the patterns of social organization, too. Indeed, the use of coins in long-distance trade during the Middle Ages provided much of the basis for the subsequent wholesale monetization of social life in Europe. Local commerce was conducted mainly by barter after the fall of the Roman Empire, so had it not been for long-range trade money pieces might have become an archaeologist's curiosity (Cipolla 1956: Ch 1). In our own century, meanwhile, a volatile international monetary situation arguably contributed to the outbreak of each of the two world wars and, by extension, to the various social changes to which those hostilities gave rise (De Cecco 1974: Ch 7; Aldcroft 1977). The weakened international position of the US dollar was among the circumstances that constrained the American Government to withdraw its troops from Indochina in 1969–73 and thereby aided the subsequent communist triumphs in Cambodia and southern Vietnam (Kolko 1985: 285–92, 313–15, 349–51). At the present time, fears that a single European currency and European central bank will undermine national institutions – and indeed national identity itself – are helping to hold back the advent of monetary union within the EC.

International financial interdependence extends beyond money itself to various pecuniary activities such as banking, share dealing, lending, income payments and insurance; and these affairs have long had important implications for social change as well. Modern cross-border financial activities can be dated back to the previously mentioned prototypical international banks of Renaissance Italy. Transnational brokerage firms including Hope & Co. and Barings linked stock exchanges of Western Europe together as early as the eighteenth century (Born 1977). Karl Polanyi describes *haute finance* as having been one of the four pillars of international order in the nineteenth century, so that, amongst other things, the international situation often strongly influenced interest rates in the various countries (1944: 9–14). By the 1880s banks based in the City of London maintained hundreds of branches in foreign lands and in the British Empire, a number that grew to over 5600 by 1914 (Baster 1929; 1935; Teichova *et al.* 1986: 233). Further internationalization of finance after the First World War prompted national central banks to institute regular mutual consultations in 1930 through a newly created Bank for International Settlements (BIS).

Yet the trend towards financial globalization has principally unfolded during the past two decades, much aided by the introduction of advanced computer technologies. For instance, international bond issues with a total value of US$ 167.3 billion were issued through the Eurocurrency markets in the single year 1985 (Gill and Law 1988: 151). Cross-border lending has also risen to unprecedented levels, as commercial banks alone (i.e., excluding public-sector institutions) arranged an average of more than US$ 300 billion per annum in new international loans during the period 1987–91 (BIS 1992: 160). As of 1988 countries of the South owed externally based financial institutions the equivalent of some US$ 1320 billion (Spero 1990: 52). The United States Government, too, now finds that a large part of its accumulated debt is underwritten by investors who reside outside the USA. Indeed, the Saudi, Kuwaiti, Japanese and German governments financed 88 per cent of the cost of US military operations against the Iraqi occupation of Kuwait in 1990–1 (Freeman 1991: 159; *New York Times*, 17 January 1993: 7). The 1980s saw the advent of twenty-four hour global share dealing; already by 1984 more than 2700 companies were listed on stock exchanges outside their base country (Hamilton 1986: 181; O'Brien 1992: Ch 5). Given this tight international interlinkage of stock markets, a major fall in share prices on Wall Street in October 1987 turned overnight into a global tailspin. Less impressive in terms of absolute figures, but no less significant for the people involved, transnational repatriation of earnings by migrant labourers is crucial to the lives of millions of families in, among other places, the Indian Subcontinent, Mexico, Southern Africa and countries bordering the Mediterranean (Cohen 1987). All told, the monetary value of financial flows between countries is now some fifty times greater than that of cross-border flows of goods (Spero 1990: 50; also Drucker 1986: 782).

Both in earlier periods and in the current era of globalization, international financial interdependence of the kinds just described has on various occasions figured strongly in transformation processes. For instance, Rudolf Hilferding maintained early this century that capital export from Europe 'enormously accelerated the overthrow of all the old social relations' and the emergence of capitalism in other parts of the world (1910: 322). To take another, more particular example, in the second quarter of the nineteenth century international debt problems constrained newly self-governing countries in Latin America to abandon ambitious economic development projects and to halt various liberal reforms (Bushnell and Macaulay 1988; Dawson 1990). This scenario has been repeated in the region several times since, including during the past decade, when hardships associated with international debt burdens have moreover fed the rise of Liberation Theology and other movements for social change in many parts of Central and South America. In the 1920s and 1930s, international payments relating to war debts and German reparations, together with the worldwide reverberations of the Wall Street crash of 1929, arguably contributed to the rise of Nazism and the eventual outbreak of the Second World War (Aldcroft 1977). As for the present day, a number of authors suggest that the marked intensification of financial internationalization in the late twentieth century is playing an important role in creating new forms of capitalist social relations (e.g., Lash and Urry 1987).

Another form of international interdependence, the aspect to which students of IR have traditionally given the most emphasis, concerns the interconnectedness of states (i.e., territorial governments). An early writer on international law, Samuel von Pufendorf, highlighted this circumstance by formulating the concept of a 'system of states', by which he meant a situation 'when more than one [state] are so held together by some special and strict bond that they appear to form one body' (1688: 1043). In the present context the mutual involvement of countries through their state apparatuses is referred to as 'diplomatic interdependence' rather than the 'states-system', as the latter concept in a broadly realist fashion limits the scope of the world system to the interrelatedness of states and separates this 'international system' from domestic conditions. In contrast, I think we should, for the reasons elaborated earlier, regard diplomatic interdependence as but one of several aspects of international interdependence, and moreover as a circumstance that affects and is affected by internal situations (cf. Rosenau 1969). The mutual involvement of states is effected through various means: visits by special envoys; exchanges of permanent missions (embassies and consulates); summit meetings between heads of government; multilateral conferences; treaties and other instruments of international law; and, as previously mentioned, intergovernmental institutions and transgovernmental activities (Bull 1977; James 1978).

Substantial diplomatic interdependence appears to have existed during various periods in history. In ancient times, intense mutual involvement between states developed on a regional scale in China under the Chou dynasty, in southern India, and in Greece between the ninth and third centuries BC (Wight 1977; Holsti 1992: Ch 2). Students of IR have also discerned geographically limited interstate interdependence amongst the Muslim *taifa* kingdoms in the Iberian peninsula in the eleventh century AD and amongst the city-states of Renaissance Italy (Mattingly 1955; Rosenberg 1992: 132n). The modern network of national states took form between the fifteenth and seventeenth centuries: largely in Europe, but also in the context of regular diplomatic interchange between Asian and European states which continued until the direct annexations of the former by the latter in the nineteenth century (Alexandrowicz 1967; Tilly 1975; Wight 1977).[4] Diplomatic interdependence on a global scale has emerged during the past two hundred years through developments such as colonialism, the worldwide establishment of national states and the proliferation of global IGOs (Bull and Watson 1984). Indeed, we have since 1960 witnessed the creation of various intergovernmental groupings that do not include the original national states as members at all: e.g., the Non-Aligned Movement (NAM) in 1961, the Organization of African Unity (OAU) in 1963, the Association of South East Asian Nations (ASEAN) in 1968, and others. At the same time, the older national states have developed mutual consultation and collaboration to an unprecedented extent: viz. through the inter-Allied Combined Boards in the war effort against the Axis Powers during the 1940s; in the OECD and its predecessor the OEEC since 1948; with the North Atlantic Treaty Organization since 1949; by means of the Conference on Security and Cooperation in Europe since 1972; through the annual Group of Seven summits since 1975; and so on. Another indicator of the extent of contemporary diplomatic interdependence is the fact that, worldwide, over 60,000 treaties were in force between national states as of 1983 (Boulding 1988: 19).

Diplomatic interdependence has over the centuries contributed to the furtherance or hindrance of a number of social transformations. Indeed, several authors have highlighted the importance of the interlinkage of states in the development of the modern state itself. In this vein Anthony Giddens has asserted that:

> 'international relations' are not connections set up between pre-established states . . . they are the basis upon which the nation-state exists at all.
>
> (1985: 263–4; also Skocpol 1985: 8; Kazancigil 1986)

Diplomatic interdependence may in addition contribute to wider social changes. For example, Hall and Ikenberry have argued that interstate competition in Europe played a key role in the rise of capitalism, the emergence of the modern military and the rationalization of administration (1989: 39–41). In the early nineteenth century collaboration amongst states through the so-called Concert of Europe quelled revolutions in Naples, Spain and elsewhere (Kissinger 1957). One hundred years later interventions into Russia by half a dozen outside states threatened the survival of the fledgling Bolshevik regime, while in the 1940s another collective effort of states quashed the Nazi New Order in Europe. Meanwhile, in recent decades socialization through participation in the conventions of diplomacy has perhaps tended to diminish momentum for far-reaching social change amongst government ministers and officials who had once, as leaders of decolonization struggles, promoted programmes of radical social transformation.

Cross-border interdependence through warfare is another to some extent distinctly international force that has long figured in world-systemic dynamics of social change. One military analyst has calculated that across nearly three and a half millennia of recorded history there have been only 227 years without warfare (Larus 1964: 137). Even in ancient times a number of military campaigns were conducted over great distances and thereby also could have long-range social effects.[5] However, the period since the twelfth century in particular has seen a marked intensification of warfare in terms of the duration and geographical scope of hostilities, the size of armies, the sophistication of weaponry, and so on (Sorokin 1937: Part Two; Howard 1976). The Seven Years War of the eighteenth century might qualify as the veritable 'first world war' insofar as it encompassed concurrent battles in Europe, North America and India. More recent times have seen the advent of so-called 'total war', whose execution involves factory workers and other civilians to such an extent that the line dividing combatant from non-combatant becomes very blurred (Aron 1954; Shaw 1988). Contemporary technology also reinforces the fact of international military interdependence, as nuclear, chemical, biological and other weapons of the twentieth century enable the parties to international armed violence to inflict unprecedented degrees of destruction upon one another.

The issue of the relationship between war and social change has occupied writers as far back as Heraclitus in ancient Greece and Livy in ancient Rome

(Dunn 1974). In the nineteenth century liberals like Comte and Bright saw warfare as the chief obstacle to social progress, while social darwinists like Steinmetz and Bernhardi conversely viewed armed struggle between competing nations as a crucial means to prevent humanity's stagnation and decline (Howard 1978: Chs 2, 3). Early in the twentieth century Werner Sombart (1913) claimed that war fostered the development of industrial capitalism, a thesis which John Nef (1950) in turn contested. More recently, Randall Collins has suggested that the phenomenon of national solidarity arose historically not from a preexisting ethnic unity of a population, but from a people's experience of having fought together against common enemies (1986: 152–5). Several authors have furthermore stressed the repercussions of warfare for patterns of gender relations. For example, Susan Jeffords (1989) has maintained that representations of America's war in Vietnam through film, television, literature and journalism served to reinvigorate patriarchal structures in the USA during the 1980s, after social movements of the preceding quarter-century had begun to undermine prevailing constructions of masculinity. Meanwhile Charles Tilly has developed the succinct thesis that 'war makes states' (1985: 170), thereby joining a substantial company of historical sociologists who have followed Otto Hintze (1906) in asserting that the demands of organized armed violence have driven state formation through modern history (e.g., Huntington 1968: 122–3; Zolberg 1986; Rasler and Thompson 1989). Whatever the merits of these particular arguments, it does seem that warfare has often encouraged major reorganizations of society to occur: at least for the duration of the military campaign, and on various occasions more permanently as well. For instance, the two 'world wars' of the present century gave impetus to, amongst other things, the emergence of various communist regimes, the advance of women's suffrage, the decolonization process, significant economic reconstructions, the growth of a 'security state' with large surveillance capacities and campaigns against racial injustice (Marwick 1974; Milward 1977; Holland 1985; Dower 1986; Higgonet et al. 1987). Thus while it would seem excessive to claim, with Trotsky, that 'war is the locomotive of history' (Hall 1986b: 5), we can assert that world-historical-sociological studies should consider the possible effects – unplanned as well as intended – of war on processes of social change.

International interlinkage of people in the area of knowledge is on the whole mentioned much less frequently in discussions of world affairs than the previously discussed environmental, commercial, diplomatic and military aspects of interdependence, but it is no less significant for having been relatively neglected. Under 'knowledge' we can include not only understanding that is derived from formal learning and academic disciplines, but also cognizance of the world in the form of 'commonsense' knowledge, spiritual awareness, emotional experience and other aspects of consciousness. It is important in studies of social change not to restrict the scope of 'knowledge' to that which currently prevailing norms treat as high learning. Knowledge is multidimensional, and also plural. Yet, as Foucault, Laing, Bourdieu and others have maintained, the multiple truths that circulate in a given social setting (world society in our case) tend to be arranged hierarchically. All too often the tag of 'knowledge' becomes reserved for dominant conceptions, which are thereby helped to gain largely unquestioned acceptance, while the potentially enlightening voices of countercultures, being labelled as 'ideology' or 'myth', are stifled before they have begun to speak. As will be elaborated in later chapters, the clash of orthodox and alternative knowledges can figure centrally in the dynamics of social change.

For the moment, though, our concern is to note the significance of international interdependence in the construction of knowledge. It was argued earlier that cross-border data flows and transfrontier movements of people have often served to diffuse new learning from one country to others. Here we suggest that, in addition, international interaction can itself help to produce frameworks of understanding in the first place. For example, proponents of a number of major religions have formulated and sustained their respective truths largely through transnational networks such as the Roman Catholic and Eastern Orthodox Churches, the Caliphate, the various Sufi orders, Protestant movements, and recent revivalist strains in several faiths. Not surprisingly, given this international interpenetration, religious knowledge has often obtained a syncretic character: for example, in the 'Hinduism' of Bali, the 'Judaism' of the falashas in Ethiopia, the 'Islam' of Mindanao, and so on. In more recent history an additional syncretism has occurred as these previously established truths have been joined by the international 'religion' of techno-scientific rationalism. The resulting confrontation of old and new faiths has given rise to developments such as Islamic modernism (Rahman 1982). Indeed, the Enlightenment discourse, which has so profoundly shaped dominant forms of knowledge in contemporary world social relations, arose in the eighteenth century largely from, as Peter Gay describes it:

> [a] coalition of cultural critics, religious skeptics, and political reformers from Edinburgh to Naples, Paris to Berlin, Boston to Philadelphia.
>
> (1966: 3; also Porter 1990)

Subsequently the various social sciences emerged in the nineteenth and early twentieth centuries in part from international academic links. Such interdependence has figured as well in the intellectual history of the field of International Relations, albeit that some commentators have – I think wrongly – treated IR in a reductionist manner as essentially a product of US academe (Grosser 1956; Hoffmann 1977; Krippendorff 1987).[6] Meanwhile, twentieth-century developments in nuclear physics, genetic engineering, information technology and the like have often involved international research teams such as the CERN complex in Geneva, the International Rice Research Institute in Manila and the ESPRIT programme of the European

Community. In a more general fashion people are 'kept informed' about world affairs in good part by international mass media conglomerates such as News Corporation (chaired by Rupert Murdoch) and Visnews (Wilhelm 1990). On the other hand, international dialogues have also stimulated the formulation of a number of alternative modes of understanding in contemporary society, including quantum mechanics, psychoanalytic theory, postmodernism and deep ecology.

The relationship between knowledge and the social order – and in particular the link between intellectual developments and social transformations – will be discussed at greater length in later chapters. A few examples at this stage will support the general point that international interdependence in the realm of discourse and consciousness can be involved in the world-systemic dynamics of continuity and change. For instance, Enlightenment ideas provided considerable inspiration to the French and American Revolutions of the late eighteenth century. One hundred years later, internationally promulgated ideas of racial hierarchy and social darwinism added stimulus to the drive for colonial expansion and contributed to the rise of institutionalized racism (Hofstadter 1944; Jones 1980). International collaboration through the Manhattan Project during the Second World War opened the door to the age of nuclear warfare in 1945. Today international debates about the definition of 'Europe' are helping to determine the inclusion or exclusion of countries from the project of European integration. Finally, to make a self-reflexive observation, this book may be part of an international dialogue that reconstructs the way that we understand social change, a development of theory that may in turn have an impact on the actual course of social transformations.

Last in this survey of forms of international interdependence, we can consider cross-border interrelatedness in the arts and entertainment, i.e., in music, dance, painting, sculpture, architecture, literature, theatre, film, sport, cuisine and so on. For centuries many individual artists have consolidated their styles as they roamed between countries; and genres including reggae music, surrealism, the Buddha figure, the novel and a host of other forms of artistic expression have each developed through international interchanges. Anthony King has produced a detailed study of the bungalow as 'a product, and symbol, of a complex yet interrelated world' (1984: 263). He shows that international interactions in the architectural profession have established the model of a physically separate, one-storey, single-family dwelling as a common form of human residence throughout the contemporary world. Mass entertainment of the twentieth century is also in many instances largely internationally produced, marketed and consumed. The spectacle of the international Olympics has been held quadrennially since 1896 and was drawing a global television audience of over one billion viewers by the time of the Montreal Games in 1976 (Varis 1985: 17). Spectator sports ranging from cycling to chess follow an international schedule, while various other games whose fixtures are organized primarily on a national basis hold periodic global and regional competitions. In the field of music, both rock bands and symphonic orchestras travel on the international entertainment circuit and issue their recordings worldwide. In this globalized situation it is difficult to identify wholly local art, untouched by international interdependence, as even the production of folk crafts is nowadays often tailored to external markets.

Although recreational activities and the arts are generally treated as falling outside the 'serious business' of social life, these matters can in fact both reflect *and shape* the organization of society. To that extent this area of international interdependence may, like the other aspects already discussed, figure in the process of social transformation. For example, the exclusion of South African athletes from most international sporting events until 1992, and the attack by Black September on the Israeli contingent at the Munich Olympics in 1972, helped to publicize the struggle against apartheid and Palestinian grievances, respectively. Other links between leisure activities and the dynamics of continuity and change are more subtle: for instance, the impact of a world cup competition in reinforcing nationalism; the influence of international fashion designs in creating and sustaining consumer capitalism; or the repercussions of depictions of sexuality in the international mass media on sexual behaviour itself. Meanwhile, twentieth-century movements in the arts such as dadaism, the *avant garde* and punk have perhaps played a part in undermining confidence in the Enlightenment promise of the continual historical improvement of society through the application of reason.

To summarize, then, people are internationally interdependent through everything from disease to the arts. In addition, a wide range of international actors are important in shaping social life and can be centrally involved in causing a social transformation to occur. This is not to say that international activity has been an all-determining force in social history, of course. According to the world system concept elaborated in Chapter 2, local and national circumstances influence the shape of international interactions, as well as vice versa. Furthermore, the precise impact of international actors and interdependencies varies at different locations in world society according to the specific local context. So international activity is only part – albeit an important and frequently unrecognized part – of world-systemic processes of social change.

$\equiv 5 \equiv$

INTERNATIONAL ORDER AND SOCIAL CHANGE

It was noted at the outset of this book that social relations are ordered; they have general patterns. Thus actors in a human collectivity do not behave in a completely random fashion, and interdependence does not take utterly haphazard forms. If this premise holds true of society as a whole, then we can expect that the international dimension of social life will also exhibit certain regularities. The following discussion indicates that international relations do indeed incorporate organizing frameworks which shape the conduct of actors and the character of interdependencies within a world-systemic condition. More particularly, these forces of international order can thereby serve either to encourage or to inhibit the occurrence of social change, and they may in addition affect the nature of the changes that do transpire.

The present chapter examines the involvement of international order in the transformation process under three headings. The first section, concerning international norms, considers aspects of international order that are fairly readily visible to us: namely, formal international regulations (discussed here in terms of international regimes) and informal international habits. Other patterns of international relations are less immediately observable and are addressed in the second section on international social structures and the third section on international trends. The guiding premise throughout this chapter is that organizing principles of international relations have a certain force of their own, with a degree of independence from, and influence upon, international activities, cross-border movements and domestic circumstances within world society.

INTERNATIONAL NORMS

Norms are ruling standards of behaviour; international norms, then, are conventions that govern the conduct of cross-border relations. These rules can be roughly divided into two categories: formal and informal norms. Many international standards take the shape of explicit regulations: i.e., they are officially formulated, administered and monitored, often through an intergovernmental organization. Nowadays such directives are frequently grouped into sets of rules and procedures that define a framework of acceptable behaviour regarding a specific issue area in international relations, such as trade or environmental protection. A package of regulations of this kind, together with the institutional apparatus that oversees its implementation, has come in IR to be called an 'international regime' (Haggard and Simmons 1987). In contrast to regimes, other international norms are more implicit, taking the form of customs, fads and other patterns of behaviour which develop internationally in the absence of a specific regulatory framework. The following paragraphs consider the involvement of formal international norms in the dynamics of social transformation, while the significance of informal norms will be addressed briefly at the close of this section.

Fully-fledged international regimes have consolidated only during the past hundred and fifty years or so, but antecedents of these sets of formal rules can be traced back many centuries. For instance, the Romans 2000 years ago united the various parts of their far-flung empire with a common official standard for the designation of time: namely, the Julian calendar with its now globally used (although not universally preferred) seven-day week and twelve-month year of 365 days with a quadrennial leap year. The Gregorian reform of this calendar in 1582 had been adopted across most of Europe by 1752, again providing an international norm of time measurement (Whitrow 1988: 65–8, 116–19). In respect of another matter, money, we have in the previous chapter noted the acceptance of the *solidus* and the *dinar* as 'international currencies' over a thousand years ago. Regarding the issue of warfare, scholars in ancient China, Greece and Rome, as well as in the early Islamic world and medieval Europe, sought to establish universally valid grounds for the resort to arms, i.e., a doctrine of the just war (Khadduri 1955; Brownlie 1963: Ch 1). Certain norms were also established in these earlier epochs for the actual conduct of war once it had been declared. For example, the Code of Manu of ancient Indian civilization in the fifth century BC and the Second Lateran Council of Christendom in the twelfth century AD prohibited the use of certain inhumane weapons, long before the Hague and Geneva Conventions of our time formalized rules of warfare (De Lupis 1987: 121). Meanwhile the norm of sovereignty in relations between states was formulated in the writings of Jean Bodin and others several hundred years before it was codified in twentieth-century international law (Hinsley 1986: Ch 5). And in the seventeenth century Dudley North (1691) and a few other anti-mercantilist pamphleteers advocated the reduction of state restrictions on cross-border commerce, a principle that has come to underlie the present-day international regime for trade.

In contemporary history international regimes in one way or another touch all of the transfrontier movements, all of the international actors and all of the areas of interdependence discussed in the preceding two chapters (cf. Luard 1977). In regard to cross-border transport, for example, regulatory regimes cover, *inter alia*, the use of international rivers, the carriage of dangerous goods by sea and air travel (Chamberlain 1923; Henry 1985; Jönsson 1987). To govern cross-boundary communications the International Telegraph Union was established in 1865, at the time when transoceanic cables were first being laid. Today, as the International Telecommunication Union (ITU), this body also administers regulations relating to telephone, radio, television and other electronic communications across national frontiers. Meanwhile the Universal Postal Union (UPU) has overseen transboundary mail flows since 1875. Formal procedures for the international prevention and control of epidemics were instituted beginning with the four international sanitary conventions of the 1890s, half a century before the creation of the World Health Organization (WHO) (Leive 1976: 16). The construction of an international regime for the registration of patents, trademarks and copyrights also began during the 1890s, with the 1891 Madrid Agreement, and is today administered through the World Intellectual Property Organization (WIPO). Internationally agreed rules regarding the cross-border movement of persons have been established to govern matters such as the use of passports and the treatment of refugees (Goodwin-Gill 1978). At the same time the International Criminal Police Organization (Interpol) has since 1923 coordinated the transboundary pursuit of lawbreakers (Anderson 1989). International monetary conferences began to take place with some frequency in the late nineteenth century and, as noted earlier, a permanently institutionalized international regime for money was installed through the IMF after the Second World War. In respect of transfrontier trade, formal international arrangements governing individual products have existed since the 1902 Brussels Convention set up a Permanent Sugar Commission to monitor sugar prices (Tacke *et al.* 1963). Eight international commodity agreements and twenty-two cartels covering a score of primary materials operated during the 1920s and 1930s (Gordon-Ashworth 1984: 72–3, 84). Such accords experienced a considerable revival during the 1970s, in the wake of OPEC's (ephemeral) success at regulating price and supply in the world oil market, before suffering major setbacks once again during the past decade (Maizels 1992: Ch 7). Covering a broader scope of international commerce, the General Agreement on Tariffs and Trade (GATT), inaugurated in 1947, has provided a permanent institutional framework for the coordinated multilateral reduction of tariffs and other statutory impediments to cross-border trade (Finlayson and Zacher 1981). Elsewhere, in the area of international production, several codes of conduct for transnational corporations have been agreed, although these norms have so far tended to take the form of general recommendations rather than specific and binding directives

(Robinson 1983). Meanwhile international instruments in respect of working conditions were by the early 1980s sufficiently numerous for the International Labour Organization to publish a 1150-page compilation (ILO 1982). In recent decades formal international norms have also been constructed to govern the use of so-called 'global commons', including the oceans, Antarctica and outer space (O'Connell 1982/1984; Fawcett 1984; Joyner and Chopra 1988). Other international regimes have emerged to cover matters such as technical standards, human rights, environmental protection and armaments, as will be noted in more detail later.

On a superficial examination, the multifaceted apparatus of international government just described may appear to be relatively weak. International institutions often lack the extent of administrative resources (personnel, offices, stores of information, etc.) that national ministries can deploy to implement and monitor agreed regulations. Indeed, a number of intergovernmental organizations are chronically short of funds. Moreover, IGOs in many cases have relatively few sanctions at their disposal to enforce compliance with international regimes. Moral pressure often has limited effect, insofar as people in the present era of nationalism tend to confer comparatively little legitimacy upon international institutions. Meanwhile expulsion of an offending party from the relevant IGO tends to accomplish little but confirm the transgression. Commercial and financial sanctions have been decreed only sparingly and have had a mixed record in achieving their declared purpose (Doxey 1987). Nor have permanent international military units been available to effect compliance through the use of armed force. Even peacekeeping contingents of the United Nations or regional bodies such as the OAU have been deployed only on the invitation of national authorities in the countries concerned (Rikhye 1984). Given such contrasts between international and domestic regulatory arrangements, some commentators have denied the existence of anything worthy of the name 'international law' (cf. Lauterpacht 1970: Ch 1; Nardin 1983: Ch 6).

Yet this negative conclusion rests on two shaky premises: (i) the use of resources as a direct measure of influence; and (ii) reference to national law as the standard of comparison. In regard to the first of these points, reliance on resources as the prime indicator of effectiveness involves confusing means with power. The two are not the same thing, as *inter alia* the American Government's debacle in Vietnam amply demonstrated. In that war the US Air Force dropped more tons of bombs than in the whole of previous history, but nevertheless failed to secure Washington's control over the country (Ambrose 1983: 291). Conversely, as was previously suggested in Chapter 4, resource limitations do not necessarily reduce an international institution to an irrelevance. Indeed, if we assess the influence of international regimes in relation to the behaviour of actors in world society, then these norms are seen to have considerable impact. After all, though some of the international regulatory frameworks surveyed above have periodically come under strain, few have actually suffered a complete collapse, especially in the period after 1945. For instance, while negotiations through the GATT to decrease trade barriers – the eight 'rounds' of talks held since 1947 – have experienced perennial stalemates, the regime has nevertheless curtailed so-called 'trade wars' for nearly half a century. In fact, the GATT organization has recently increased its membership with the accession of most communist and former communist-ruled states as contracting parties. Other IGOs such as the UPU, WIPO and WHO execute their responsibilities largely without controversy or challenge. In the great majority of cases the participants in an international regime have perceived it to be in their interest to comply with the rules; hence the need for explicit persuasion, threats of expulsion, financial punishment or armed coercion has not arisen. In this way, for example, most foreign-exchange dealers unthinkingly respect international monetary rules, airplanes fly through the skies in the official internationally designated manner, the vast majority of passport checks at border crossings follow agreed international principles, and so on. There is a tendency for this day-to-day adherence to international regimes to go unremarked, whereas the relatively infrequent transgressions grab the headlines. Yet unchallenged regulations – those that require no deliberate enforcement – are in many cases the strongest laws.

Moreover, some IGOs do in fact have access to quite far-reaching measures with which to ensure compliance with international regimes. For example, several of these agencies have a court or an arbitration panel that rules authoritatively on violations of international norms, e.g., the European Court of Human Rights of the Council of Europe and the Permanent Court of Arbitration of the United Nations. The European Court of Justice can in addition impose severe financial penalties for transgressions of EC regulations. For its part the IMF has over the years despatched staff missions to a number of national capitals to design and monitor the implementation of a 'stabilization programme' when a country has run into serious problems with its international payments. On these occasions the international institution rather than the member government in question has had the initiative in national policymaking (Knieper 1983; Killick 1984). At certain other times popular pressure has helped to enhance the effectiveness of an international regime. For instance, a host of non-governmental organizations have supplemented official agencies in monitoring compliance with international human rights standards (Weissbrodt 1984; Armstrong 1986). Indeed, grassroots agitation has now and then directly prompted the creation of new international legal instruments. For example, campaigns of the International Baby Foods Action Network against sales promotion practices by transnational corporations in the infant milk sector stimulated the WHO to formulate the 1981 International Code of Marketing of Breast-Milk Substitutes (Chetley 1986).

A second questionable premise that is commonly invoked when evaluating international law is the presumption that the national state is the model of effective regulation and thus sets the standard for assessment. However, the preceding discussion suggests that international regimes have brought a considerable degree of legal order to international relations without having the national state's attributes of territoriality, centralization, constitutional sovereignty and direct control of tools of armed violence. Perhaps, then, we need to reconceptualize the state in an age of globalization, taking distance from such hallmarks of the classical Weberian definition (Weber 1922a: 56). It is indeed curious that most sociologists who have developed an interest in the international have continued to conceive of the state solely in national terms (e.g., Giddens 1981: 190; Evans *et al.* 1985; Mann 1986: 37; Tilly 1990: 130–1). However, several other authors have reformulated their notions of statehood by suggesting that international regimes have introduced an additional dimension of governance into contemporary society (cf. Cain 1983; Cox 1987: 253–65; Picciotto 1988; 1991).

It might therefore be suggested that, as part of our shift from national conceptions of society to a world society idea, we ought to replace the conventional notion of the state as national state with the concept of a world state. Drawing on the world system principle, we would then regard the state as a world-scale phenomenon with interlocking global, regional, national and local branches. From this perspective, official agencies at the various levels of government effectively form one complex of regulation, even though they are constitutionally discrete. The national state should therefore not be examined in isolation, but in the context of formal norm construction on a world scale. In this way we again reject the traditional separation of the international and the intra-national, as here expressed by Ernest Barker, the first Professor of Political Science at the University of Cambridge, when he asserted that:

> international government . . . goes beyond the area of government in the domestic sense . . . and it belongs to the sphere of another inquiry.
>
> (1942: v)

Indeed, why should we assume a sharp division of international regimes from national governments? After all, in many cases there is quite intense open collaboration between institutional arms of the world state at the different levels. For example, crime in the twentieth century has often been tackled through the combined efforts of the international organization Interpol, national agencies such as the FBI, and local police forces. To cite one rough indicator of the extent of this coordination, Interpol exchanged 280,000 telegrams with partner agencies in the year 1977 (Freese 1979: 31). Likewise, monetary policy has been devised in contemporary world society through constant exchanges between national finance ministries and international bodies such as the IMF and BIS. In addition, regulation on a world scale can also transpire with little if any multilateral consultation. For example, a world norm of monogamy has come to be enshrined in the national statutes of most countries without any deliberate international planning to that end. More recently, national states the world over have individually pursued what has in effect become a global policy of privatization (Clutterbuck 1991).

Of course the various qualifications enumerated in Chapter 2 in regard to the general world system principle apply equally to the more specific world state notion. Thus, for example, world law is not reducible either to international regimes or to municipal statutes, but involves an interrelation and mutual determination of the two (cf. Hopkins 1976). Furthermore, world law is by no means completely homogeneous: the world regulatory framework exhibits uniformity in some respects and differences of principle in others (cf. Bozeman 1971). Regulation through the world state gives rise to conflict as well as cooperation: disputes can arise within an international institution, within a national government, within a local council, or between agencies at the international, national and local levels. Moreover, the world state is not an egalitarian set-up: some parties in world society on the whole have greater access to, and reap greater benefits from, the regulatory agencies than others. Bearing such qualifications in mind, we can suitably view regulation, like social change, as a world-systemic phenomenon.

But what connections exist between international regimes, as part of a wider world-state apparatus, and the process of social transformation? The links can be intimate, insofar as social change involves a fundamental reconstruction of the social order, and regulations constitute a formal expression of an existing or desired overall social organization. Broadly, then, if an official rule conforms with the prevailing social order, it may serve to perpetuate that arrangement. On the other hand, a regulation that runs counter to entrenched social practices may help to undermine them and encourage the emergence of radically different circumstances of social life. Thus, for example, laws concerning property either: (i) could help to establish capitalist social relations in a previously non-capitalist context (e.g., a land registration law which denies peasants tenure and compels them to become wage labourers); or (ii) could serve to reinvigorate a capitalist order under strain (e.g., measures facilitating widespread home ownership, which help to secure workers' continued acquiescence to capitalism); or (iii) could have the effect of undermining capitalism (e.g., the revocation of patent laws). In a similar fashion international regimes may reflect prevailing organizing principles of social life and thereby tend to reproduce that order, or they may promote new norms and thereby help to produce a social transformation. The construction (or reconstruction) of official international norms can therefore play an important role in stimulating and/or blocking social change, as the following illustrations indicate.

To take one example, the emergence during the past hundred years of an international regime of technical standardization has given considerable impetus to one of the principal historical trends of our time, the globalization process. Cross-border exchanges can be greatly hampered when the countries involved use different scales of measurement, diverse modes of classification, multiple types of equipment, and so on. For instance, international efforts to prevent famine in Asia in 1946–7 faced major problems insofar as articles of food were weighed, graded and packaged in widely varying manners throughout the continent. It was therefore difficult to determine with precision where shortages were most critical, and in the end a special international conference was held to standardize methods of gathering and presenting statistics across the various countries (MAF 1948). This meeting at Singapore was one of many efforts towards global harmonization that have been undertaken during the past hundred and more years. In 1884 an international conference in Washington DC agreed to make Greenwich Mean Time the common reference point for clocks throughout the world (Whitrow 1988: 161–5). Harmonization of documentation in cross-border trade was established in 1890 with an international agreement on a common form for bills of lading (Rudolf 1926). Official efforts at international standardization of electrical apparatus began through the International Electro-Technical Commission in 1906. A current major challenge in this field is the establishment of common international standards in computerized telecommunication equipment (Survey 1987; Brown 1988). Already, the different parts of the world largely share the metric scale, the ISBN classification of published books, the same twenty- and forty-foot containers for freight transport, the Celsius scale of temperature, and so on. An International Organization for Standardization was established in 1946 to oversee the whole process of technical harmonization (White 1951: 96–100; ISO 1982). Mundane as this enterprise may be, the construction of an international standardization regime has, with little public notice, made an important contribution to the sea change of globalization in contemporary history.

An area of norm construction with a higher political profile which has helped to reshape social life in many parts of the world is the international human rights regime (see generally Meron 1984). The transnational campaign against slavery mentioned in Chapter 3 culminated in the conclusion between 1841 and 1956 of seven intergovernmental conventions against the practice (Sawyer 1986). Other international accords and institutions have sought to halt illicit cross-border traffic in women and children. Opposition to racism has been formalized in international instruments including the ten minority treaties in the Paris Settlement after World War I, the United Nations Convention on Genocide after World War II, and the 1965 International Convention on the Elimination of All Forms of Racial Discrimination (respectively, Rosting 1923; Harff 1984; Lerner 1980). More comprehensive international bills of rights have appeared in the form of the European Convention on Human Rights and Fundamental Freedoms (which came into force in 1953), the two international covenants on human rights of the United Nations (1976), the American Convention on Human Rights

(1978), and the African Charter on Human and Peoples' Rights (1986) (Sieghart 1983). In all, international standards of human rights were by the late 1980s enshrined in over three dozen intergovernmental legal instruments as well as a host of IGO resolutions (Guest 1988).

True enough, international norms of human rights do not enjoy universal, constant and complete respect. Moreover, philosophers and statespersons have argued ceaselessly about the precise nature of human rights: e.g., whether these principles have a fundamentally political or economic character; whether they relate in the first place to the individual or to the collective; whether they are universally applicable or culturally diverse; and so on (respectively, Cranston 1973; Crawford 1988; Pollis and Schwab 1980). However, the crucial point to note here is that, whatever its practical and philosophical shortcomings, an international human rights regime has in fact come into place and has on various occasions contributed to a process of social change. These activities of norm construction have brought practices ranging from summary execution to female circumcision under a critical international spotlight. In the light of human rights considerations, the Tanzanian-led invasion of Uganda and the consequent overthrow of President Idi Amin in 1979 met with worldwide approval. More generally, international human rights conventions have helped to spread ideologies of individual freedom and egalitarianism throughout contemporary world society, placing violators of these principles on the defensive even if their transgressions have not been wholly eliminated.

A more recent trend in international norm construction, the development of an international regime for environmental protection, may also turn out to have implications for fundamental social transformation, e.g., a possible change in the direction of a post-industrial society. International conventions to protect certain species of wildlife date from the turn of the century, but ecological issues mainly began to attract attention in international official circles during the 1970s (Boardman 1981: 27–30; Caldwell 1984). A UN Conference on the Human Environment at Stockholm in June 1972 resolved to create a special United Nations Environment Programme (UNEP). Other international meetings in the 1970s addressed problems of population growth, food, human settlements, eutrophication, harmful effects of pesticides, deforestation, desertification, the depletion of mineral resources, marine pollution, the development of renewable energy sources and so on (El-Hinnawi and Hashmi 1982). A number of international conventions concerning environmental protection were formulated in the process (UNEP 1985). In the 1980s questions of ozone depletion and global warming rose to the top of the international ecological agenda, prompting *inter alia* the conclusion of the Vienna Convention for the Protection of the Ozone Layer in 1985 and the creation of an Intergovernmental Panel on Climate Change (IPCC) in 1988 (Kemp 1990; Caldwell 1991). In tandem with UNEP activities the World Bank and other IGOs have declared it a priority to pursue policies of 'sustainable development' which incorporate a heightened sensitivity to ecological matters (IBRD 1992; UNCTC 1992).

It is perhaps too early to assess the long-term effects on overall social organization of the emerging international regime for the environment. Some observers see these initiatives as part of a fundamental shift in the orientation of international organizations at the end of the twentieth century (Kostakos *et al.* 1991). However, others are more sceptical: for example, describing the World Bank's Office of Environmental Affairs as a 'token' agency (Hayter and Watson 1985: 274). Ecology activists were certainly disappointed in the results, such as they were, of the highly publicized 1992 UN Conference on Environment and Development (UNCED), or 'Earth Summit', at Rio de Janeiro. Indeed, official international initiatives such as UNCED and the IPCC may ultimately have the effect of diluting the radical potential of green politics. Other critics have dismissed much of environmentalism as scare-mongering ideology which, like fears of a red tide in the days of the Cold War, effectively diverts attention from pressing social ills of patriarchy, capitalist exploitation, the authoritarian state and so on (Tucker 1980; Burton 1981). Yet whether one greets the ecology movement with enthusiasm or distrust, it is clear that, for the moment, efforts to expand the international regime for the environment have become a focal point of a number of strivings for social transformation.

Other attempts at social change through international regulation have to date given still less cause for optimism. For example, a hundred years of attempts to establish international controls on weapons stockpiles and the arms trade have thus far had only the most marginal effect of demilitariz-ation. General intergovernmental disarmament meetings began with the Hague Conferences in 1899 and 1907 and continued through the League of Nations Disarmament Conference in 1932–4, a sequence of Geneva disarmament committees after 1960, and Special Sessions of the UN General Assembly on Disarmament in 1978, 1982 and 1988 (Groom and Guilhaudis 1989). However, world wars did not prompt the creation of a permanent International Disarmament Authority in the way that world depressions encouraged the development of the Bretton Woods framework. Half a dozen multilateral treaties restricting the use of various weapons of mass destruc-tion have come into force since 1959, but little has been achieved towards the objective of 'general and complete disarmament' (GCD) which was placed on the agenda of the UN General Assembly in the same year (Sims 1979; Goldblat 1982). On the contrary, the quarter-century after 1945 saw a fourfold increase in real terms of world military spending, and during the period between 1960 and 1976 world cumulative military spending was more than twenty times greater than the total of official aid transfers (Harris 1983: 217). In the case of disarmament, then, the failure to construct a wide-ranging and effective international regime may be seen as part of a broader failure to effect a transformation towards a demilitarized social order. On the other hand, past frustrations may still give way to success, so that future historians could come to see twentieth-century efforts at regime formation as halting first steps in a long revolution of disarmament.

In other instances social change has been pursued through the reconstruction of existing international regimes, but campaigns to this end have generally made little headway. The unsuccessful initiatives of the 1970s to create a New International Economic Order have been mentioned in previous chapters. Associated proposals to develop a New World Information and Communication Order (NWICO) through UNESCO provoked an even more explicit and concerted counterattack from established interests, culminating in the withdrawal of funds and membership from the organization by the United States and British Governments in 1985–6 (Wells 1987). There is to this day only very limited international regulation of transborder information flows, which, as we saw earlier, constitute one of the main modes of international transaction and interdependence.

In another quarter the United Nations Decade for Women (1976–85) aroused less controversy than the NWICO project, but the Decade involved only modest efforts with modest funds towards the modest aim of raising awareness of women's issues in intergovernmental agencies (Ashworth 1985; Pietilä and Vickers 1990). Tellingly, perhaps, the initiating conference in Mexico City was chaired largely by men (Percy 1975). The UN Decade ended without the establishment of an autonomous international agency for women's affairs, and no drive of note towards a feminist reconstruction of international organization is apparent at present. On the other hand, women's associations have lobbied quite effectively through the European Community to obtain an Equal Pay Directive in 1975 and Equal Treatment Directives in respect of employment opportunities in 1976 and social security entitlements in 1978 (ROW 1983).

In sum, then, formal international norms can, depending on the particular circumstances in question, either help to uphold the existing social order or contribute to a process of social reconstruction. As we might expect, given the general interrelation of change and continuity, international regimes can often be seen to have a mix of both transformative and conservative effects. For example, the IMF has arguably fostered the internationalization of capital while at the same time checking challenges to capitalism. In the light of evidence such as that presented above, it does not seem possible to generalize about the relationship between international regulation and social change except to say that connections between the two are indisputably important and have become particularly significant in the twentieth century.

Other norms – namely, the informal conventions mentioned at the beginning of this chapter – have become embedded in international relations with little if any direct monitoring and control by official agencies. Informally generated international customs such as certain clothing styles (miniskirts), haircuts (dreadlocks) and eating habits (the fast food restaurant) may subtly reflect and contribute to deeper social changes. For example, a shift in many parts of the world from familial to institutional care of the elderly may manifest and reinforce a deeper social process of bureaucratization, and may also in the long run have implications for birth rates and population growth, as children become less of a focus of social security in many circles of society.

An area of informal international norms that would seem to have particularly far-reaching social consequences is rules of language. Verbal expression embodies patterns of thought which in turn relate to the overall organization of social life. For example, gendered language forms part of gendered social relations. Meanwhile anthropomorphism of the national state, but not of intergovernmental organizations, arguably reflects and helps to sustain the former's legitimacy: do we ever hear the UN or the GATT referred to as 'she' in the way of 'mother Russia' and the like? In such ways an informal 'international regime' of language, too, can serve as a principal vehicle for the reproduction or, potentially, the reconstruction of fundamental patterns of social life.

For one thing, the emergence of international languages has greatly facilitated the globalization process. In earlier epochs, on a smaller geographical scale, Latin brought linguistic unity to Christendom, Arabic linked the Islamic world, and Malay served as an international *lingua franca* in the harbours of insular South East Asia. It is true that, in the twentieth century, specially designed global languages such as Esperanto have gained little currency (Glossop 1988). However, certain national tongues have achieved a distinct international status. According to a UNESCO estimate, more than two-thirds of the printed materials in the world now appear in English, Russian, Spanish, German and French (MacBride *et al.* 1980: 49n). The English language in particular has become a means of global communication, with at least 750 million speakers worldwide. English is an official language of countless IGOs and INGOs, currently dominates both popular culture and academic research, figures in three-quarters of the world's post and cables, and provides the language medium for eighty per cent of the information stored in computers across the globe (McCrum *et al.* 1986: 19–20). English has thereby acquired an international significance as a tool of power; those who have command of that language have relatively privileged access to information and policymaking processes in world society.

International linguistic norms also have less immediately apparent, but more fundamentally significant, impacts on the social order, insofar as surface differences of national vocabulary and rules of grammar may obscure what are in fact common underlying constructions of meaning. Thus, for example, English and other dominant tongues arguably reflect and reinforce broadly shared patterns of patriarchy, individualism, militarism and other social structures. To that extent the international currency of these primary languages helps to spread and sustain the social order which is embedded in their deeper linguistic structures on a world scale.

An international dynamic of this kind may also affect languages whose usage is largely confined to a single national arena. To take one vivid example, a new Indonesian language has been constructed in the course of the twentieth century to replace both Dutch, the language of elites in colonial times, and the disparate local tongues that dot the archipelago. Yet although *bahasa Indonesia* has been developed with a view to promoting an Indonesian national identity and unity, its designers have at the same time also consciously sought to make the new language conform with dominant patterns of meaning in world society. As one of the principal architects of *bahasa* has argued:

> the Indonesian language itself must express the concepts and ideas of modern culture, otherwise the Indonesian people will not be able to participate in the progress of modern society.
>
> (Alisjahbana 1976: 117)

In this instance, then, language has been deliberately used as a tool of social transformation, i.e., to promote the national ideal and to advance a broader (and worldwide) modernization process. Thus apparent differences in national languages can disguise deeper international linguistic norms which in turn have repercussions on the overall social order.

To summarize, then, the foregoing discussion indicates that international relations can be involved in social change not only in terms of a multitude of movements and interdependencies across national frontiers, but also in the context of distinct international rules that govern those cross-border contacts. Both formally and informally, and with reference to a full range of issues, international relations contain standards of conduct which may have far-reaching implications for the course of social history both within and between the countries of the world.

INTERNATIONAL SOCIAL STRUCTURES

As noted at the beginning of this chapter, and as indicated again in the preceding discussion of language, norms are but one aspect – the more visible face – of international order. Yet such official regulations and day-to-day informal habits at the same time manifest, as well as help to sustain, deeper and more encompassing principles of social order. These macro-organizational configurations are examined under the present heading of structures and in the next section on trends. In this discussion structures are viewed as 'vertical' frameworks which mark the social order at a particular moment in time (e.g., a given class pattern or industrialism), whereas trends refer to 'horizontal' regularities which organize social relations through time (e.g., class dialectics or technology cycles). Needless to say, and as this pair of examples indicates, structures and trends are, as parts of a systemic whole, closely interrelated. Some authors in fact understand the term structure in a wider sense that covers both vertical and horizontal aspects of the underlying social order.

Since academics conceive of 'social structure' in a variety of ways, and often quite loosely, it is necessary to devote some paragraphs to the general notion before discussing its more specific importance in regard to international relations of social change. John Thompson rightly observes that 'few concepts in the social sciences are more basic and essential, and yet more ambiguous and contested, than that of structure' (1989: 62; see more generally Blau 1976). Some authors alternatively use phrases such as 'social formation', 'social fact', 'social organization' and so on to convey the idea that social life is structured, i.e., that relations between persons in a collectivity incorporate certain broad ordering principles. Anthony Giddens characterizes structures as 'principles of organisation implicated in those practices most "deeply" (in time) and "pervasively" (in space) sedimented in a society' (1981: 54–5). For Fernand Braudel, structure is 'an organization, a coherent and fairly fixed series of relationships between realities and social masses' (1958: 31). Zygmunt Bauman declares that ' "structure" connotes merely the regularity with which the allocation of social positions and actions tends to reproduce itself over time' (1989: 44). Structures, then, align social events and circumstances into particular patterns, establishing a general ordering framework for the actions of and interdependencies between persons in society. Due to structures (in combination with norms and trends) social activities do not proceed completely at random.

Social structures encompass more than, and therefore need to be carefully distinguished from, institutional 'structures'. Thus when we speak, for example, of a 'class structure' we are referring to more than trade unions, peasant associations, chambers of commerce and other such bodies. These formal organizations can be viewed as outward manifestations of class, but the structure itself is a more comprehensive phenomenon. As a fundamental ordering principle of social relations, class in some way touches all aspects of people's lives, including educational opportunities, state of health, family situations, use of language, leisure pursuits, level of income, etc. Likewise, the scope of a structure of militarism extends well beyond institutions such as the armed forces and weapons factories; in addition, militarism may be manifested in musical and literary genres, children's play, journalists' construction of the news, and so on. In a similar fashion, democracy as a social structure involves not simply political parties, but a wide range of laws, attitudes and behaviour patterns, of which election campaigns are just one example.

As the illustrations just given suggest, social structures may be conceptualized in a number of specific ways. Indeed, the identification of structural properties, and the determination of the relative importance of different structures vis-à-vis one another, have over the years constituted *the* central concerns of sociological research. Accordingly also, disputes over the nature of structure have lain at the heart of the most fundamental debates in Sociology.

A number of 'schools of thought' on the character of social structure can be distinguished. For their part, Marxists have defined structure first of all in terms of class. On this principle they have divided history into epochs according to the prevailing 'mode of production' (e.g., feudalism, capitalism, etc.) and its associated class structure (e.g., landlord/tenant, bourgeoisie/proletariat and so on). From an orthodox Marxist perspective, class is the underlying source of all other configurations of social interaction, such as race, gender, kinship patterns, nationality, democracy, militarism and so forth. In contrast, social theorists including Saint-Simon, Comte and Durkheim have developed a broad tradition of Sociology which treats industrialism as the primary structure from which other frameworks of action in modern society are derived. According to this conception, structural features such as capitalism, urbanism and nationality are all by-products of a principal social fact of mechanization and mass production. Alternatively, what some would loosely characterize as the Weberian perspective presents rationality as the core structure of modern social life. From this point of view, an all-pervading techno-scientific, pragmatic, problem-solving mode of knowledge has been the wellspring of secondary structural features such as capitalism, industrialism, secularism and bureaucracy. For their part, feminist theories have turned the sociological spotlight on structures of gender, in particular on the patriarchal configuration which is held to be central to the organization of contemporary social relations. Some feminist analyses moreover view patriarchy as a social force which has given rise to subsidiary structures such as bureaucracy, industrialism and militarism (Boulding 1975; Merchant 1980; Elshtain 1987). Adopting contrary approaches, other social theorists have stressed the importance of race as a prime structure of modern life, still others have focused on militarism, and so on.

Taking a rather different tack (one that, as later remarks will indicate, I myself tend to favour), some recent sociological research has rejected the tradition of attempting to grasp the entirety of social structure in one concept and a fixed hierarchy of forces. Instead, writings in this vein posit the existence of a multiplicity of structural configurations which intersect with one another in varying combinations across space and time. For example, Anthony Giddens has argued that 'there are no prime movers in human history' and has regarded capitalism, industrialism, the military order and the surveillance state as each being 'irreducible dimensions' of the structure of modern society (1985: 5, 8, 310–14; 1987: 26–9; 1989: 252–3). In a broadly similar fashion Silviu Brucan has maintained that each of the structures of class, nation and state has a drive of its own (1978b: 10–14; 1980: 757). Mary Kaldor (1982b) has suggested that social relations are structured by a 'mode of warfare' as well as a mode of production. For his part, Michael Mann (1986) distinguishes four transhistorical sources of structural power, each with an autonomous logic. Such arguments have been criticized in some quarters for advancing 'an unnecessarily complicated theory of history' (Sanderson 1988: 311). Yet proponents of multidimensional conceptions retort that social structure is 'far more messy' and 'complex' than the older theoretical traditions supposed (Giddens 1989: 293; Tilly 1990: 14).

Admittedly, the foregoing fleeting survey of some of the main notions of social structure oversimplifies the different points of view. However, these summary descriptions suffice for the moment to indicate that the analysis of structure is steeped in controversy. In short, it is one thing to assert that social life is structured; it is quite another to specify the nature and hierarchy of structural features.

Yet although different theorists characterize social structures differently, few sociologists would deny their importance. Indeed, these underlying patterns of social order are not merely the product of other aspects of social relations, such as actors, interdependencies and norms. Structures also have a significance in their own right, so that they, too, exert a notable influence on events and the wider conditions of social life. The question of the exact causal relationship between actors and structures is so fundamental to explanations of social change that Chapter 7 will be specifically devoted to that issue. For the moment we consider the more general point that what can be called 'structural power' is integral to social relations. According to this premise, structures have an important effect in moulding the perceptions, objectives and decisions of actors and in shaping the character of regulations and customs in society. To take an obvious example, a gender structure produces feminine and masculine modes of behaviour and experience that both women and men find difficult to avoid. Social structures in this sense have what Michael Mann calls 'diffused power', which:

> spreads in a more spontaneous, unconscious, decentered way through-
> out a population, resulting in similar social practices that embody power
> relations but are not explicitly commanded.
>
> (1986: 8)

Indeed, a social structure may be so deeply entrenched in a given historical context that people are scarcely aware of its existence and power. Steven Lukes stresses this sometimes 'invisible' quality of structures, noting that:

> structural constraints can work . . . in the form of ideological limi-
> tations, internalised values and beliefs, setting pre-set limits to what is
> even conceivable by agents.
>
> (1977: 11)

Thus, for example, we may not be conscious of racism in our behaviour, or, even if we are alert to the influence of this structure, we might be unable to conceive of a strategy – or even the very possibility – of replacing racism with a non-racial social organization. In a similar fashion, the structural power of bureaucracy might cause us to suppose that administration can only be conducted on bureaucratic lines, blinding us to the option of making policy, say, on a small scale, without formal offices and in a non-hierarchical fashion.

Structural power may at times even produce outcomes that run counter to the conscious aims and expectations of the actors involved. For example, a man's offer to walk a woman home at night may, insofar as the act involves a relationship of female dependence on male 'protection', subtly result from, and serve in turn to reproduce, a structure of patriarchy, even though neither party intended this transaction to have such an effect. Likewise, charitable aid to the destitute might, as an emergency measure that only just prevents the worst disasters of poverty, be instrumental in perpetuating a structure of liberal capitalism under which the needy in fact lose far more through debt repayment, low wages, tax charges and so on than they gain from the occasional donation. Yet neither the well-meaning donor nor the grateful recipient will have perceived this structural significance of their interaction.

Although stressing the importance of structural power, the foregoing remarks are not meant to imply that structures are unitary, all-encompassing, consistent and unchanging forces in social relations. On the contrary, not one but a plurality of structures or sets of structures may be present in a given social context. For example, some Marxists have discerned situations in which different modes of production coincide and 'articulate' with each other (Wolpe 1980). Similarly, as mentioned in Chapter 1, theories of dualism analyse settings where 'traditional' and 'modern' structures exist side by side. In much the same way, some sociologists characterize the present historical moment as a transition period in which features of 'modernity' and 'postmodernity' are found together (Turner 1991). Thus to say that social relations are structured is not necessarily to say that all actions, interdependencies and norms in a given historical context fit into a single underlying framework.

Nor are structures all-embracing forces in social life, in the sense that they compel each actor, any interaction and every law in a society to conform to a particular pattern. For example, although social relations may be structured on gender lines, individual men and women tend to respond to the general organizing principle in different ways, and some persons may largely defy prevailing masculine and feminine modes of behaviour. By the same token, conscientious objectors may surface under overall conditions of militarism; co-operative enterprises can emerge in a generally bureaucratized society; under a structure of nationality a minority of individuals may refuse to declare a national affiliation; and so on. In other words, although social structures are omnipresent, and although structural power has great force, some persons and circumstances may nevertheless deviate from the dominant pattern. (In fact, such exceptional behaviour often helps us to become aware of the ruling configuration.) Hence a structure is a general but not exclusive pattern of social relations.

Indeed, the various structures in a given social situation can between them have contradictory implications. The conceptualizations of structure cited earlier may have suggested that a set of social structures constitutes a coherent package, e.g., around one fundamental principle, such as rationality or capitalism, or through combinations of several forces in the ways that Giddens and others posit. Likewise, a functionalist variant of feminist theory might discern only mutually reinforcing relations between patriarchy and secondary structures such as industrialism, militarism and bureaucracy. Yet structures can have incompatible as well as complementary logics. For example, the force of nationality may clash with the force of capital on occasions: say, when a firm with a particular national affiliation discovers opportunities for greater surplus accumulation in 'foreign' lands than in its 'home' country. Meanwhile the egalitarian logic of democracy is often difficult to reconcile with the hierarchical nature of bureaucracy. Structural contradictions can emerge even at the level of an individual: for instance, a black female business executive may experience contrary influences of race, gender and class forces. In short, when we say that structures bring order to social life, this is not to say that they produce stability and harmony. On the contrary, structural forces can induce considerable volatility and conflict in social relations.

Being plural rather than unitary, far-reaching but not all-embracing, contradictory as well as complementary, structures are not so thoroughly and securely entrenched in social relations as to be unchangeable. Quite the reverse, as illustrations throughout this book have indicated, structures are the objects of fundamental reconstructions of social life. Social transform-ation involves, for example, altering gender relations, transcending militar-ism, replacing bureaucracy with alternative decision-taking principles and so on. True, given the substantial power of social structures, it can be very difficult to shift them, particularly in the short term. Nevertheless, structures do change, and the aim of world-historical-sociological research is to establish how and why they undergo transformations.

Indeed, our principal concern at this juncture is not the issue of structural power in general, but more specifically the involvement of structural forces in the dynamics of social change. In other words, are these ordering principles implicated in the process as *causes* as well as objects of transformation? Given that structures have a certain autonomy from other social forces, like actors and regimes, does 'structure' constitute an *explanatory* as well as a descriptive concept in the study of social change? If so, then rearrangements of structures, shifts in norms and so on would emanate – at least in part – from structures themselves. Such a possibility is accepted by Marxists, for example, when they explain transitions from one mode of production to another as a consequence of contradictions in class structure. Alternatively, we might speculate that ecological disasters consequent upon industrialism could in the future help to unravel the structure of industrialism itself.

Furthermore, a case could be made that the nineteenth-century rise of the nationality principle encouraged the concurrent deepening of racism, and vice versa. In each of these scenarios, structures are impulses to, as well as outcomes of, a process of social change.

Having made a long but necessary detour through basic sociological issues, we can return to the main line of discussion and incorporate the notion of social structure into an understanding of international relations of social change. If structures are integral to social life, then we should expect that international relations, as one of the key dimensions of society, contain general ordering principles of this kind no less than social phenomena in national and local contexts. After all, there is no reason why structural forces should recognize territorial boundaries and remain confined to one or the other 'level' of social life. Thus cross-border activities, too, are structured in terms of gender, race, class, nationality or whatever other organizing principles might prevail in social relations. Structural power affects the behaviour of *international* actors, the nature of *international* interdependence and the character of *international* norms no less than it shapes actors, interdependence and norms inside countries. This observation hardly seems an earth-shattering revelation; yet, due to the conventional separation in social theory of the domestic and the international spheres, researchers have rarely pursued this insight. In the prevailing academic division of labour, sociologists have traditionally directed their investigations of structure to local or national settings, whereas international relationists have generally assumed that social structure was a matter of national 'societies' and therefore fell outside the immediate scope of IR research.

In contrast, by breaking down the domestic–international division, world-historical-sociological studies regard structures as features of world society, which encompasses both the various countries and the international relations between them. In this light structure becomes a question of *world* social order, and structural forces are examined as part of world-systemic dynamics of continuity and change. Of course, the sorts of qualifications enumerated in Chapter 2 regarding the general nature of a world perspective on social relations also apply to the more specific notion of world social structures.

Thus, for one thing, the reach of a world structure is not delimited on strictly geographical lines. This principle can be read into Mahatma Gandhi's comment that 'there is no such thing as Western or European civilization, but there is a modern civilization' (1909: 293). In other words, modern structures are spread across world society and cannot be identified on a one-to-one basis with particular territorial domains. Similarly, divisions between Islamic and non-Islamic social structures,[1] between capitalist and non-capitalist formations, and so on do not fall neatly on geographical lines. Hence we ought perhaps to speak not of, for example, industrial and non-industrial countries, but of a world structure of industrialism which crisscrosses borders and has an irregular spatial impact both within and between countries.

Indeed, a given social structure rarely extends to every corner of the planet, i.e., a world structure is not necessarily a universal structure. Hence we can treat bureaucracy as a world-scale social configuration even though there are few visible signs of it amongst those bush people in the Kalahari Desert who continue to pursue a nomadic existence. Likewise, the nuclear family may be regarded as a structure of world society, even though different kinship patterns are more prevalent in some areas.

Nor is a certain structure likely to be embedded to an equal extent at all of the locations in a world social circumstance that it does touch. For example, nationality is, on the whole, not as entrenched in Somalia as it is in Japan, nor in the villages of India as much as in that country's urban centres. Meanwhile militarism appears not to run as deep in Costa Rica as it does in the USA (Aas and Høivik 1986).

In addition, a particular social structure can manifest itself in a variety of guises at different points in world society. This possibility was suggested earlier, in the discussion of surface language contrasts which may mask common underlying linguistic structures. For instance, the specific character-istics of bureaucracy, capitalism and militarism were far from the same in the former communist bloc and the West, but a number of commentators have argued that broadly the same fundamental structural forces shaped both areas, as well as the relations between them (Binns and Hallas 1976; Hegedus 1976; Kaldor 1982a). Likewise, a structure of patriarchy can be said to exist on a world scale even though the particular laws and habits through which women are subordinated show considerable variety between, say, sex tourism in Bangkok and the reservation of the priesthood for men in Rome.

The preceding remarks have indicated that world social structures do not present a pattern of global uniformity, but a panoply of both similarities and contrasts. Moreover, the fact that a number of structures have made impacts across long distances has to date not resulted in a situation of world community. On the contrary, structures such as race and militarism would seem sooner to have bred conflict than cooperation in world social relations.

Structural forces reside in both international relations and domestic circumstances within the world society as a whole, but for reasons elaborated at the end of Chapter 2 the present discussion concentrates first of all on the international manifestations of social structure. In particular, we consider how structural power, as mediated through international transactions, can figure significantly in the world-systemic dynamics of social change. Struc-tures are to some extent created by, embedded in, and reproduced through international actors, international interdependence and international norms. In addition, structural forces conveyed through cross-border activities can help to effect transformations in local and national settings as well as to alter patterns of international relations themselves. Conversely, of course, struc-tural forces contained within domestic activities may have transformative implications for international relations, although this reverse direction of the internal–international interplay is not addressed in detail here.

The following paragraphs explore the involvement in the process of social change of several specific structures. For reasons of space only two fundamental ordering principles – capitalism and nationality – are examined from amongst the numerous structural properties that might be discerned in contemporary international relations. The choice of these two particular structures is a largely arbitrary one. In other words, my purpose in the present context is to use the examples of capitalism and nationality to establish the general point that structural power figures significantly in international relations of social change. I am not seeking to propound a specific structural theory of transformation in world perspective. Hence I will not be explicitly assessing the relative merits of Marxist, Durkheimian, Weberian, feminist and other arguments concerning the hierarchy of structural properties in contemporary society. (My own present inclination is to conceive of dominant world social structures in a fivefold fashion – in terms of intersecting forces of nationality, capitalism, rationality, patriarchy and the liberal/surveillance state. However, to elaborate that conception would require a separate book in itself.)

One frequently mentioned structural force in international relations is capitalism. Definitions of capitalism and theories to explain its development are numerous and vary widely (cf. Bottomore 1985). Yet liberals, Marxists, world-system theorists and others who highlight the importance of this structure broadly agree that social life takes a capitalist pattern when it is infused with a process of surplus accumulation. Under a capitalist framework, social behaviour is largely orientated towards the acquisition of ever-greater amounts of surplus, i.e., resources in excess of the minimum that people require for subsistence and biological reproduction. Actors, interactions and norms fall into a capitalist configuration insofar as people are involved in constant efforts to retain, and preferably to increase, stores of surplus value. Money plays a central role in this process of accumulation, since wages, prices, taxes, usury, currency revaluations, balance-sheet accounting techniques and other financial manipulations are especially instrumental in facilitating the expansion of production and the concentration of surplus value in the hands of the powerful. In this light Marx characterized money as 'the universal commodity' of capitalist society: 'the reflex, thrown upon one single commodity, of the value relations between all the rest' (1867: 89–90).

Capitalism has structural power in that it sets a framework of social relations which individuals and groups find difficult to avoid, let alone to challenge. The structure has become so entrenched that most of the people it touches take it as given that the attainment of 'growth' and 'productivity' are primary indicators of society's success. Indeed, capitalism has come to be unquestioningly accepted as a 'natural' part of the social order. The structure thereby has far-reaching and fundamental significance in shaping cultural, psychological, economic, political and ecological conditions in the affected (critics would say afflicted) historical contexts.

In modern world society the structure of capitalism has encompassed international as well as intra-national social relations. As noted in Chapter 1, Karl Marx in his pioneering analysis of capitalism recognized that this structure had an important international quality. Following the expansion of foreign direct investment and cross-border financial transactions in the late nineteenth century (charted in Chapters 3 and 4), writers including Hilferding (1910), Luxemburg (1913), Kautsky (1914), Bukharin (1915) and Lenin (1917) stressed the international dimension of capitalism even more strongly. During the past two decades the accelerated globalization of money markets, share dealing and factory production has prompted many Marxists again to emphasize the international qualities of capitalism (Mandel 1972; Poulantzas 1974; Palloix 1977; Hymer 1979; Szymanski 1981; Brett 1983; Berberoglu 1987; Cox 1987; Miliband and Panitch 1992). Some of these authors have also highlighted the role of intergovernmental organizations in promoting the internationalization of capital, while other writers have investigated the allegedly deepening transnational nature of class relations. For example, Ralph Miliband has asserted that:

class analysis . . . is as relevant to the international context . . . as to the national one . . . international relations since 1917, and particularly since 1945, have been shaped by class struggle on a world scale.
    (1987: 339–40; see also Krippendorff 1975c; Pijl 1984; Sklair 1991)

Outside orthodox Marxist circles, too, a number of researchers have in recent years drawn attention to the international dimension of capitalism. For instance, proponents of world-system theory have posited the existence since the sixteenth century of a capitalist world-economy with a core, periphery and semiperiphery as 'classes' of countries (Chase-Dunn 1989). From a different perspective, John Hall has argued that 'nation-states . . . operate within the larger society of international capitalism' (1986b: 13). Bryan Turner has also suggested that 'the global features of capitalism' figure centrally in the dynamics of social transformation (1981: 248–56).

Turner's observation broaches the issue that is of principal interest to us here: namely, the involvement of capitalism as a structure of international relations in the process of social change. On this subject Theda Skocpol has proposed the general thesis that the onset, course and outcome of social revolutions has historically been closely related to the 'internationally uneven spread of capitalist economic development' (1979: 19ff). In regard to more specific social changes, Carolyn Vogler (1985) has affirmed that the acceleration of the internationalization of capital in recent decades has fundamentally altered class relations within the various countries that the structure has touched. One can also argue that international-structural forces of capitalism have contributed to the emergence of the newly industrializing countries discussed in Chapter 4. It might in fact be suggested that capitalism has to some extent been a self-expanding force, so that the structure has partly through its own power and momentum in international activities helped to create capitalist social relations on a global scale.

On the other hand, international capitalism has in certain contexts placed a brake on transformative impulses, too. For example, a number of writers have concluded that international forces of capitalism constrained and eventually frustrated socialist experiments in the (former) Soviet Union and elsewhere in the 'Second World' (Frank 1976; Chase-Dunn 1982). Meanwhile previously mentioned transnational activities by the CIA, the IMF and other bodies to 'stabilize' potentially revolutionary situations in newly decolonized countries may also have been structured by capitalism to one degree or another.

As noted earlier, Marxists tend to reduce all structural forces in contemporary history to capitalism and associated patterns of class; however, other theorists put the primary emphasis on one or more different ordering principles, or see capitalism at work in international relations in combination with one or several additional configurations. Here we consider just one of these possible other international structures, i.e., the nationality principle.[2] Like capitalism and other purported social structures such as militarism, patriarchy, bureaucracy and so on, nationality has been defined and explained in many different ways (Smith 1983). For present purposes we can broadly characterize it as a structure that establishes nationhood as the chief basis for organizing human community in a given social context. In other words, under the influence of the national idea people in modern times have constructed their collective identity and their bonds of group solidarity in the first place in terms of nationhood. Thus Rupert Emerson has described the nation as the 'terminal community' which prevails 'when the chips are down' (1960: 95–6); and Reinhold Niebuhr has spoken of the nation as 'the most absolute of all human associations' (1932: 83).

But what exactly is a nation? The circumstances which seal a national bond are so variable, obscure and mythical that Benedict Anderson (1991) has concluded that nations are 'imagined communities'. On one occasion or another, national identity and solidarity has been said to derive from, *inter alia*: a shared language, a territorial homeland, bonds of religion, a common personality makeup or 'national character', a unique genius, a distinctive set of customs, similar racial features, a common heritage, a shared historical destiny, joint economic interests and/or collective self-government through a nation-state. Amidst this confusion about what exactly constitutes nationhood we can discern three fairly consistent broad themes. First, a nation generally encompasses a larger population and a wider territory than other communal units, such as hunter-gatherer bands, kin groups, neighbourhoods, city-states and tribes. Second, nationality is based on a claim of uniqueness and difference, e.g., a distinct language or whatever. Third, a nation tends to be a relatively closed community and generally maintains a defensive posture towards outsiders in order to preserve the geographical, cultural, political and other boundaries that divide it from the 'not-nation'.

As a structural force, nationality exerts its own power over social relations. In contemporary history a person is born into a national identity and finds it extremely difficult to defy nationality as the fundamental basis for organizing human community within the world society. Indeed, most people today accept the national idea unquestioningly, treating it almost as a 'natural' (and thus unalterable) principle, rather than as a pattern of social order that is bound to the particular historical circumstances in which we live. True, much conflict has arisen over the years between competing nationalist visions: e.g., between Pan-Arabism and various territorial nationalisms in the Middle East; between Bosnian, Serbian, Yugoslav and other nationalisms in the Balkans; and so on. Is a resident of San Sebastián a Basque, a Spanish or a European national? Yet in structural terms there is no dispute between those who accept prevailing identifications of nations, those who pursue macro-nationalist integration programmes and those who support mini-nationalist secession movements. Such arguments are about where to draw national lines and do not call into question the nationality principle; on the contrary, they are steeped in it.

Of particular interest to us here, however, is the fact that the structure of nationality is embedded in international as well as domestic affairs. Nationality has an obvious international quality in one sense, insofar as this framework of social activity has spread across borders to become lodged to one degree or another around our planet. Like the development of capitalism, the reorganization of social life in terms of nations has unfolded as a long and eventually global revolution. In addition, though, the structure of nationality has become rooted in international relations themselves and serves as a primary ordering principle for cross-border activity. Indeed, nationality has during the past two centuries generally been a major consideration in the establishment or alteration of the geographical borders of countries, even though territorial states and national populations have rarely if ever obtained a one-to-one correspondence. Nationality has also made a substantial impact on foreign policies (pursued in name of the 'national interest', whatever that might be) and on the construction of international institutions (as epitomized in appellations such as the League of *Nations* and the United *Nations*). IGOs as a rule draw their members from *national* states and are generally constrained by formal injunctions not to infringe upon *national* sovereignty. The force of nationality has furthermore affected international trade and military rivalries, the organization of the world's money (i.e., mainly in terms of national currencies) and so on. In academic International Relations and other social sciences, the structural power of nationality has been manifested in the habit – decried throughout this book – of conceiving of society in national terms and reifying the distinction between the national and the international.

It is indeed a paradox that, as noted in Chapter 2, the emergence, spread and deepening force of the national idea, with its emphasis on particularity, has unfolded in world society simultaneously with the globalization process during the past two hundred years. In this light Hans Kohn has advanced the seemingly self-contradictory thesis, also propounded by Eugene Kamenka (1973: 3), that 'the age of nationalism represents the first period of universal history' (Kohn 1944: vii). However, a world-systemic analysis perhaps reveals a logic behind these two apparently incongruous developments. Various commentators have followed Max Weber (1922a: 385–98, 921–6) in noting that national identities have been established largely by means of drawing contrasts between insiders and outsiders on the world stage, between collaborators and opponents in international affairs. Thus the principle of nationhood emerged in Western Europe largely in the international context of struggles between Protestants and Catholics as well as through mercantilist competition (Hayes 1926: 38–40; Heckscher 1955; Kohn 1965: 13–22). Similarly, Balkan nationalisms rose to a considerable degree as a result of opposition to imperial domination from Constantinople and Vienna, while the principle of Arab nationhood developed as much as anything in reaction to intrusions from 'the West'. Likewise, anti-colonialism and subsequent protests against 'neo-colonialism' have provided a major impulse to the construction of nationalities in the Americas, Asia, Africa, the Caribbean and the Pacific. In this sense international relations have created and sustained nations as much as vice versa, and in consequence of this world-systemic interplay increasing cross-border contacts could in fact encourage an intensification rather than, as many people presume, a reduction of nationalism.

Hence in considering the significance of international forces of nationality for social change we might point first of all to the role of international relations in the emergence and spread of the principle itself. Halvdan Koht hints at such a dynamic when he suggests that it 'cannot be a simple coincidence' that 'a truly national consciousness . . . burst forth almost simultaneously in many of the European countries' (1947: 266). Anti-colonial nationalism of the twentieth century, too, has been fed in part through international activities: e.g., transnational communist support for national liberation movements; Japanese promotion of 'Asia for the Asians' between the 1920s and 1940s; intercontinental Muslim support for national resistance efforts in colonized parts of the *umma*; anti-colonial agitation by Pan-African and Pan-Asian coalitions; and previously mentioned United Nations initiatives (Elsbree 1953; Queuille 1965; Pischel and Robertazzi 1968).

More generally, constant *inter-national* conflicts in one or the other part of the world, together with pervasive tensions between globalization and the nationality principle, can help to produce a volatile situation in which space is opened up for a variety of other social transformations. For example, anti-colonial nationalist struggles have frequently provided an occasion for the rise of women's movements, with the result that decolonization has in a number of instances been accompanied by the introduction of new family laws and other measures which improved the position of women (Davies 1983; Jayawardena 1986). Peasant strivings for land reform and pro-grammes of religious revival have also sometimes gained strength by linking themselves to an anti-colonial struggle (Wolf 1969; Peters 1979).

In other situations, however, international structural forces of nationality have placed a brake on impulses towards social transformation: namely, by dividing and weakening a transnational movement for change. For example, although the Bolsheviks played the national card to their advantage in the early period following the October Revolution, in later years the inter-national socialist 'community' collapsed *inter alia* under the strain of national fractures (Connor 1984; Munck 1986). Likewise, Islamic revolutionaries have to date been unable to persuade many of their fellow Muslims to abandon national allegiances in favour of a transnational religious coalition, as events such as the Iran–Iraq Gulf War of the 1980s have shown.

The examples of capitalism and nationality demonstrate that the consider-ation of structural power is of central importance to a study of international relations of social change. A number of additional structural forces could also be examined to reinforce this point further, but space limitations preclude a detailed discussion of the whole gamut here. Briefly, it can be noted that other research has explored the role in international relations of social structures such as militarism (e.g., Kaldor and Eide 1979; Mann 1988), race (e.g., Thorne 1982; Smith *et al.* 1988; Pieterse 1990: Ch 11), gender (e.g., Ward 1984; Mies 1986; Enloe 1989), the family (e.g., Smith *et al.* 1984), urbanism (e.g., Timberlake 1985), secularism (and its possible decline) (e.g., Robertson 1985; Robertson and Chirico 1985), industrialism (e.g., Pettman 1979: 182–91) and bureaucracy (e.g., Rizzi 1939; Burnham 1941).

Whatever specific structure or structures we identify in international relations, however, these underlying organizing frameworks of social life can affect a process of transformation in several general ways. On the one hand, structural forces contained in international relations may influence recon-structions indirectly: that is, by shaping the behaviour of actors, the nature of interdependencies and the character of norms, all of whose involvement in the dynamics of social change has been considered in earlier sections of this book. International activities are thus, at least in part, structurally generated. Second, a given change in the social order can result to some extent from the self-propelling power of the structure in question. For example, the accumulated force of secularism might promote a further entrenchment of that structure. Conversely, the decline of a certain ordering principle in society may be due partly to self-reinforcing weaknesses of that structure. On these lines it was suggested earlier that industrialism might recede in the face of the ecological damage it causes. Third, structural power may figure in a transformation process when one configuration of social forces encourages the development of other new structures. In this vein it was proposed above that the nationality principle might have contributed to the emergence of other features of contemporary social organization such as racism. Fourth, structures can affect the dynamics of change when one structural force helps to displace another, previously dominant, social framework. For instance, as illustrated in Chapter 3, matrilineal structures have been undermined in certain parts of the world following the insertion, through international contacts, of patriarchal patterns into these locales. Finally, structural forces can figure in international relations of social change when the interplay of several existing structures gives rise to new configurations of social life which deviate from each of the preexisting patterns. For instance, it might be argued that interrelations in the early twentieth century between structures of liberal capitalism and incipient communism shifted the former in the direction of corporatist welfare-state capitalism and reshaped the latter into state socialism. In any or all of these ways – several of which may operate simultaneously – structural power lies at the heart of international relations of social change and the wider world-systemic dynamics of which the international is a part.

INTERNATIONAL TRENDS

It was mentioned at the beginning of the previous section that some social theorists use the term 'structure' to refer to both vertical and horizontal regularities in the deeper organization of society. In the current discussion, however, the concept of structure has been reserved for the relatively 'stationary' patterns of social relations at any one point in time, while the notion of underlying developmental patterns of international relations through time is examined under the present heading of 'trends'. The general premise here, then, is that social life is ordered in part in relation to 'rhythms' of history, that the world system is among other things a 'moving' system. Braudel had such a postulate in mind with his idea of *conjonctures* (recall Chapter 1), while other writers have encapsulated this notion of embedded historical regularities in phrases such as 'secular movements', 'developmental tendencies' and, most strongly, 'laws of motion'.

Of more specific concern to us in the present context is the proposition that trends – as contained in international relations as well as in domestic conditions – may figure alongside actors, interdependencies, norms and structures in the world-systemic dynamics of social change. In other words, can developmental tendencies exert a distinct 'pressure of history' which may help induce fundamental reconstructions of social life to occur and influence the course that these transformations then take? Might trends reinforce or undermine the existing social order, and promote or check the rise of new organizing principles of social life? Four general types of longitudinal configurations of social relations are assessed in this light here: namely, linear, cyclical, equilibrating and dialectical trends.

The notion that linear historical movements might affect the process of social change was already intimated in the final paragraph of the preceding section. These unidirectional trends involve the progressive broadening and deepening of the impact of a given social ordering principle or, conversely, the continual contraction and attenuation of a particular social force. The rise or decline of the social pattern in question thus develops a certain momentum of its own. Walt Rostow (1960) conveys this idea graphically (albeit in relation to national 'societies') with his postulate of a 'take-off' stage to self-propelling economic growth. In a broadly similar fashion, Talcott Parsons and his followers have treated modernization as a linear developmental trend through which an industrial, rationalist, democratic pattern of social life comes in time to encompass more and more countries and localities in the world, as well as more and more areas of social life. From a contrary perspective, orthodox Marxists have variously argued that capitalist social relations have inherent tendencies towards the expansion of the accumulation process, the concentration of surplus holdings, the cartelization of firms and the internationalization of the structure of capitalism itself. Proponents of world-system theory, too, posit the existence of a linear advance towards the extension and pervasive intensification of the forces of capitalism on a global scale, through what these authors term progressive 'mechanization', 'contractualization', 'commodification', 'interdependence', and core-periphery 'polarization' (Hopkins *et al.* 1979: 483–5). In the present book repeated references have been made to a broadly linear development of general globalization in contemporary world society, a trend that has often encouraged or hampered other social transformations. In each of the cases just described, a social development is said to have something of a juggernaut-like quality, acquiring a momentum of its own which is difficult to slow, let alone to stop or reverse.

Other trends affecting social change which are contained in and conveyed through international relations may take a cyclical pattern. According to this general principle, social order is manifested *inter alia* in the form of a sequence of distinct phases of development which broadly repeats itself over time. Cyclical conceptions of history have been held since well before the advent of modern social science, but during the past century a number of such ideas have been linked more specifically to international relations and the world system as a whole.

For example, a number of Marxists (such as Mandel), world-system theorists (such as Wallerstein) and liberal economic historians (such as Rostow) have concluded that the modern world economy experiences a so-called 'long wave' of expansion and contraction at roughly fifty-year intervals (Barr 1979). This trend is often called a Kondratieff cycle, after the researcher who during the 1920s first documented this apparent long-term regularity of upswings and downswings in wholesale prices, interest rates, wages and industrial production (Kondratieff 1926; Day 1976). As well as helping to cause periodic decelerations of accumulation which weaken the structure of capitalism, the long wave in the world economy is said by some authors to have had implications *inter alia* for the rate of technological innovation, the incidence of anti-semitism, the onset of major wars, and the expansion and contraction of colonial empires (Bergesen and Schoenberg 1980; Freeman 1983; Goldstein 1985).

Meanwhile other writers have in various ways suggested that international relations are marked by a cyclical rise and decline of successive preponderant national states. For example, George Modelski has argued that a four-phase 'long cycle of world leadership' has repeated itself four times since 1494 (Modelski 1987; Thompson 1988). A company of other authors have developed related notions, also on broadly realist lines, of alternating periods of 'hegemony'[3] and capability deconcentration in interstate relations (Gilpin 1981; Kennedy 1987; Mann 1990). From a different perspective, researchers in world-system theory have traced a succession of three cycles of alternating hegemony and rivalry in relations amongst national states in the capitalist world-economy since the seventeenth century (Bousquet 1980; Wallerstein 1983; Arrighi 1990). Drawing on one or the other of these approaches, authors have variously claimed that this cyclical movement of hegemony (or world leadership) has affected shifts from colonialism to neo-imperialism, moves between liberal and social-democratic forms of state, the course of technological development, and other social changes. Joshua Goldstein (1988) has taken the further step of analysing social history in terms of an interpenetration of the two long cycles just discussed, Kondratieff and hegemony cycles.

A number of further variations on the general theme of cyclical trends also appear in the literature on social change in world perspective. For example, Arnold Toynbee has offered an account of world history in terms of a cycle of civilization, where emergence, growth, decline and breakdown are determined by a civilization's ability or failure to respond creatively to internal and external challenges (K.W. Thompson 1985: Ch 1). Daniel Chirot (1986) for his part has divided the course of modern world history into a series of five industrial cycles, i.e., triggered by successive technological revolutions in the production of textiles (1780s–1820s), iron and railways (1840s–70s), steel and chemicals (1870s–1910s), mass consumer goods (1920s–70s), and services (1970s–present). Meanwhile Geoffrey Blainey observes some link between upswings in business cycles and the outbreak of war, with all of the social changes that large-scale armed conflict can bring (1988: 91–6).

It should be noted that none of the various theories described above concerning cycles of history has won universal acceptance in academic circles. For example, William Thompson (1982) has rejected the thesis that a significant correlation exists between business cycles and the incidence of warfare. Indeed, many regard the very idea of cyclical regularities in history with scepticism. However, incredulity in itself provides insufficient grounds to dismiss such propositions out of hand.

A third class of trends that may be involved in international relations of social change are equilibrating movements. Arguments in this vein follow the general structural-functionalist premise that all systems (and thus the world social system, too) have an inherent tendency towards balance and stability. For instance, Parsonian sociologists have suggested that modern society evolves in a gradual and smooth fashion, as institutions and behaviour patterns are continually adapted to maintain the vigour of the underlying social structures (Parsons 1966: Ch 2). Meanwhile, some international theorists assert that forces of equilibrium mould the course of interstate relations by means of a balance-of-power mechanism, which allegedly operates to prevent any one national state from absorbing the rest and creating a universal empire (Morgenthau 1948: Ch 11).[4] However, given their preoccupation with interstate competition per se, realist writers have not, as far as I am aware, related the balance-of-power thesis to questions of social change. Indeed, the very notion of equilibrating tendencies suggests that rhythms of history work against fundamental transformations: certainly in the short and medium term, if not in the long run, too.

In contrast, theorists who conceive of trends in terms of dialectical movements posit that social relations have essentially unstable and dynamic historical qualities. The notion of dialectics posits that the tension created by the interrelation of contradictory parts of a social system generates major forces of transformation. Marxist notions of class dialectics are perhaps the best-known version of this sort of argument: namely, it is alleged that a fundamental clash of interests between the dominant and subjected classes within a given mode of production provides the primary impulse for the transcendence of that social order. Silviu Brucan has reconstructed this classical Marxist thesis by seeking to explain social change in the light of a dialectical interplay between national conflict and class struggle, or what he calls a 'see-saw of class and national motive force in world affairs' (1984: 106). From another angle, Wim Wertheim has formulated what he calls a 'counterpoint hypothesis', which suggests that deviant value orientations continually emerge in society in opposition to dominant sets of values, creating a dialectical dynamic which provides the chief impetus for social change (1974: 105–18). From this perspective anarchism, communism, fascism, radical feminism, pacifism, religious fundamentalism and so on could be seen as counterpoints which might in time – through both local and transnational activities – help to undo one or several currently dominant social structures such as bureaucracy, capitalism, democracy, patriarchy, militarism and secularism.

Yet whether trends have a linear, a cyclical, an equilibrating or a dialectical character, as aspects of the social order they have a causal significance which, as in the case of norms and structures, is not reducible to social forces at the level of units. In other words, these historical patterns of social relations are not only produced by actors and their various bonds of interdependence; embedded developmental tendencies also to some extent constrain social activities to take the forms that they do. Like 'stationary' structures, secular movements have a force that the people affected by them find difficult to resist. Indeed, actors may in many cases not even be aware of the trends which affect, and are sustained by, their actions.

Needless to say, the sorts of specifications and qualifications that were earlier attached to the notion of structural power also broadly apply in regard to the force of longitudinal movements. Thus, for one thing, trends do not recognize country boundaries: they are facts of world society which affect international relations as well as intra-national conditions. However, this is not to say that these historical patterns are universal phenomena, in the sense that they touch all places and all people in the world. For instance, Kondratieff cycles presumably made no significant impact in the Australian outback and other isolated areas during the early nineteenth century. In addition, a given trend may be manifested in different guises at the different locations that it does affect. For example, a 'counterpoint' to techno-scientific rationality may appear in the form of Hindu revivalism in one corner of the globe and Liberation Theology in another. Moreover, it is possible that several developmental tendencies may be operative concurrently in a given socio-historical context, shaping the course of social change through their complementary and/or contradictory implications. Hence, for example, a Marxist analysis might simultaneously incorporate notions of the linear concentration of capital and long cycles of accumulation and class dialectics.

Finally, it is important to stress that the concept of deep trends of social life does not necessarily entail a premise of historical determinism. Thus to say that social relations exhibit regularities through time is not in itself to say that the course of history follows predetermined and irreversible 'laws': it might be possible to 'buck the trend'. In this view a developmental tendency is indeed but a 'tendency' and can – albeit perhaps only with difficulty – be avoided or even superseded. For instance, Karl Marx in this vein suggested that the class dialectic could be overcome in a future classless society under communism. This key distinction between determination and determinism will be discussed at greater length in Chapter 7.

RECAPITULATION: INTERNATIONAL RELATIONS AND WORLD-SYSTEMIC RELATIONS

The present chapter has explored the involvement in the process of transformation of three forms of social order, particularly as manifested in international relations, i.e., 'visible' norms and 'deeper' structures and trends. Earlier, Chapters 3 and 4 charted, respectively, the importance of transfers between countries of new frameworks of social life and the significance of cross-border activities themselves in triggering and shaping social changes. With a host of illustrations, these three chapters have established that international forces do indeed lie at the heart of the causes, courses and outcomes of transformation processes. Evidence suggests that the involvement of international relations in the dynamics of social change can be traced back over many centuries, but also that the international dimension has become especially prominent during the present era of globalization. Moreover, all current signs suggest that globalization will persist and even accelerate in the years to come, making it all the more vital to incorporate international relations into our understanding of social change.

As was stressed in Chapter 2, the focus in the present writing on international actors, international interdependencies, international norms, international structures and international trends is not informed by a premise of international determinism. Rather, the bias in the foregoing discussion has been taken in reaction against conventions of endogenism in the study of social change. The aim has therefore been to fill a gap rather than to create a new one. Having now established the importance of international relations alongside local and national circumstances in the dynamics of transformation, we can – and I think should – proceed to abandon once and for all the false dichotomy between internal and external realms of social life. A world-historical-sociological perspective on social change achieves this end by transcending, on the one hand, fields of International Relations and International History, which have studied 'international society', and, on the other hand, fields of Sociology and History, which have investigated 'national society'.

Although world-systemic analysis marks a departure from long-established conventions in the study of social transformation, this enterprise confronts some of the same core problems of theory that have faced the traditional approaches. Hence continuity is mixed with change in the study of social change, too! The remaining chapters of this book therefore examine the notion of world-systemic explanation in regard to three fundamental questions of social enquiry: namely, the relationship between different facets of social life (politics, economics, culture, etc.); the relationship between agency and order; and the relationship between theory and practice. This discussion is all the more important for those participants in the world-historical-sociological project who might be drawn from International Relations as, in contrast to practitioners of other social sciences, most researchers in IR have until recently neglected to address these metatheoretical issues with the care that they require.

═ 6 ═

FACETS OF WORLD-SYSTEMIC
SOCIAL TRANSFORMATION

In Chapter 2 we reformulated the analysis of social change in terms of the world system concept. It was proposed that we should alter our conceptualization of social space from one based on the notion of different 'levels' – with the implication that there are separate international and domestic societies, and hence discrete international and internal causes of social change – to a holistic conception constructed around the idea of a single and 'layerless' world society. For analytical purposes a conceptual distinction between international and intra-national dimensions of social life was temporarily retained in Chapters 3 to 5, although readers may have noted that this artificial separation was progressively relaxed as that discussion proceeded. The remainder of the book will address questions of world society and world-systemic relations without focusing on international–national connections, whose existence can in the light of preceding chapters henceforth be taken as a given.

Instead, the present chapter will concentrate on a different analytical slicing of the world-systemic whole: namely, between what will be called the various 'facets' of social relations – politics, economics, culture, psychology and ecology.[1] This matter of facets was raised indirectly in Chapter 4, when it was noted that international interdependence takes ecological, ideological, commercial, military, artistic and other forms. (By extension the same kinds of mutual involvement between people pertain in local and national settings within world society, of course.)

However, the issue of the causal status of the different facets vis-à-vis one another was not directly addressed at that stage. In other words, where amongst the cultural, political, psychological, ecological and economic aspects of world social relations are the forces of transformation generated?[2] For example, which of these facets caused the decline of Amerindian civilizations several hundred years ago, which prompted the advent of total war in the twentieth century, which has sparked the ongoing information revolution, and so on?

Three broad types of answers to this fundamental question about the dynamics of social change can be distinguished. A first approach is to establish a hierarchy of forces in which one of the five facets just named is posited to lie at the root of the other four. In such arguments the process of transformation is said to be, at base, politically driven, or economically propelled, or culturally determined, or psychologically triggered, or ecologically stimulated. A second perspective on the question of facets focuses on a more general distinction between matter and consciousness and holds that change is either a result of material forces (politics, economics and ecology), or an outcome of ideal causes (culture and psychology). Meanwhile a third position – the one that is advocated here – takes distance from both single-facet explanations and the materialism/idealism debate in favour of an understanding of social transformation in terms of simultaneous cause–effect connections between all five facets. In this view world-systemic relations involve not only a co-determination of international, national and local dimensions of social life, but also the mutual constitution of economics, psychology, ecology, politics and culture. Thus the causal dynamics of social change are held to be multifaceted as well as multidimensional.

The three parts of this chapter examine each of these broad approaches in turn. The first section reviews explanations of social change that have been couched in politicism, economism, cultural determinism, psychologism and ecologism. The second part assesses materialist and idealist accounts of social transformation in world perspective, before the third and final section elaborates a case for adopting a five-faceted conception of the dynamics of change.

SINGLE-FACET EXPLANATIONS

Politicism

As just mentioned, some accounts of change treat reconstruction of the social order as being primarily a political process. Social relations have a 'political' quality insofar as they involve the distribution and exercise of power, where social power is the capacity to affect the behaviour and experience of persons and groups in their relationships with other individuals and associations. The political facet of social life is often conceived narrowly in terms of the affairs of state alone, but of course the pursuit, consolidation, maintenance and application of power also occurs in many social contexts outside government. There are politics of the firm, politics of the church, politics of sexuality, politics of sport, politics of student-faculty relations and so on. In this light Maurice Duverger has rightly objected that 'to study power only within the framework of the state without comparing it with power elsewhere is restrictive' (1964: ix). Indeed, politics is a ubiquitous phenomenon: every social act, any case of interdependence, each norm, any social structure and every trend in some manner entails the establishment, reproduction or realignment of power relations. In this sense social life is inherently political, and the purported distinction between 'politicized' and 'apolitical' situations refers only to the degree to which the operation of power is overt and contested, as opposed to tacit and perhaps even unrecognized.

Matters connected with the distribution and exercise of power invariably have the effect of promoting or blocking social change. Earlier chapters of this book have illustrated the frequent importance in the transformation process of pressure-group campaigns, official regulations, international and civil wars, interventions by transnational corporations, and so on. Thus social change is not only a question of creating new power relationships in society, but politics is itself a force of transformation, too.

Politicist arguments, however, take the further step of affirming that politics provides the first and foremost impetus to social change. Politicism, the reduction of social life to its political facet, was noted in Chapter 1 to be a characteristic feature of realist international theory. Although realists have generally shown little interest in questions of social transformation, certain historical sociologists and social historians have taken a politicist line in their explanations of continuity and change in social life. For instance, the title of Michael Mann's magnum opus, The Sources of Social Power, reveals a principal preoccupation with politics; his model of historical development defines social relations in terms of four power networks and organizations of social control (1986: Ch 1). In regard to a more specific transformation, John Hall (1987) and Geoffrey Parker (1988) rank amongst a number of authors who have tended to explain 'the rise of the West' primarily in terms of the emergence of modern military forces and their overwhelming strength in combat with other armies. Indeed, Hall has characterized 'competition' as the main (and transhistorical) spur to social development (1985: 189). Meanwhile John Breuilly and Silviu Brucan have adopted a premise of political determinism in their accounts of the growth of the nationality principle: Breuilly viewing this structure as a by-product of competition for state power (1982: 1–2); and Brucan treating nationhood as an outcome of struggles for social power generally (1978a: 20).

These and other arguments suggest that political forces lie at the root of the dynamics of social change. Yet it is one thing to say that politics is important, and quite another to reduce the world system to world politics alone. Politicist premises become untenable when note is taken of economic and other facets of the transformation process.

Economism

Economistic approaches to the issue of change are on the whole more prevalent in the literature than politicist accounts, and indeed are perhaps the most frequently encountered type of single-facet explanation of social history. Economics refers, in the words of Lionel Robbins, to 'the forms assumed by human behaviour in disposing of scarce means . . . which have alternative uses' (1935: 15–16). Thus social relations have an economic quality insofar as they involve the management of resources for the creation of value. Economics encompasses matters of production (the transformation of one or several objects of value into another source of value), distribution (the movement of resources across space), trade (the exchange of one source of value for another), storage (the retention of resources for later use) and consumption (the extraction of value from resources). The 'scarce means' that are produced, transported, exchanged, saved and consumed include primary commodities, manufactures, labour, technology, knowledge, information, money, experiences (i.e., concerts, travel, etc.) and health. Economics typically involves combining and recombining these various kinds of resources in order to create other forms of value. It should be noted that this conception of economics ranges more widely than the definitions which generally inform Economics textbooks or business news bulletins. In those contexts the focus is put on the kinds of resources that tend to fetch the highest value in contemporary world social relations: namely, industrial goods, high technology and financial instruments. Yet economics in practice touches every corner of social life, including housework (as a form of labour, often unwaged), sleep (as a use of time), spiritual reflection (as a means of producing knowledge) and friendship (as a valued experience for which other resources will be foregone). Moreover, each social structure has an economic aspect. Thus, for example, race has consequences for employment opportunities, secularism affects the share of resources in society held by clerics, etc. In one way or another, then, all social relations are in part economic relations, and all social change is in part economic change.

Previous chapters have included ample evidence that economics often figures in social relations as a force as well as an object of change. For example, we noted in Chapter 4 that the pursuit of raw materials and investment opportunities gave an impetus to many nineteenth-century imperial policies, and that these interventions often set full-scale social transformations in train in the colonies, as well as in semi-colonies such as China and Thailand. In addition, technological innovation has been a principal spur across the globe to industrialization and urbanization. A number of researchers have examined the significance of taxation practices and public debt for the emergence of the modern state (Tilly 1975/1990; Rasler and Thompson 1989). Meanwhile uneven distributions of resources between different circles in society have provided an important stimulus to the rise of women's associations, trade unions, anti-apartheid campaigns, pensioners' groups and other social movements. In these and countless other instances, social change has had economic causes as well as economic effects.

Some authors take this widespread evidence as reason to adopt an economistic perspective on social change, i.e., to treat economics as the root cause of historical discontinuities. Amongst modernization theorists, for example, Walt Rostow (1960) has explained contemporary social change in terms of 'stages of economic growth', while Marion Levy has assessed modernization as a function of the ratio of inanimate to animate sources of energy in the production process (1972: 3). Wilbert Moore, too, has treated modernization in terms of technological shifts, the expansion of material production and the associated social organization to which these economic developments give rise (1974: Ch 5).

Economism has also characterized much analysis of social change that carries the Marxist label. The writings of Karl Marx himself sometimes suggest an economistic approach, for example, in statements such as 'changes in the economic foundation lead sooner or later to the transformation of the whole immense superstructure' (1859: 21). Intimations of an even narrower, technological determinism appear in Marx's quip that 'the hand-mill gives you society with the feudal lord; the steam-mill, society with the industrial capitalist' (1847: 122). Friedrich Engels likewise was prone to make assertions like 'the economic structure of society always furnishes the real basis . . . of a given historical period' (1892: 41). That said, he on other occasions vehemently denounced those who 'twist [the materialist conception of history] into saying that the economic element is the only determining one' (1890: 381). Certainly Marxists normally treat the *mode* of production as something that encompasses much more than the *means* of production, and some Marxists have undertaken considerable research on cultural conditions of capitalism (e.g., Gramscian investigations of ideology as a brake on revolutionary politics). Nevertheless, Marxist analyses of social change have on the whole shown at least an economic bias, if not full-blown economism.

Much work in world-system theory has rested on economistic premises, too. This research explicitly takes the capitalist world-*economy* as its principal object of investigation. Particularly in their early writings, Wallerstein and his colleagues reduced world society to a world market and treated its main divisions (core, periphery and semiperiphery) in the first place as economic zones. As we noted in the discussion of international trends in Chapter 5, world-system theorists have during the past fifteen years given some attention to politics, in connection with the problem of hegemonic cycles. Moreover, a number of their recent writings have raised the issue of 'metaphysical presuppositions' in the capitalist world-economy, as well as questions of 'global culture' (King 1991; Wallerstein 1991a). That said, though, an economistic tendency continues for the most part to hold sway over world-system theory.

So explanations of social change have exhibited several variants of economism; yet are any of these arguments sustainable? After all, although every event and circumstance in world society can be seen to have an economic aspect, we saw earlier that the political facet was equally pervasive in social life, and the following remarks will establish that culture and other forces are also omnipresent (and influential) in processes of transformation.

Cultural determinism

A third type of single-facet reductionism in the study of social change places culture in the position of prime mover. The word 'culture' rivals 'structure' for the diversity and ambiguity of its usages. In the present context the term refers to that aspect of social life which entails the construction, communication, circulation and consumption of meaning.[3] Culture is the process whereby people in their interactions with one another continuously establish, reaffirm, reassess and alter values and beliefs – namely, by creating signs and symbolic representations, by transmitting meanings to others, and by interpreting signifiers received from others. Cultural practices are most conspicuous in activities related to literature, music, dance, drama, oratory, religion, philosophy, journalism, advertising, sculpture, painting, photography, film, fashion and architecture. More broadly, however, any utterance, bodily gesture or handling of an artefact involves a conscious or implicit attribution of meaning, and hence an assessment of values and interests. In this sense every social phenomenon has a cultural quality. Each transaction between persons in some way includes a communication of values and beliefs, and each structure and trend organizes meaning at the same time that it arranges relations of power and production in world social life.

Remarks in earlier chapters concerning cross-border cultural diffusion and the international production of knowledge have already indicated that culture can figure centrally in the process of reproduction and/or reconstruction of the patterns of social life. We have noted the impact on various transformations of, for example, the historic religions, the principle of instrumental rationality, different artistic genres, racial consciousness, the deification of money under capitalism, and so on. In this vein, too, proponents of the cultural imperialism thesis have maintained that the global construction of dominant patterns of belief – particularly through international mass media conglomerates – has been a driving force of social history in the contemporary 'Third World' (Tomlinson 1991). The general suggestion, then, is that the emergence of new ways of understanding and discussing social relations lends important weight to the overall transformation process. As Kenneth Boulding puts this point:

> When communication is part of the system we are communicating about, then communicating about it will change the system itself.
>
> (1985: 138)

Extending the notion of cultural determination to an extreme, certain authors have actually reduced the dynamics of transformation to cultural forces, so that changes in values and the construction of meaning are held to be the root cause of rearrangements of social life. For example, Talcott

Parsons openly declared himself to be a cultural determinist, arguing that 'the normative elements are more important for social change than . . . material interests' (1966: 113). Taking inspiration from Max Weber's thesis concerning the Protestant ethic and the rise of capitalism (1904–5),[4] Parsons argued that modernization had its origins in Christianity and, more particularly, in a new world view which emerged in Europe during the Renaissance and the Reformation. Moreover, normative cohesion was for Parsons the key to the maintenance of the modern social order. Robert Bellah (1965), Shmuel Eisenstadt (1968) and others have similarly explained the occurrence or absence of modernization in the various parts of the world in terms of locally prevailing religious conditions. Meanwhile Cyril Black (1966: 7) has rooted the process of modernization in the development of techno-scientific knowledge.

In contrast to the works just mentioned, which broadly endorse modernization as a progressive historical development, other cultural determinists, writing in the trends of 'postmodernism' and 'poststructuralism', have taken a fundamentally critical stance towards the modern social order.[5] Poststructuralists and postmodernists typically highlight the importance of language as the ultimate source of social organization and its changes. ('Language' here refers less to verbal expression per se than to a more general and deeper framework of meaning, which these writers also variously call a 'discourse', 'narrative' or 'text'.) For example, Michel Foucault (1966) has divided the history of Western Europe into epochs of knowledge, each of them grounded in a distinctive 'episteme': namely, the Renaissance episteme, which held sway until the early seventeenth century; the Classical episteme, which structured knowledge between the mid-seventeenth and late eighteenth centuries; and the modern episteme, which became dominant in the early nineteenth century. In postmodernist eyes, then, the social order is reducible to a structure of meaning, and social activities are essentially a matter of 'language games' and 'text readings'. From this perspective world history is seen to unfold as a function of the institutionalization of some meanings and the simultaneous exclusion or marginalization of others (Der Derian and Shapiro 1989; Ashley and Walker 1990). Thus most 'voices' speak in harmony with, and thereby reproduce, the prevailing patterns of social order, while alternative frameworks of meaning tend to be suppressed. Following poststructuralist logic, change in language holds the key to social transformation, as radical discourses challenge prevailing narratives to give history a dynamic character. Donna Gregory takes such a line in her foreword to a recently published collection of postmodernist International Relations essays, suggesting that:

> we do shape our world somehow in accord with our discursive structures . . . changing the latter might help us to change the former.
>
> (1989: xvii)

The possibilities of reconstructing social relations would accordingly be enhanced insofar as people listen to and 'celebrate' voices on the margins.

Undoubtedly there is a strong case for exploring cultural aspects of the world-systemic dynamics of social change; however, the 'textualism' of Roland Barthes, Jacques Derrida et al. (Harari 1979), the religious-determinist tendency in work by the likes of Bellah and Clifford Geertz, and other forms of cultural determinism constitute oversimplifications of the transformation process. As social relations have integral political and economic qualities alongside omnipresent cultural aspects, it is difficult to see how the forces of culture can be isolated from, and treated as a prior cause of, politics, economics and the other facets of the dynamics of social change still to be discussed.

Psychologism

Most arguments concerning the purported 'base' of social relations pit political determinists, economic determinists and cultural determinists against one another. In addition, however, a smaller number of psychological determinists have advanced single-facet explanations of social change which treat mental apparatuses as the primary engine of social processes. The psychological aspect of world social relations encompasses conditions of the human mind, such as personality, conscious and unconscious motivation, cognition and the person's general sense of being. Together these circumstances constitute the self.

Sociologists and psychologists alike have often regarded social make-up and psychic make-up as separate questions, but in practice the distinction between the two dissolves. On the one hand, the individual's experience is always constructed in the context of social interaction, social interdependence and social organization. Conversely, social life is steeped in conditions of the self such as anxiety, stress, sexual desire, anger and human bonding. Indeed, psychological circumstances in some way touch every social act and each feature of the social order, even if the connections do not always seem immediately apparent. For example, various theorists have linked national identification with the psychological dynamics of personal identity (Bloom 1990). Others have discerned relationships between capitalism and alienation, between industrialism and anomie, and between militarism and sexuality (cf. Marx and Engels 1846; Durkheim 1893; Enloe 1989). Thus at the same time that the self never exists outside of a social context, no social situation exists independently of psychic conditions either; and any social change involves, in part, a transformation of the self.

Given the pervasive nature of the psychological facet of social relations, we might reasonably hypothesize that forces connected with personality structure, modes of perception, motivational drives and so on shape world-systemic dynamics of social transformation no less than forces of economics, politics and culture. For example, the rise of fascism in the second quarter of the twentieth century is explained by some as being not only a result of weak constitutions, material hardship and propaganda, but also a consequence of a particular form of mass psychology which developed in conjunction with those political, economic and cultural conditions (Reich 1933). On a similar premise, the dismantling of patriarchy would require a reconstruction of the self on the part of both sexes as much as it would entail altered depictions of men and women in the mass media, the equalization of rates of pay, and large-scale promotion of women to positions of public leadership.

Some authors take such insights to the point of adopting a postulate of psychological determinism in the study of social change, reducing the transformation process to psychological causes. For instance, psychoanalytic theory has generally explained social life as an outcome of conscious and, especially unconscious motivations, so that the social order is said to be rooted in psychic structures. On this premise Sigmund Freud in his later writings (e.g., 1929) understood history in terms of an interplay of life and death instincts, while Wilhelm Reich (1949) and others have reduced social relations to the libido. Following such logic, progressive social change essentially becomes a question of liberating the self from neuroses, although Freudians, Jungians and other factions within psychoanalytic circles have disagreed profoundly on the design of therapies that might effect such an emancipation.

From a very different perspective certain modernization theorists have explained the transcendence of 'traditional society' primarily in psychological terms. For example, Inkeles and Smith (1974) have identified fourteen personality traits as engines of modernization. More specifically, David McClelland (1961) has affirmed the need for an 'achievement orientation' as a prerequisite for the transition to modernity, while Everett Hagen (1962) has concluded that a propensity for innovation is vital.

Regrettably, questions of psychology have often been excluded *a priori* from studies of social change, and indeed these issues are almost universally ignored in works that explore the international dimension of transformation processes. That said, however, psychological determinism surely constitutes an overcompensation. Links between the self and world society warrant careful attention, but they exist simultaneously with – and need to be assessed in relation to – the political, economic, cultural and ecological facets of social life.

Ecologism

A final form of single-facet explanation considered here, ecologism, reduces society to nature and regards social change as an outcome of biospheric forces. Ecology is that aspect of social relations which concerns conditions for life in a particular environment. As such, it encompasses questions of biomass (i.e., the concentration of living matter in a given space), climate and weather conditions, properties of the earth's waters, features of land masses, demography (size, distribution and other circumstances of human population on the planet), epidemiology (the incidence of disease amongst humans and other species) and so on.

Like the connections between society and the self, the society–nature nexus has often been overlooked in social research. Indeed, ecology is to this day often thought to concern natural processes as something separate from social relations. A bifurcation of academic endeavour into social enquiry on the one hand and natural science on the other became entrenched during the Renaissance (thus several centuries before the development of specialized disciplines further fragmented the study of social life) (Leiss 1972: Chs 2–4). Under the influence of this dichotomy social theorists – and students of social change amongst them – have generally regarded the living world as something that falls outside the scope of their central concerns.

However, an alternative methodology which rejects this society–nature separation has survived on the margins of modern thought: for example, in the seventeenth-century writings of Spinoza (Naess 1977). Early in the present century Georg Lukács reaffirmed the position that 'nature is a societal category . . . nature's form, its content, its range and its objectivity are all socially conditioned' (1919: 234). The reverse could equally be said, of course – namely, that society is naturally conditioned. Recent research in the emerging field of 'social ecology' has made substantial inroads into the orthodoxy of separating natural and social studies (Bookchin 1986).

Indeed, ecology is a pervasive facet of social life. Every social activity in some way either sustains, enhances or degrades the quality of life. Ecology figures very dramatically in social relations on the occasion of droughts, oil spills and epidemics, but it also has a more subtle involvement in situations such as urban crowding and the day-to-day exploitation of a multitude of natural resources. Social structures, too, have ubiquitous ecological consequences. For example, industrialism has altered the chemical composition of the earth's atmosphere, land mass and seas, with implications for life processes that remain in many respects unclear. Nationality has had the ecological effect of encouraging drives to increase population in a number of countries, including France after the world wars and Rumania under the Ceauşescu regime. Militarism has done violence not only to humanity, but also to the living planet generally. In a word, then, ecology is no less integral to social relations than politics, economics, culture and psychology; and every social change is in some respect an ecological change.

In the light of this circumstance we might expect that ecology can be a force as well as an object of social transformation. William McNeill has argued explicitly that 'a fuller comprehension of humanity's ever-changing place in the balance of nature ought to be part of our understanding of history' (1976: 5). Biospheric conditions may, depending on the situation, either encourage or inhibit a reconstruction of the social order. For example, malnourishment and disease might add to discontent with a given framework of social relations, although such afflictions might also cause a population to be physically too weak to mobilize for change. Meanwhile mounting adverse ecological developments in contemporary history may, as suggested in Chapter 4, prompt major world-scale reorganizations of social life in the coming decades or centuries.

This may be so, but a number of environmentalists have allowed their worries about biospheric damage to lead them into arguments of ecological determinism. For example, over the past two hundred years each successive generation has heard Malthusian predictions of impending social breakdown due to overpopulation. In a recent revival of this proposition, Garrett Hardin (1977) has called for the application of 'lifeboat ethics' in world social policy, i.e., suggesting that some proportion of humanity should be sacrificed to famine and disease in order that life itself can be salvaged in the long run. Yet the actual course of history has thus far defied Malthusian forecasts, as developments in economics and other facets of social life which are underplayed by eco-determinists have allowed ever-larger human populations to be accommodated on the planet. This is of course not to say that demographic trends are unimportant – only that Malthusian views are oversimplistic.

From another angle, and in a milder tone, James Lovelock (1979) has advanced the so-called Gaia hypothesis, which suggests that the biosphere is a single living organism whose self-regulatory dynamics – mediated *inter alia* through humanity and its social relations – have the effect of keeping the earth fit for life. Eco-fundamentalism also informs 'deep ecology', with its advocacy of 'biospheric egalitarianism' amongst all species on earth (Devall and Sessions 1984). In different ways, each of these theories holds that social development has an underlying ecological dynamic.

Yet ecological determinists seem to have escaped the Scylla of anthropocentrism only to fall into the Charybdis of naturalism. It is one thing to recognize the often neglected society–nature nexus and the ecological forces that affect the course of social history; but it is quite another thing to allow environmentalist sentiments to blot out the other facets of social life. Like politics, economics, culture and psychology, ecology constitutes only one aspect of world-systemic dynamics of social change, not the whole force of transformation.

HISTORICAL MATERIALISM AND HISTORICAL IDEALISM

So far in this chapter we have established the inadequacy of single-facet explanations of social change, whether they focus on ecology, on politics, or whatever. In contrast, other theories account for transformations of the social order in terms of a combination of two or more facets, e.g., adopting a political economy or a psychocultural approach. As indicated at the beginning of this chapter, my own position is that we need to examine social change in terms of a fivefold interplay of political, economic, cultural, psychological and ecological forces. However, other researchers have conceived of causality more narrowly in materialist (political, economic and/or ecological) or idealist (cultural and/or psychological) terms. Such arguments are attractive for their simplicity relative to the concept of five-faceted world-systemic relations, so they warrant careful consideration before we opt for the less easily manageable premise of material–ideal interconnections.

The postulate of historical materialism locates the causes of transformation in the 'objective realities' of the social context in question. A materialist premise underlies politicist, economistic and naturalist arguments of the sorts considered in the preceding section, as well as explanations discussed below which combine these facets: for example, theories of political economy (i.e., those that genuinely combine politics and economics[6]); ecological-economic accounts; and geopolitical arguments.

The separation of politics and economics is now widely accepted to be no more than an analytical distinction (cf. Barratt Brown 1984; Staniland 1985). In fact, a number of analysts today refer to world society as the 'world political economy'. On one side of the political-economic interrelation, politics is intrinsically a function of economics. In other words, the alignment and exercise of power is always in part contingent upon access to resources obtained through production, exchange and consumption. True, as we saw earlier, in the course of discussing international regimes, resources do not automatically yield power; however, no power develops in the absence of resources either. Concurrently, economics is equally a function of politics. That is, power relations invariably affect what is produced in a society, how the resulting products are allocated amongst the population, and to what ends they are used. In a word, then, neither politics nor economics comes before the other; they are co-determining in social relations.

Authors across quite a wide spectrum of theoretical persuasions have adopted the view that social change is largely if not wholly a political-economic process. For example, Marxists explain social transformation as a consequence of the quintessentially political-economic question of 'ownership (read, control) of the means of production'. Outside Marxist circles, Daniel Chirot has highlighted 'the interaction between economic change and global political relationships' as the causal dynamic behind reconstructions of the social order in the modern era (1986: 226). For his part, William McNeill has urged that the gap between military and economic history should be closed, given that, in his view, a 'merger of the military with the commercial spirit' in Europe was a key reason for 'the rise of the West' (1982: 64, 116, 143). A host of other writers including Otto Hintze (1929), Theda Skocpol (1979), Charles Tilly (1981; 1990), Michael Mann (1986) Aristide Zolberg (1986) and Anthony Giddens have developed the political-economic argument that social change has in modern history been driven by mutually determining forces of capitalist development and the growth of the modern state. Giddens describes these 'two great transformative agencies' as 'intersecting processes, both intrinsically globalizing, neither of which can be reductively explained away in terms of the other' (1989: 267; 1990: 174).

Another two-sided materialist formulation of the dynamics of social change – namely one that highlights the mutually constitutive nature of economics and ecology – has to date attracted considerably less attention than theories of political economy. Yet the connections between resource management and biospheric conditions are no less intimate than relations between politics and economics. On the one hand, economics is inherently an outcome of ecological forces. Demography, topography, climate and other conditions of the natural environment determine what can be produced, how long it can be stored, and so on. As André Gorz puts this point:

> all productive activity depends on borrowing from the finite resources of the planet and on organizing a set of exchanges within a fragile system of multiple equilibriums.

(1975: 13)

Conversely, economics always affects and can in some instances fundamentally change the character of those ecological 'equilibriums'. Human management of resources cannot but in some way shape biospheric conditions: either neutrally, or for better, or for worse. This insight has recently given rise to a spate of literature promoting so-called 'sustainable development' as a guiding principle for social relations across the globe (cf. Redclift 1987).

From another materialist perspective, geopolitical theories have for more than a century propounded explanations of history which focus on inter-relations between power struggles and the natural environment (Kristof 1960). For example, Halford Mackinder at the start of this century and Colin Gray more recently have argued that command of the Eurasian 'heartland' was vital to protect 'the West' from purported 'yellow perils' and 'red threats' in 'the East' (Mackinder 1919; Gray 1977). In regard to a more general issue of social change, both Randall Collins and Charles Tilly have explained the historical emergence of the modern state largely in geopolitical terms. Tilly has for his part affirmed that 'states always grow out of competition for control of territory and population' (1990: 4; also Collins 1981: 4).

Without necessarily endorsing these particular arguments, we can recognize that politics and ecology are intrinsically interconnected in social affairs. For one thing, ecology in some way shapes all power relations in society. Thus the spatial distribution of mineral deposits has yielded so-called 'oil power' and the like. Both short-term weather variations, such as storms, and long-term climate changes, such as the greenhouse effect, may bring re-arrangements of power alignments in their train. For example, inept handling of the 1972 earthquake disaster in Nicaragua, together with widespread corruption in the ensuing rebuilding programmes, gave a major spur to opposition that eventually overthrew the Somoza regime in 1979 (Close 1988: 28–9, 66). Demographic developments such as a rising proportion of young persons in a population can also have political consequences, e.g., helping to promote Islamic revivalism in Algeria in recent years. Conversely, and simultaneously, politics also affects ecology, insofar as the organization and exercise of power helps to determine whether social activity will undermine, preserve or enhance conditions for life. In short, then, political-ecological interrelations lie at the heart of transformation processes as much as ecological-economic and economic-political inter-connections.

Each of the various types of materialist arguments just surveyed tend to accord only epiphenomenal status to cultural and psychological facets of world social relations. These 'subjective' aspects of social life are thereby regarded as outcomes – without substantial causal significance in themselves – of underlying 'objective' forces of social transformation. However, in diametric opposition to materialist notions, the postulate of historical idealism reverses this hierarchy of facets and explains continuity and change in social relations as a consequence of developments in the realm of thought. In other words, history is held to have primary ideational (i.e., psychological and cultural) causes which produce material (i.e., political, economic and ecological) effects.

In the first part of this chapter we considered cultural determinism and psychologism as single-facet versions of the idealist premise, but other explanations of social change also highlight the importance of interrelations between cultural and psychological forces. For example, some post-modernists emphasize the importance of feeling, instinct, personality and other conditions of the self in shaping the way that texts are read and 'deconstructed'. In this vein, too, Michel Foucault focused in his account of the history of ideas on how 'the human being, consciousness, origin, and the subject emerge, intersect, mingle and separate off' (1969: 16). Jürgen Habermas in his theory of 'lifeworlds' and communicative action (1981) also posits a crucial interplay in the transformation process between self-identity and the construction of meaning. (Recall from Chapter 1, however, that neither Foucault nor Habermas have developed their arguments with explicit reference to world society and world-systemic processes (cf. Mészáros 1989: 23–4).)

Although we might object to the idealist extreme in explanations of social change, it is clear that culture and psychology have important mutual effects in social relations. On the one hand, conditions of the self are invariably culture-bound. Among other things, prevailing values and beliefs shape the character of human motivations and the way that they are expressed. Hence, for example, homosexuality was generally accepted and overtly practised in ancient Greece, whereas this drive has been widely repressed under the force of values prevalent in large parts of contemporary world society (Dover 1978). The construction of meaning through language and artefacts also profoundly affects cognition: that is, how people perceive their social situation and the ways that it might be changed.

On the other hand, and at the same time, psychology has significant consequences for culture. After all, meaning cannot be interpreted in the absence of cognitive processes. In addition, beliefs are in part an expression of psychological needs for a sense of identity, coherence and so on. Artwork reflects the state of the soul as much as the prevailing political and economic order. In a word, then, neither culture nor psychology exists in the absence of the other, and each is a pervasive aspect of world social relations.

MULTIFACETED WORLD-SYSTEMIC DETERMINATION

In the first part of this chapter we established the central importance of political, economic, cultural, psychological and ecological forces in the dynamics of social transformation, while noting that none of these facets could be regarded as the prior cause of the others. In the second section we furthermore determined that power relations, resource management and environmental conditions are inseparable from one another, and that culture and psychology are similarly two interwoven strands in a single social fabric. However, neither materialism nor idealism provide a sustainable basis for a theory of social change in world perspective, as the following remarks indicate. Explanations of social transformation must therefore attend to a complex fivefold interplay of conditions relating to power, production, belief, the self and the biosphere.

Although historical idealism and historical materialism differ radically in their assignment of causality, in another fundamental respect they share an underlying assumption – namely, the separate existence of consciousness and physical circumstances. Idealist arguments maintain that continuities and changes in social life are caused by developments in human consciousness, while materialist explanations affirm the primacy of political, economic and ecological forces in social relations. However, both of these general approaches presume a dichotomy between the experiential realm (the subject) and the physical realm (the object).

On the whole, materialist notions hold greater sway in contemporary social thought than idealist perspectives. Indeed, in our everyday vocabulary we tend to equate the word 'objectivity' with 'truth' and 'the real world', while the terms 'perception' and 'belief' are treated as antonyms of 'reality' and 'fact'. In this sense values and the soul are not regarded as 'real', and on those occasions when a causal connection is drawn, consciousness is assumed to be constituted by, and not constitutive of, material conditions.

However, it has been suggested through earlier comments and illustrations in this chapter that ideational forces do in fact make 'real' impacts on social transformations, just as, conversely and concurrently, ecology, economics and politics shape the psychological and cultural aspects of social life. Hence neither the material nor the ideal appears to be reducible to the other in social relations, and both, as a combination, have causal status in the process of social change. In this light Anthony Giddens discusses social relations in terms of what he calls symbolic orders/modes of discourse, economic institutions, modes of sanction, and political institutions (1977a: 81–111); and Theda Skocpol suggests that the key transnational contexts affecting history are geopolitical relations, the international communication of ideals and world economic patterns (1985: 8). Each of these formulations suggests that, while an analytical separation of experiential and physical forces can be helpful to an investigation of social transformation, the distinction must not be reified.

For one thing, politics and culture are 'in reality' inseparable from one another, as is well captured in the Foucauldian dyad 'power/knowledge' (Foucault 1980).[7] On the one hand, the alignment and exercise of power in world society is always in part a function of the construction of meaning. A power relationship is established and sustained through myths, symbols and – most convincingly – a process of legitimation whereby a population comes to believe that the forces which exercise power over it do so rightfully. To take a readily apparent example, the power of the nationality principle is maintained by, among other things, artefacts, such as flags and emblems; rituals, such as national holidays and customs checks at frontiers; literature, such as nationally orientated accounts of history; and a host of other cultural practices. By the same token, the deconstruction and reconstruction of meanings can radically alter the nature of politics. Thus, for example, the development of black consciousness has helped to mobilize many struggles against racism. In a word, then, power does not exist independently from *empowerment* through cultural forces.

Conversely, and simultaneously, politics shapes the construction of meaning: race politics have produced black consciousness just as they have been affected by this ideology. We have already noted, in Chapter 4, that the definition of 'knowledge' is an inherently political question. Power relationships are a key determinant of what becomes accepted as 'rational' and 'meaningful' in a given social context. Pierre Bourdieu has in this regard distinguished between the *doxy* (the range of normal and permitted discourse) and the *doxa* (the realm of the unspoken and undiscussed) in each social setting (1972: 164–71). For example, Galileo would have moved freely in the *doxy* of twentieth-century world society, but in his own day he had to struggle to assert his construction of knowledge from a position in the *doxa*. By the same token, whereas pacifist values are generally dismissed as impracticable today, they may come to command the realm of 'commonsense' in the politics of tomorrow.

The material–ideal divide is also crossed in the causal relationship between economics and culture. On the one hand, economics is intrinsically a cultural process. People cannot 'dispose of scarce means which have alternative uses' unless they have a framework of values in relation to which they can articulate and rank-order their wants. Constructions of meaning influence what is produced, where it is moved, on what terms it is exchanged and to what ends it is consumed. Culture has a profound effect on what will qualify as 'good health', 'appropriate technology', an 'essential raw material', a 'real job', a 'rewarding experience', a 'just price' and so on in a given historical context.

On the other hand, economics is also integral to culture. The instruments through which meaning is formulated and communicated (books, icons, films, etc.) must all be produced, exchanged and consumed. Moreover, the deployment of resources in education is crucial to the reproduction or reconstruction of prevailing values in society. The economic quality of culture is well captured in Bourdieu's phrases 'the production of belief' and the 'economy of symbolic goods' (1980). There is thus an economic side to culture as much as there is a cultural side to economics. In this respect, too, thought and material processes exist in combination rather than separately in social relations.

Other interconnections between the material and the ideal prevail between ecology and culture and between psychological and physical aspects of social life. In regard to the relationship between belief and the biosphere, for instance, ecological conditions in a given social setting are in part a function of the prevailing framework of meaning. When nature is understood as a threat to be conquered, ecological circumstances are quite different than when nature is regarded as an omnipotent god to be feared, or as a source of life to be cultivated. Conversely, the natural environment shapes the myths that circulate in social relations, the sorts of dress that are worn, the ornaments that are fashioned from available raw materials, and so on. Meanwhile, material forces affect psychology in that, for example, cognition is a function of physiological processes as much as cultural conditions. Likewise, the sense of self is irrevocably bound up with material circumstances such as health, wealth and power. Conversely, psychology has material effects insofar as, say, territorial impulses in human motivation can help to define the dynamics of politics and so on.

To summarize, then, the preceding remarks indicate that studies of social change in world perspective cannot be based on either materialist or idealist premises, any more than they can rest on politicism, economism, cultural determinism, psychologism or ecologism. Social relations are political-economic-cultural-psychological-ecological relations. The reconstruction of the social order is therefore not a question of economics *or* psychology *or* culture *or* politics *or* ecology; but a process combining ecology *and* psychology *and* culture *and* economics *and* politics. Without politics there is no economics, without which there is no culture, without which there is no psychology, without which there is no ecology and so on. All five facets are involved concurrently and in conjunction with one another in each and every social transformation.

We must therefore reject any unilinear construction that extracts one or several facets from the combination and accords them primary causal significance. Every such explanation takes part of the world system to constitute the whole, much as, in relation to a different slicing of world social relations, endogenous models and notions of international determinism seek to isolate causation at one or the other 'level'. However, the notion of a system posits that causality lies in interrelations rather than in individual parts. In world-systemic dynamics of social change each facet is simultaneously determined by and determining of the others: nature, self, meaning, production and power concurrently yield each other.

This inseparability is plain when we examine any concrete social event. History cannot be split into five neat categories of cultural, ecological, political, psychological and economic occurrences, albeit that we are encouraged to do so by an academic division of labour which fragments social enquiry between anthropologists, geographers, political scientists, psychologists and economists. In practice every transaction between people in some way contains a combination of all five qualities. For example, an everyday routine such as shopping concurrently involves economics (an exchange of resources), politics (the relative power of buyer and seller), culture (notions of value which shape the price), psychology (the interpersonal transaction between the parties) and ecology (insofar as the traded goods are a product of human relations with the rest of nature). Thus processes of aligning power, developing the self, relating with nature, managing resources and attributing meaning are analytical divisions of the concrete unity of the social act.

Similarly, any feature of the social order has a multifaceted character. Thus, for example, capitalism is not a narrowly economic structure so much as a social ordering principle which at one and the same time constitutes a structure of power, a structure of production, a structure of meaning, a structure of being and a structure of ecology. Likewise, militarism is not only a political structure, but also a pattern of resource allocation, a state of mind, an organization of values, and a way of relating to the biosphere. In these and other ways the social order is inherently a political-economic-cultural-psychological-ecological order.

It follows, then, that a social transformation is a process with multifaceted causation and multifaceted effects. World-systemic dynamics of social change involve a combination of ecological, psychological, cultural, economic and political forces which alters a combination of power relations, production patterns, value frameworks, constitutions of the self, and biospheric conditions. Like the distinction of international, national and local dimensions of social relations, the distinction of facets of social life involves an analytical differentiation which should not be reified as an actual separation.

=7=

ORDER AND AGENCY IN WORLD-SYSTEMIC DYNAMICS OF CHANGE

Since establishing the fundamental principle of world-systemic causation of social change in Chapter 2, we have made a series of different analytical cuts into world society in order to examine several kinds of interconnections that generate forces of transformation. First, Chapters 3 to 5 discussed the interplay of the international with other 'dimensions' of world social relations. Then Chapter 6 considered the intersection of material and ideal 'facets' of social history. As a result, we now have a conception of social change as an internal—external, political-economic-cultural-psychological-ecological process within a world-systemic whole.

This perspective marks an important shift from the endogenous and often single-facet approaches that have traditionally dominated the fields of Social History and Historical Sociology. However, the postulates developed so far need to be supplemented with several others before we will have a sufficient basis on which to undertake more substantive research. To this end the present and next chapter advance critiques of two further types of reductionism which have frequently marred studies of social change.

One of the core issues that previous chapters have touched on, but not adequately clarified, is the causal relationship between action and order in the world-systemic transformation process. Chapters 4 and 5 made separate examinations of international activity and international order as influences on social change, respectively. Even at that juncture, though, it was stressed that the distinction between the two sets of forces was an artificial one. The main purpose of those earlier sections was to indicate the wide range of international circumstances that can play a part in rearranging patterns of social relations, and to that end it was useful to survey actors, interdependencies, norms, structures and trends in succession, without at that stage elaborating on the connections between social action and social order. Now we bring the latter question to the fore. Where is the fundamental impetus for social change generated: amongst actors and their purposeful decisions; or in deeper forces of structures and trends; or from action and order in combination?

We are here touching on a central issue of social theory, one that is implicated not only in the study of social change, but in all social research. It is often called 'the agent–structure problem', where the term 'structure' in this context generally encompasses all aspects of social order, i.e., norms and trends as well as the somewhat more restricted notion of 'structures' discussed in Chapter 5. In the present chapter the word 'structure' will in most cases be used in this wider sense. Alternatively, a number of authors refer to the 'wholes–parts' relationship, or to the 'individual–collective' connection, or to the difference between holism and reductionism. In general the terminology of agency and structure (or action and order) will be favoured here over those other characterizations.[1] It is not possible in the present writing to delve fully into the intricate philosophical debates that surround the agent–structure question, arguments which have been developed at length in a voluminous literature (cf. O'Neill 1973; James 1984; Wendt 1987; Hollis and Smith 1991). However, as every student of social change must take a stand on this matter, we need in this book at least to outline the main contending points of view and to suggest a general way through the methodological difficulties involved.

Traditionally, the question of causal links between order and action has divided academic circles into two broad groups. One side has taken the position that has variously been called 'individualism', 'actionalism', 'reductionism' or 'voluntarism'. The opposing perspective has been known by a range of labels including 'collectivism', 'structuralism', 'historicism', 'functionalism' and 'determinism'. In a word, methodological individualism maintains that social phenomena are essentially the outcome of actor properties. On this premise, social change is held to result from consciously designed and deliberately pursued policies of individuals, pressure groups, political parties, firms, governments, religious associations and/or other agents. In contrast, arguments of structural and historical determinism explain social conditions and their transformations in terms of forces emanating from the social order, where these powers exist prior to and independently of decisions and control by actors. According to a structuralist perspective, the course of social change is imposed on agents, who have no choice but to act out roles that larger 'outside' forces have scripted for them.

In this way the agent–structure debate has generally been conducted on the premise of a separation of cause and effect. Voluntarists and determinists alike share this basic assumption, although they differ fundamentally in where they assign causality: with actors in the case of individualists; with structure in the case of collectivists. Such a separation of cause and effect – and the consequent practice of isolating causality in one or the other part of a social whole – also underlies previously discussed arguments between internalists and externalists, as well as divisions between idealists and materialists.

In contrast to this chicken-or-the-egg approach to the problem of social causation, the notion of systemic relations which guides the present book holds that social forces arise in the first place from the intermeshing of different aspects of world society, rather than from one or several separate parts of the whole. Viewing the agent–structure debate in the light of this axiom, we take action and order to be co-determining phenomena in world social relations, much as we have previously posited that the international and the domestic are mutually constitutive, and that different facets concurrently form one another. The notion that structure and agency form a dynamic unity has *inter alia* been captured in Anthony Giddens' concept of 'structuration'. Adherence to this postulate has already been broadly intimated in earlier chapters, insofar as actors, interdependencies, norms, structures and trends were at those points *all* characterized as social forces. Moreover, the social order was qualified in Chapter 5 as being a significant but not all-determining force in the process of social change. Now we need to consider the nature of this unity of structure and action more precisely.

To clarify the general structuration principle, the body of the present chapter is divided into three sections. The first two parts review the distinct importance in transformation processes of both action and order, thereby establishing that neither of these aspects of social relations can be reduced to the other. However, agency and structure do not exist separately from one another either, and in this light the last section of the chapter elaborates a case for adopting the postulate of co-determination through structuration.

ACTION AND INDIVIDUALISM

The terms 'actor' and 'agent' are used here interchangeably to designate what Kenneth Boulding has alternatively described as 'behavioural units': that is, individuals, informal groups and formal organizations which engage in social interaction (1968: xix). It was established in Chapter 4 that a wide range of actors can be involved in the process of social change: transnational corporations, non-governmental associations, intergovernmental organizations, migrants, revolutionaries, authors and so on. Although the focus at that stage was on international actors more specifically, the principle of international–national interlinkage suggests that persons and groups who remain confined inside one country can equally be party to world-systemic dynamics of transformation. Thus, for example, the advance of human rights norms has been furthered (or frustrated) by national and local governments as well as by intergovernmental agencies. Similarly, so-called 'de-industrialization' in a number of former manufacturing centres has generally involved a combination of investment decisions by transnational, national and local firms. Meanwhile international televangelists, national church leaders and local *imams* alike have in recent times advanced religious revivalism in various faiths on a global scale. In short, social change can implicate any number of kinds of actors at all 'levels' of world society.

The concept of action, though, suggests that individuals and corporate bodies are not caught up in social change in a passive manner, but that they do positively *act* to bring about reconstructions of the social order. On this premise, film companies, charities, police forces, banks – indeed, any sort of actor – can in principle initiate, promote, slow or block a given social transformation. Thus the incidence, nature and speed of change is held to be a function, at least in part, of the visions that individual and group actors have for the future, the goals that they choose, and the ingenuity and perseverance which they employ in pursuing selected objectives.

On the one hand, action theories of social change take the intentions and personality characteristics of individuals to be crucial determinants of the success or failure of an attempted reorganization of social relations. For example, the specific ideas and initiatives of Mary Wollstonecraft and Marcus Garvey might be regarded as having been significant, if not indispensable, in the rise of feminism and black consciousness, respectively.

In addition, action theories view the attributes of group actors (their internal organization, corporate spirit, resources and so on) as key forces of social history. For instance, it might be concluded that the cohesion and drive of the Chinese Communist Party was a major cause of its triumph in the October Revolution of 1949, or that the initiatives of the Solidarity trade union were vital to the decommunization of Poland and the rest of Eastern Europe during the 1980s.

The proposition that agents constitute a significant force of change is particularly important in relation to social movements, insofar as these groups are 'characterised by the spontaneous development of norms and organisation which contradict or reinterpret the norms and organisation of the society' (Banks 1972: 9). More than any other kind of actor, social movements have an explicit and focused commitment to effect transformations of the social order. The women's movement, the peace movement, the environmentalist movement, the student movement, the civil rights movement and the like have all made it their primary and deliberate aim to pursue social change of some kind. In addition, peasant organizations have been created specifically to accomplish land reform, 'new age' groups to promote spiritual revival, pensioner associations to improve the lot of the elderly, anarchists to disband the state, 'Third World' solidarity organizations to halt underdevelopment, and so on. James Rosenau has, in a recent book (1990: 249–71), suggested that transnational social movements are gaining increased importance in the 'multi-centric' world society that, in his view, is currently emerging in the place of the state-centric international politics of old.[2] Writers in world-system theory have of late also shown increased interest in the activities of what they call 'antisystemic movements' (Arrighi *et al.* 1989). Meanwhile Alain Touraine has for several decades focused his 'sociology of action' on such groups, asserting that 'at the heart of society burns the fire of social movements' (1978: 1).

The postulate of methodological individualism takes such notions of actor significance to the point that agency is assumed *fully* to determine the course of continuity and change in society. Social explanation is then constructed wholly in terms of the beliefs, desires, decisions and other properties that are specific to actors (Lukes 1968; Elster 1982). World-systemic dynamics are reduced to a question of agency, and 'rational choice' is elevated to a position of being the guiding force of history. On the premise of methodological individualism, the social order results from an aggregation of deliberate actions: i.e., structure is purely an outcome and has no causal significance of its own. Articulating this postulate of 'actor determinism' in relation to Political Science, James Buchanan has affirmed that 'the political structure is . . . something that *emerges* from the choice processes of individual participants' (1966: 26). In the field of International Relations, meanwhile, Kenneth Waltz has contradicted his avowed structural approach by positing that:

> Changes in, and transformations of, systems originate not in the structure of a system but in its parts . . . Systems change, or are transformed, depending on the resources and aims of their units.
>
> (1986: 343)

Although the preceding paragraphs and several earlier chapters in this book have with ample illustration indicated that actors and their strategies can exert important influences on the process of social change, the notion that agents are entirely self-determining – and thus the root force of history – is an altogether different proposition. As Eric Hobsbawm has stated, 'the evident importance of the actors in a drama . . . does not mean that they are also dramatist, producer, and stage designer' (cited in Skocpol 1979: 18). We have seen in Chapter 5 that norms, structures and trends have a significance which is in some sense autonomous from, and to that degree imposed upon, the actors whose behaviour manifests those patterns. Individuals are born into a historical context that is not of their making and thus have no choice but to take this prevailing situation as the starting point of their action. Thus, for example, a goal of national liberation would hardly have made the running a thousand years ago, when the absence of the nationality principle meant that there were in effect no nations to liberate. Indeed, it is probable that no one in the tenth century even conceived of the idea of national self-determination. Closer to our own time, Adolf Hitler's initiatives elicited a huge response in 1930s Germany; however, if the classic Monty Python sketch is to be believed, the aspiring *Führer* would have been a laughingstock in 1970s Britain. In short, actor decisions are taken from a historically delimited range of available options, and the individual's 'rational choice' is defined largely by the historically variable contours of what counts as 'rational'. Purposeful behaviour may affect the timing, speed and character of social change, but agents do not wholly generate their own actions. Social activity needs to be understood in relation to the prevailing social order.

ORDER, STRUCTURALISM AND HISTORICISM

As was indicated in Chapter 5, the social order encompasses an array of directly observable regulations and customs, or norms, as well as deeper structures and trends. Social behaviour falls into patterns: both at the level of codified laws and, less visibly, in line with more fundamental and longer-term frameworks of activity. In the present epoch of world history the dominant underlying principles of social relations are variously said to include secularism, nationality, industrialism, capitalism, militarism, patriarchy, bureaucracy, race, democracy, Kondratieffs, hegemonic cycles, globalization and so on. Other rules of social organization are also found within contemporary world society, but alternatives of the kind practised by uncompromising Islamic revivalists, radical feminists, full-scale post-modernists and various so-called 'traditional peoples' remain on the margins for the most part. Prevailing orthodoxies dismiss these alternative frame-works of social relations as 'backward' or denounce them as 'extremist'. Indeed, these secondary patterns tend to be *kept* at the margins by the greater force of ordering principles such as industrialism and secularism.

Whether dominant or subordinate, however, properties of the social order exert a certain influence of their own, or 'structural power' (again, used here in the more generic sense of the word 'structure'). Thus, to recapitulate points made in Chapter 5, these organizing principles impose constraints on the forms that social behaviour is likely to take. In other words, the social order tends to delimit the range of actions that are contemplated and practicable in a given historical circumstance. To that extent agents are not, as Milton Friedman's individualist manifesto would have it, 'free to choose' (1980). Norms acquire a life of their own, operating somewhat autonomously from the actors who put the rules into place and subsequently observe, monitor and enforce them. Deeper structures, too, substantially affect personalities, mould perceptions and influence actors' conceptions of their interests and goals. And trends have a certain power which is not reducible to the attributes and decisions of the agents whose behaviour exhibits these linear, cyclical, equilibrating and/or dialectical patterns of history. In short, social order is not simply an outcome of social action, but also helps to produce that activity.

Hence social order has a distinct causal significance in the world-systemic dynamics of social change. Structure as much as action may stimulate, advance, hinder or block transformations within world society. If we accept the premise of structural power, then it is not only the conscious and concerted efforts of agents that determine the timing and direction of social change. For example, forces of militarism and capitalism may have been as crucial in propelling the Industrial Revolution as the inventiveness of James Watt and Eli Whitney. The world-historical forces of nationalism and democratization may have advanced the process of decolonization as much as the campaigns of the Indian National Congress, the FLN in Algeria, Frelimo in Mozambique and other national liberation movements. The momentum of a hegemonic cycle may have encouraged the decline of *Pax Britannica* as much as particular policy decisions taken in Whitehall and other seats of government. In such ways agents are not in full control of transformation processes.

Some social theorists take the postulate of structural power to the point of proposing that the social order wholly determines action. From a structuralist perspective actor properties have no causal significance whatsoever in the process of social change. The choices, decisions, tactics and strategies of agents are said to be wholly effects and in no sense causes of the course of history. Functionalist arguments posit that even the beliefs and campaigns of seemingly spontaneous and self-propelling social movements are irrelevant except as consequences of structural and historical forces. For example, from a structuralist viewpoint the rise of *perestroika* in the former USSR after 1985 was not connected with the person of Mikhail Gorbachev as such. Likewise, structuralists would maintain that recent moves to undo the apartheid regime in South Africa have taken place without any real initiative from bodies such as the ANC. The premise of structural determinism holds that actors have no effective possibility themselves to create or increase opportunities for social transformation. World-systemic forces are reduced to structures and trends; indeed, such arguments tend to use the words 'structure' and 'system' interchangeably.

Structuralist explanations have taken a variety of specific forms and attracted substantial academic followings especially during the 1960s and 1970s (cf. Kurzweil 1980). For example, some modernization theorists at this time advanced the so-called 'structural-functionalist' premise that action performs what Robert Merton (1968) termed a 'latent function' of maintaining social institutions and organizations, regardless of whether this outcome is intended by the agents concerned. On the assumption that social structure has this self-perpetuating quality, these authors concluded that social change unfolds in the modern era by means of gradual structural evolution rather than through revolutionary activity. The Marxist epistemology of Louis Althusser also rested on a notion of structural determinism, albeit from a perspective that was otherwise radically opposed to modernization theory. In Althusser's view:

the structure of the relations of production determines the places and functions occupied and adopted by the agents of production, who are never anything more than the occupants of these places.

(Althusser and Balibar 1968: 180)

Nicos Poulantzas employed an Althusserian interpretation of Marxism in his studies of the modern state, asserting with what Ralph Miliband has described as 'structural super-determinism' that the capitalist social system 'in no way depends on the motivations of the conduct of managers' (Poulantzas 1969: 71; Miliband 1970: 57). Some realist international theory has also exhibited a structuralist streak: namely, by affirming that interaction between national governments follows an unassailable logic of the states-system. In this vein Fred Northedge argued that 'in its fundamental character and operations [the international political system] is relatively resistant to purposive reform' (1976a: 32). From the preceding examples it is plain that notions of structural determinism are not distinctive of any one theory of social change, but inform certain liberals, Marxists, realists and others alike.

Some determinist explanations of social change also have an explicit historicist quality. In other words, the transformation process is said to be governed by unalterable 'laws of history' to which actors have no choice but to submit (cf. Berlin 1954; Popper 1957). Certain arguments moreover link such notions of inevitability to a postulate of teleology: that is, the premise that social developments are moving inexorably towards some predetermined end state. In this view, as Jon Elster describes it, history is moulded by 'a purpose without a purposive actor' (1982: 454). For example, a number of world-system theorists have posited that structures and trends of capitalism foredoom the modern world-economy to deepening crisis and eventual collapse (Wallerstein 1974b; Amin 1982; Bergesen 1983). In a broadly similar train of thought, Karl Marx in some writings propounded a secular millenarian vision that social transformations would lead ultimately to a classless communist society in which structural contradictions would be permanently resolved. Meanwhile modernization theorists have generally assumed that so-called 'less-developed countries' are, as if by a 'natural' progression, following the lead of the West. Such a presumption has recently led Francis Fukuyama (1989) to announce 'the end of history' with the demise of state socialism and the alleged final triumph of a US-led liberal world order, as though social change has with these events become a redundant question.

But can social transformation be explained with a structuralist and/or historicist formula? Do forces of the social order constrain agents so completely that actor intentions, decisions and designs have no effect on the way that social relations develop? Although, as was established in the first part of this chapter, the agent–structure axis of world history does not turn on the pole of actors alone, it does not follow that a process of social change rests one-sidedly on the other pole of structure. On the contrary, each end of an axis exists and moves by virtue of its connection with the other. Putting Hobsbawm's previously cited metaphor another way, the evident importance of stage and set in a drama does not mean that they are also the play that is enacted amidst the props. The social order sets the scene into which individuals are born, but it is dependent upon those actors for its repro-duction – or indeed transformation. Militarism needs soldiers; business cycles need businesses. Patriarchy will not be dismantled in the absence of women and men who negotiate new relationships with one another. To say that the time and place had to be ripe for Hitler is not to say that Hitler himself was unimportant. In short, it is one thing to assert that structure defines broad contours of human consciousness and limits the range of practicable courses of action in a given historical context, but it is something else to dismiss the notion of purposeful activity altogether.

STRUCTURATION

The preceding remarks suggest that we need to address the agent–structure problem in a different way than it has traditionally been posed. Dualistic arguments of actor versus order, agency versus structure, voluntarism versus determinism have become quite sterile. Methodological individualism clearly lacks an adequate account of structure, and structuralism just as obviously lacks an adequate account of agency. Moreover, both postulates rest on an artificial separation and polarization of cause and effect which contradicts a systemic approach to social explanation.

In contrast, the notion of 'structuration' offers an alternative conceptualiz-ation of the agent–structure problem that fits well with the general principle of world-systemic causation of social change. The term was coined by Anthony Giddens in the mid-1970s to denote the maxim that, in his words, 'social structures are both constituted *by* human agency, and yet at the same time are the very *medium* of this constitution' (1976: 121).[3] Much of Giddens' prolific writing since that time has been devoted to the elaboration of this basic proposition (especially Giddens 1984; for commentaries see Cohen 1989; Thompson 1989; Bryant and Jary 1991). In a recent restatement of the postulate he summarizes that:

> the structurationist approach . . . does not 'begin' either with the individual or with society . . . the core concern . . . is with recurrent social practices and their transformations . . . how actors are at the same time the creators of social systems yet created by them.
> (1991: 203–4; note Giddens' use of the term 'system' to mean 'structure' here)

From a structurationist perspective, then, order and agency are treated as interconnected aspects of social relations, neither of which has an existence without the other. Action and structure are posited simultaneously to cause and be caused by the other. Dynamics of social change therefore involve a world-systemic interrelation, or what Nicholas Onuf (1989) has called 'co-constitution', of structural properties and unit properties. Each is an important determinant of the course of history, but only by virtue of its links with the other. Activity is structured while it at the same time reproduces or transforms the configurations of social life. Personal and group choices erect, reaffirm, undermine and/or reconstruct patterns of social order at the same time that the social order delimits and constrains those choices. Actors do take significant decisions, though not under circumstances of 'free will', as prevailing structural conditions encourage certain options to be chosen while tending to rule out other alternatives. In short, says Zygmunt Bauman, the notion of structuration is intended:

> on the one hand, to dethrone the concept of 'structure' as an external, pre-existing determinant of action; on the other hand, to deny the random or entirely self-propelled character of actors' behaviour . . . 'Structuration' refers to the agents' mediation between 'unacknow-ledged conditions' and 'unintended consequences' of action, which in their turn become . . . conditions for the further activity of the agents.
>
> (1989: 42)

Relating the structuration principle to a substantive problem of social change, we might argue that, for example, the contemporary issue of militarization versus demilitarization needs to be understood in terms of a conjunction of agency and structural properties. Today's actors have entered into a world society in which armed violence and associated behaviour forms are a pervasive feature of social relations: that much is an unalterable given. Militarism has deeply shaped the patterns of politics, economics, culture, psychology and ecology that these actors have – without any choice in the matter – inherited. In this sense the structure, militarism, has a head start over agents in determining the course of current history. However, this organizing principle has depended in part on an accumulation of previous actions to reach its present position of entrenchment in the social order; in this sense militarism embodies agency as well as structure. Actors had to invent weapons, to compose battle hymns, to prepare and execute war plans, etc. In other words, the structure is a product of the actions . . . that it has helped to produce. Today, too, militarism remains dependent for its perpetuation on actor decisions *inter alia* to manufacture weapons, to sing battle songs and write new ones, to pay taxes towards the maintenance of armed forces, to make and implement declarations of war, and so on. At the same time, however, customs and laws that mediate the structural power of militarism make it difficult for actors not to participate in the reproduction of this feature of the social order. Refusal to enter the arms factory might spell unemployment, failure to sing the battle hymn will probably evoke censure from peers, non-payment of taxes will be countered with legal sanctions, and opposition to a war effort is likely to elicit name-calling and possibly physical punishments. Hence deliberate defiance of prevailing structural forces can normally be accomplished only with considerable difficulty, and it is likely to come at a substantial cost to those individuals and groups who adopt such a course. Militarism therefore places heavy constraints on actors' choices and makes it unlikely that the (in principle) ever-present opportunity to transform the structure will be exploited. That said, at certain historical junctures the space for transformative activity is widened. For example, recent upheavals in Eastern Europe have opened new possibilities, both within those countries and in the world at large, for a reduction of threat perceptions, a diminution of military establishments, a large-scale conversion of arms industries to civilian production, and the launch of efforts to construct an as-yet ill-defined structure of peace in the place of the structure of militarism. In this way imagination and initiative can, especially under historically auspicious conditions and with politically astute strategies, shift the same structural bounds that otherwise may tend to suppress policies of transformation.

Social theorists across a wide spectrum have in recent years endorsed the general structurationist response to the agent–structure problem, although they have not necessarily called the idea by that name (Outhwaite 1989). For example, Alain Touraine has urged:

> Let us turn away . . . from the tempting illusions of analyzing actors without any reference to the social system, on the one hand, and of describing the system without actors, on the other.
>
> (1984: xxiii)

Pierre Bourdieu has blended notions of structural causation with a theory of social action, as did Michel Foucault in his later writings. Steven Lukes has promoted the structuration principle by declaring that:

> social life can only properly be understood as a dialectic of power and structure, a web of possibilities for agents, whose nature is both active and structured, to make choices and pursue strategies within given limits, which in consequence expand and contract over time.
>
> (1977: 29)

More succinctly, R.W. Connell has spoken of 'an active presence of structure in practice, and an active constitution of structure by practice' (1987: 94).

The structuration principle has also entered explicitly into some studies of social change in world perspective. For example, Charles Tilly has emphasized the need to steer a course between 'the blank wall of randomness' and 'the crevasse of teleology' (1990: 33). Immanuel Wallerstein, too, has on occasion taken distance from his frequently determinist predilection to state that:

> an individual, a group is caught in some web not of their own making and out of their control . . . [which] is in turn formed by the sum of

wills that are in turn formed by the structural conditions (constraints) – a perfect circle.

(1986b: 332)

Meanwhile Robert Cox has in his analysis of social forces and world order rejected the notion that 'people are merely bearers of structures' and has argued on the contrary that while:

> structures are prior to individuals in that children are born into societies replete with established and accepted social practices . . . these practices . . . are . . . made by collective human activity and transformed through collective human activity.

(1987: 4)

In sum, then, the distinction between action and order is, like that between dimensions and that between facets, ultimately only an analytical separation. We distinguish agency and structure in order to highlight several important aspects of social relations, but in practice the two forces are one in the dynamics of social change. Transformation occurs through an interrelation of order and action: not through one or the other; not through one plus the other; but through one and the other in a unity that may be called structuration. Again the postulate of systemic causation holds that parts of the whole are simultaneously cause and effect in their relations with one another.

Of course the structuration principle offers no more than a general guideline for studies of social change in world perspective. It does not in itself provide a specific explanation of transformation processes. Before that objective can be realized we need to undertake thorough theoretical and empirical research towards identifying the ordering principles and activities – and especially the relations between them – that shape the particular question of change that we are investigating. Indeed, given the deeply entrenched habit in traditional social enquiry of separating action and order on cause/effect lines, researchers need consciously to guard against collapsing structure into agency or vice versa. Thus, as David Jary has pointed out, we should not underestimate the difficulties involved in operationally accomplishing social analysis in structurationist terms (1991: 147).

=8=

THEORY/PRACTICE AND TRANSFORMATION IN WORLD SOCIETY

The agent–structure problem just considered, the question of relations between knowledge and politics examined in Chapter 6, and the matter of international academic relations noted in Chapters 3 and 4 are all relevant to the final issue which is highlighted in this book on social change in world perspective: namely, the relationship between theory and practice. In the previous chapter we established that actors play a positive role in reconstructing the social order, albeit that their decisions and strategies are invariably formulated in the context of the norms, structures and trends of their time. Now our discussion turns to the particular kind of action in which we ourselves are professionally engaged, academic research. What relationship does this activity – including indeed the writing of this very text – have with the other forces that are involved in world-systemic dynamics of social transformation?

Like many earlier parts of the present book, this final chapter raises an issue that tends to be overlooked in conventional studies of social change. In fact, explicit reflection on the links between theory and practice is missing from most historical, sociological and international relations enquiry generally. Methodological orthodoxy across the social sciences has it that academic work is – and rightly strives to be – an exercise in sober, detached, apolitical observation and disclosure of facts. If this were so, if research were conducted in the proverbial ivory tower, and if there were in consequence no substantive connections between theories of social change and concrete transformations of the social order, then the present chapter would be superfluous.

However, a number of the points discussed earlier in this book suggest to the contrary that intellectual activity is deeply enmeshed in processes of social transformation. For example, we noted in Chapter 3 that student exchanges and transnational academic communications have provided important conduits for the cross-border transmission of social change. In addition, it was indicated in Chapter 4 that internationally constructed knowledge has in cases such as the world religions and the Enlightenment contributed significantly to inducing major discontinuities in social history. In Chapter 6 it was stressed that the social construction of meaning – in which academia figures centrally – is intimately connected with other facets of the transformation process. All of these observations suggest that theories of social change cannot be divorced from transformative practices in the world-systemic dynamics of social reconstruction, any more than the international can be separated from the domestic, the economic from the political, or agency from structure. Hence to theorize about social change is in some way, unknowingly or deliberately, to swim amongst the tides of continuity and transformation that are flowing at the moment in history when the research in question is being conducted. We need therefore to ask how understanding of social change can help us to 'stay afloat' amongst the push and pull of structural forces, and how knowledge of social change might increase our capacity purposefully to influence the course of the tides – irresistible though they may seem at times – in a constructive way.

Like the agent–structure problem, the question of theory–practice connections involves fundamental issues in the philosophy of social explanation which cannot be given full attention in the present writing (cf. Bernstein 1976; 1983; Lapid *et al.* 1989). This final chapter offers no more than a summary assessment of several general epistemological stances that can be taken in the study of social change. The first section outlines and rejects positivist notions that knowledge of social life can be certain, exact, indisputably verified and value-free, with the implication that researchers can and should provide definitive and objective accounts of the transformation process. A second section considers the subjectivist response to critiques of positivism and finds this ultra-relativism to be no less wanting as an approach to the theory–practice problem. Instead, as is argued in the third part of the chapter, studies of social change in world perspective should centre on the principle of praxis, i.e., the proposition that theory, a reflection of the historical conditions of its production, also feeds back into history and can alert social movements and other agents to the possibilities afforded by their structured situation for effecting a positive reconstruction of the prevailing social order. Students of social change need therefore to maintain a keen sensitivity to the duality of subject (themselves) and object (the world-systemic relations of which they are a part) and on this basis can nurture creative links between academic investigation and wider programmes of action for progressive transformation.

OBJECTIVISM

One important reason for the neglect of the theory–practice problem in many past studies of social change is the positivist tradition of mainstream research, which has in effect recognized no such 'problem'. The authors concerned have usually not deliberately excluded discussion of the interplay between academic investigations and social transformations; they have simply assumed that there are no significant links between the two. This supposition has allowed many theorists in good (but misplaced) faith to claim – explicitly or tacitly – to hold an 'objective' viewpoint on questions of social change.

Positivist conceptions of knowledge are understood here to rest broadly on four core propositions: (i) the singularity of reality; (ii) the possibility of constructing a social theory that grasps this single truth; (iii) the reliability of empirical observation as the means of securing absolute knowledge; and (iv) the necessity and feasibility of expunging values from theory in order to obtain a viable social explanation. Together these articles of faith, which are elaborated in turn below, suggest that the true scholar stands outside the rough and tumble of the world-systemic relations that produce continuity and change in social life.[1]

For one thing, then, positivist epistemology rests on the premise that social knowledge has a singular character: that there is one truth about each social circumstance. Positivism therefore holds out the prospect that social reality can, in principle, be definitely and definitively understood. In this conviction countless researchers have aimed to discover certain and incontestable facts about the process of social change. The objective has been to establish a full and final explanation for, say, the emergence of total war or the rise of the information society. Likewise we should, according to positivist dictates, aim to determine, precisely and incontrovertibly, the repercussions of UNEP initiatives for global environmental change, or the consequences of state formation on race relations in colonial areas, and so on. In short, positivism maintains that there are definite facts about social change waiting 'out there' for academic discovery.

Second, positivist perspectives on science hold that human knowledge can be developed in such a way that it grasps the absolute facts of social life. The goal of social science is therefore to develop a theory that makes these definite truths comprehensible to the human mind. Positivists purport that a social explanation, when verified, achieves an exact and total correspondence between the analyst's abstraction and the concrete social circumstance that is under investigation. Such a match constitutes 'true knowledge'. When guided by positivist principles, studies of social change seek to develop unambiguous and incontestable concepts. For instance, orthodox Marxists have affirmed that ideas of 'mode of production', 'class' and 'capitalism' provide a non-ideological characterization of social reality. Proponents of world-system theory have advanced similar claims for notions such as the core–periphery relationship. Meanwhile Talcott Parsons made his bid to match the abstract and the concrete by using concepts of 'pattern mainten-ance', 'integration', 'goal attainment' and 'adaptation' to describe the essential dynamics of social development. In each of these cases the theorists in question have assumed that human consciousness can acquire an understanding which captures the singular realities of social change.

Third, a positivist method of social science is characterized by empiricism: that is, the premise that social theory is to be formulated and verified through sensory perception. Academically trained empirical observation is said to offer the means to acquire certain knowledge of absolute social facts. Careful monitoring of evidence received through sense perceptions will, it is claimed, give the researcher access to the indisputable truth about the object of inquiry. A study of social change might, for example, rely on a time sequence of professionally designed public opinion surveys to chart shifts in gender relations. Archival documents, newspaper clippings, television footage, diary extracts, museum artefacts, commercial statistics, musical recordings and other empirical data are said to contain within them the incontestable truth of a social situation, one that awaits discovery by the perceptive observations of the trained social scientist. For a positivist, sensory input provides both the promptings of hypotheses and the evidence against which theories can be definitively tested.

Fourth, a positivist epistemology holds that social knowledge is value-free, that theory building and empirical observation can in principle be undertaken without the involvement of normative judgements. Positivism enjoins the student of social change to cultivate detachment, to eliminate opinions and to suppress emotion in order to obtain the true understanding of the situation under scrutiny. Values are regarded as a contaminant which distorts perception and invalidates theory. Judgement and explanation are treated as separate, with the former having no place in scientific enquiry. Bias is said to block real, 'objective' knowledge of problems such as international debt management, disarmament and other issues which lie at the heart of contemporary debates concerning social change. Like psychoanalysts to-wards their clients, or econometricians towards their statistics, students of social change have been urged to approach their object of research with detachment in order to uncover the 'real truth' of the matter.

The above remarks provide a crude but, for present purposes, adequate summary of what has on the whole been the ruling epistemology in the study of social change, and contemporary social enquiry generally. To recapitulate, positivism purports that there is one truth about the course of social develop-ment in any given historical context; that a clear distinction can be drawn between 'logical' and 'mythological' accounts of social change; that empirical observation provides the whole essential link between human consciousness and social reality; and that facts and values are discrete elements of thought, with social science incorporating the former without the latter.

Running through each of these four points is an assumed separation of theory and practice. It is supposed that social reality in some sense can exist apart from human knowledge of it; that theorization can occur separately from other social activity; that the theorist can observe social reality from the outside; and that theory gains validity by being divorced from politics. In a word, understanding of social change and the process of social change are treated as two different phenomena.

Numerous remarks in earlier chapters, where we have repeatedly located intellectual developments within wider social continuities and changes, are incompatible with the positivist conception of knowledge just outlined. On the contrary, the epistemology which has guided this book holds that theory is, intrinsically, both relative in its content and biased in its effects. Like any other exercise in conceptualization, then, academic knowledge of social change is invariably contingent and partial. The positivist goal of constructing a single, definite and objective understanding of the dynamics of social transformation is a chimera of modern social science. Even if we were to accept the proposition that reality has a singular character – and recent developments in theoretical physics such as quantum mechanics may throw even this assumption into doubt – there would seem to be no way to establish a single and fixed understanding of world society and the changes that occur within it. As Edward Said has stressed, 'no one has ever devised a method for detaching the scholar from the circumstances of life' (1978: 10). Knowledge of social change, like any other object of academic enquiry, is inherently relative and limited in at least nine interconnected ways.

For one thing, knowledge is always relative to the questions that are raised for study. Given the human mind's limited capacities for conscious awareness, a researcher can consider only a restricted number of problems. Academics make a judgement of priorities when they accord attention to one issue and thereby downplay or exclude others. For example, if we focus our research on the world-historical development of nationhood in the nineteenth century, our study of social change will to that extent perforce be distracted from shifts of gender relations in the contemporary global context. In the light of the inevitably biased nature of research agendas, a student of social change needs not only to ask 'what is the answer?', but equally to consider what other questions could have been raised.

Similarly, knowledge of social change is unavoidably slanted insofar as a researcher can only examine part of the masses of available evidence. For instance, to the extent that our source material relates to transformations that have occurred in Western Europe we remain ignorant of social reconstructions that have transpired in other parts of world society. Even when empirical observation is undertaken with a conscious effort to range widely and remain impartial, there will always be a limit to the amount of documentation and other indicators that can be evaluated.

Third, as we have seen repeatedly in earlier chapters, knowledge of social change is always relative to the key concepts that a researcher invokes. A liberal's focus on economic growth, a Marxist's focus on class, a feminist's focus on gender, a religious fundamentalist's focus on divine revelation, a realist's focus on the state, a postmodernist's focus on text – each approach yields a radically different understanding of the social order and its changes. Moreover, theories often rely on different criteria of validity and contrasting methods of verification, so that it is impossible to establish the relative merits of the contending arguments, except by arbitrarily imposing methodological standards that one or several of the theories in question do not accept.

Knowledge is also relative to the verbal, visual and other symbols with which it is constructed and communicated. Such a bias is especially evident when, for instance, one writer employs terms such as 'terrorism', 'extremism' or 'fanaticism' to describe a social movement that another author character- izes as 'visionary', 'progressive' or 'emancipatory'. However, cultural partiality also extends more subtly to all vocabulary, to the way that maps and graphs are drawn, to the illustrations that an author selects, and so on. Hence, at some level, every description contains within it an explanation, a judgement and a prescription, even if these deeper meanings are not openly asserted and recognized.

Fifth, knowledge of social change is invariably time-bound rather than timeless, as the positivist ideal would have it (cf. Carr 1961). Thus, for example, studies of social transformation written in the 1990s are far more likely to address ecological issues than those undertaken half a century ago, when environmental degradation was not generally viewed as the pressing problem that it is widely considered to be today. Likewise, an apparent decline in the world status of the USA during the 1970s and 1980s occasioned a spate of work on the purported cycle of hegemony discussed in Chapter 5, when earlier theories of social transformation had given no attention to the subject and had discerned no such trend. Hence an explanation of social change is always to some extent relative to the historical moment of its construction.

A sixth type of contingency that undermines positivist notions of fixed and final knowledge is the relativity of space. In other words, comprehension of social change tends to vary in accordance with the geographical location from which the issue is analysed. Although contemporary globalization has greatly reduced effective distance between even the most far-flung spots on the planet, accounts of social transformation still tend to vary depending on the place where they are composed. For example, it might be suggested that new deployments of nuclear weapons in Europe during the 1980s helped to prompt increased work on militarism by historical sociologists in the NATO countries at this time. In contrast, writers in Latin America and Africa at this juncture generally continued to focus their studies of social change on issues relating to the underdevelopment that they witnessed in their vicinity.

Knowledge of social change is also contingent rather than positive insofar as it is related to the theorist's position in the social order. Gender, class, race, nationality and occupation can all profoundly influence a person's appre- hension of history. This is not to suggest that each woman, each peasant, each black person, each Pakistani and each accountant will hold the same conception of society and its historical dynamics as every other woman, peasant, black person, Pakistani and accountant. But it is to say that such social categories can have an important formative effect on the observer's understanding of social change. There is consequently a danger, insofar as published academic studies of social change have largely come from the pens of white middle-class men, that many alternative perspectives on social transformation have thereby been marginalized, excluded or even actively repressed.

The psychological circumstances of theorists also colour understandings of social change. For example, as my own preface to this book intimated, certain of a researcher's previous life's experiences are peculiar to that individual and may affect her/his account of social transformation in ways that are unlikely to be replicated by any other person. More general psychological consider-ations may also affect the construction of knowledge, e.g., the author's age and corresponding developmental stage of life. Academic work is also affected, subliminally if not consciously, by the writer's state of health, domestic circumstances and other immediate conditions of the self. On these counts, too, positivist notions of objective analysis are unsustainable.

Resource contingencies constitute a ninth barrier to the realization of positivist criteria of knowledge. For one thing, there is a political economy of theories of social change insofar as, for example, development economists have often gained major research grants while postmodernists have generally had to make do with paltry funds. Similarly, theorists in Europe and North America have had far more financial backing than their colleagues elsewhere, with the result that Anglo-Saxon and continental writings dominate the literature. Regarding another type of resource bias, the presence or absence of empirical evidence can have a telling influence on knowledge of social change. For instance, research into the so-called Boxer Rebellion of 1900 in China perforce has to rely chiefly on accounts given by the foreigners who intervened to shore up the Ch'ing Dynasty, as the mainly illiterate rebels have left no testaments. More generally, the elaboration of a world-systemic perspective on social transformation is hampered when most social indi-cators are calculated on a national basis, when most archives are designed with national and local history in mind, and so on.

The preceding critique suggests that positivist epistemology is irretrievably flawed, that all knowledge is tentative rather than final, uncertain rather than definite, and value-laden rather than value-free. Nothing in the study of social change can be unambiguous and impartial in the manner that positivism prescribes: not the researchers who investigate the problem; not the empirical evidence which relates to the issue; not the students and activists who in turn might consult the research. All are steeped in philosophical, cultural, historical, geographical, structural, psychological and other contingencies. Knowledge of social change is not singular, but plural; not given, but interpretive; not universal, but contingent; not fixed, but fluid. Theorists no less than openly politicized activists have a biased involvement in questions of social change.

SUBJECTIVISM

What are we then to make of the nature and prospects of knowledge of social transformation in world perspective? It is one thing to point out the weaknesses of positivist orthodoxy, but quite another matter to plot a more satisfactory epistemological course. Unqualified empiricism and objectivism are widely dismissed in the social sciences today, but many researchers implicitly continue to follow broadly positivist rules since they have not as yet been able to conceive of a viable alternative (cf. Biersteker 1989).

Meanwhile certain other social researchers have set themselves in diametric opposition to positivist tenets. This position might be described as radical postmodernism: 'radical', since what Pauline Rosenau (1990) calls 'moderate' postmodernist authors would not go to the extremes of subjectivism that are described below.

Whereas positivism presumes a singular social reality which is external to the theorist, radical postmodernists posit that 'reality' is entirely a creation of the subject. Hence the very idea of a reality 'out there' is rejected. Knowledge is said to emanate wholly from the person who constructs it, so that every account of social change (or of any other issue for that matter) will be different from all the rest. For subjectivists the goal of academic work is not to discover the single truth, but to nurture creativity with abandon and celebrate a proliferation of contrasting perspectives.

In line with this promotion of pluralism, radical postmodernists do not seek to construct a theory of social change as such. All definition is rejected as imposing a constraint on the infinite possibilities of human insight. Subjectivist epistemology not only welcomes a diversity of knowledges, but furthermore asserts that the relative merits of the various accounts cannot be determined except in accordance with ephemeral judgements of personal taste. All interpretations are said in principle to be of equal interest and validity. In reaction against the positivist goal of attaining absolute understanding, these sceptics go to the ultra-relativist extreme of declaring the impossibility of gaining any security of knowledge whatsoever. 'Truth' is regarded as a bogus concept.

Systematic empirical observation has no place in the radical postmodernist approach to knowledge either. 'Evidence' becomes a meaningless concept in a method of enquiry that locates reality entirely within the subject. Moreover, for ultra-relativists any claim to academic expertise is a sham; if all accounts are equal, then there is no need for research training. From a subjectivist viewpoint, knowledge is based on imagination rather than observation. Hence all accounts of social change are inventions and wholly arbitrary.

Subjectivist epistemology also rejects the positivist notion of the possibility and desirability of value-free understanding. On the contrary, and as previous paragraphs have suggested, knowledge is held to be suffused with the biases of the subject who creates it. But in their pursuit of pluralism and their refusal to rank-order accounts, radical postmodernists take a further step and maintain that all opinions have equal validity (and invalidity). Any moral claim is thus dismissed.

What should we make of this philosophical void? True, radical post-modernism advances some important criticisms of positivism. It alerts us to the variability and relativity of knowledge and urges us to be sceptical of academics' often exaggerated claims to special insight into the workings of social relations. However, the weaknesses of positivist orthodoxy can be highlighted without lapsing into subjectivism. It is of course important to question accepted truths, but it does not follow that truth-value itself ceases to be an important issue.

Indeed, the ultra-relativism of radical postmodernism has unacceptable consequences for academic and wider social practices (cf. Callinicos 1989; Harvey 1989). Complete scepticism produces nihilism, which in turn has two implications for the dynamics of continuity and change, both of them deplorable. On the one hand, this epistemology tends to immobilize social movements by depriving them of conviction and direction. In this way subjectivism has the effect of dissipating resistance and essentially shores up the existing order. Alternatively, nihilism can encourage blindly destructive agitation, deconstruction without reconstruction, critique without a care-fully conceived alternative vision. Historically, such 'radical' activity – for example, by the Situationist International in the 1960s (Plant 1992) – has tended rather quickly to run out of steam, with little to show for itself in the way of far-reaching and lasting social transformations.

Recently the political bankruptcy of subjectivist epistemology was illus-trated by the radical postmodernist response to the 1990–1 military contest over Kuwait. A leading writer in these circles, Jean Baudrillard, asserted at the close of coalition operations to reverse the Iraqi takeover that 'the Gulf War did not take place'. In his eyes the hostilities had been no more than a media-produced event, an elaborate video game. As a result, Baudrillard alleged, no adequate criteria for the establishment of the truth of the matter were available, and:

> All ideological or political speculations amount to a form of mental deterrence (stupidity) . . . practical knowledge of this war . . . is out of the question.
>
> (cited in Norris 1992: 193)

Following this radical postmodernist formula, then, we are urged to respond to uncertainty in social theory with an attitude of 'anything goes' and to treat our relationship to historical transformations as that of a spectator who waits to be entertained. One shudders to imagine the outcome had such an attitude held universal sway, for instance, in response to fascism in the middle of this century. And what consequences will follow if we adopt such an approach to currently pressing issues such as sexism, racism, ecological degradation, the fragility of community, pervasive intolerance, and indeed widespread nihilism, of which radical postmodernism is a telling symptom in many present-day academic circles?

THEORY/PRACTICE: KNOWLEDGE AND THE POLITICS OF CHANGE

The first two sections of this chapter have indicated that the issue of knowledge about social change poses major philosophical challenges. We have also seen that the difficulties are not resolved by ignoring the question of truth, as subjectivists propose, or by seeking refuge amongst the ruins of positivist epistemology. We therefore need an alternative understanding of the relationship between theory and practice, one which transcends both objectivism and subjectivism. The notion of praxis offers a third and more satisfactory – albeit still highly problematic – approach.

In spite of their major differences in other respects, objectivism and subjectivism share a fundamental starting point – namely, the supposition that social theories (and hence explanations of social change) are somehow ontologically separate from social practices (and thus the structuration processes that produce transformations). For their part, positivists maintain that knowledge is derived from the object of enquiry, which is held to be independent of the researcher who enquires into it. Meanwhile radical postmodernists posit that knowledge is derived from the subject of the theorist, who is treated as being independent of any social forces. Needless to say, such separations of cause and effect between theory and practice run counter to the premise of systemic interrelation that has underlain the whole of this book.

In contrast, the notion of praxis posits that the process of social change is marked by a duality of knowledge and the other aspects of reality. From this perspective, theory does count in social practice, and vice versa. Thus knowledge reflects the conditions of its construction and, simultaneously, this understanding reverberates back into and helps to shape the circumstances that are producing it. In the Gulf War of 1990–1, for example, a negative reading of appeasement policies towards Nazi Germany in the 1930s was coupled to a 'theory' that likened Saddam Hussein to another 'evil dictator'. This interpretation of the situation arguably encouraged the rapid and full-scale international military response to the Iraqi Army's invasion of Kuwait. Similarly, the purported 'lessons' of economic depression in the 1930s played a key role in the construction of the multilateralist Bretton Woods framework. In these ways knowledge of history has been constitutive of history (cf. May 1973).

Deliberately or tacitly, then, theories of social change have implications for the process of transformation itself. Reality is not separate from theory as positivism asserts, nor is it reducible to theory as subjectivism suggests. Instead, theory is a part of reality, and one that interrelates with its other parts as both cause and effect in a unity captured by the term 'praxis'. In this light Anthony Giddens has affirmed that 'all forms of social life are partly constituted by actors' knowledge of them' (1990: 38).

In some instances theory, as a part of praxis, may be a force for continuity of the existing social order. For example, we might ask whether realist international theory has itself contributed to the reproduction of inter-state rivalry. In this sense Michael Smith has suggested in his intellectual history of realism that 'to treat all politics as inexpiable struggle is to propound a self-fulfilling prophecy' (1986: 48). Similarly, modernization theory has over the years provided a rationale for policies of 'development' in many countries. A number of widely read writers on modernization have moreover lent academic endorsement to the *Pax Americana* in the second half of the twentieth century. For example, Talcott Parsons triumphally characterized the USA as the 'lead society' of contemporary history (1971: Ch 6). Daniel Bell likewise declared at a time of large-scale decolonization and 'Cold War' tensions that the USA, by concurrently increasing living standards, raising cultural levels and maintaining freedom, was 'a society that is now providing one answer to the great challenge posed to Western – and now world – society' (1962: 38). More recently, Francis Fukuyama's study of social change has designated the USA and other industrial liberal democratic countries as the 'post-historical' world which is showing the way forward for those 'still stuck in history' (1992: Ch 26). In these cases a theory of social change can become a vehicle for generating consent with the status quo.

On other occasions, however, theories of social transformation have formed part of challenges to dominant patterns of social organization and indeed have been consciously incorporated by social movements into their strategies for change. In this respect we previously noted, in Chapter 4, the impact of Enlightenment thinking on the French Revolution. In fact, the 'Preliminary Discourse' in the *Encyclopédie* of d'Alembert and Diderot stressed the necessity of constructing new knowledge for a new world. During the past hundred years Marxist theory has inspired many revolutionary programmes. More recently, 'moderate' postmodernists in the vein of Foucault have called for an end to the 'totalizing narratives' of mainstream social theory, insofar as this form of knowledge is said to sustain a number of repressive practices that are distinctive of modernity. In the field of International Relations, meanwhile, bodies such as the Institute of World Order and journals such as *Alternatives* have emerged during the past two decades with the object of linking theoretical innovations to on-the-ground transformative politics (Mendlovitz and Walker 1987). In each of the cases just cited *critical* theory is meant to assist in the reconstruction of social practices.

Hence, both when it serves to reproduce and when it serves to reconstruct social conditions, knowledge of social change has an important political quality. As Robert Cox states, 'theory is always for someone and for some purpose' (1981: 128). An exploration of theory is therefore necessarily also an exploration of politics. Sometimes the connection between the two is obvious: Walt Rostow's subtitle, 'a non-communist manifesto' (1960), is none too subtle. On other occasions the political implications of knowledge are less immediately apparent, e.g., the effects of social darwinism and racial theories in helping to create circumstances conducive to colonialism in the nineteenth century.

Thus the 'truth' of a theory lies partly in the values that it promotes and the interests that it serves. There is an alternative to positivist notions of absolute truth and subjectivist denials of truth: namely, a critical theory stance which recognizes the union and mutual constitution of knowledge and practice, and then seeks to exploit that awareness to promote progressive social change. Theoretically informed action, or praxis, can facilitate the attainment of social transformation. Although it is not sufficient in itself, the reconstruction of knowledge is an important part of a process of social reconstruction.

Producers of theories of social change therefore bear a certain responsibility in regard to the politics of social change. Academics, as actors, and their theorizing, as an activity, are involved in the dynamics of continuity and change no less than any other group of persons and their actions. Academic understanding is both a reflection of and an insertion into the world of which academics are a part. Accepting this premise, I have sought in this book to (re)formulate knowledge of social change in ways that might contribute to progressive transformations in world society.

CONCLUSION

Change is one of the core facts of social life and, correspondingly, one of the core concerns of social science. Moreover, just as we today face major social ills – of violence, of inequality, of injustice, of anomie – which positive transformations of the social order could alleviate, we also currently face major shortcomings in mainstream academic investigations of social change. Arguably these two problems are interconnected, so that reconstructions of theory constitute a necessary and important part of the overall process of reconstructing social relations.

In this book I have proposed a six-point general reformulation of the study of social change. First, I have joined those who reject academic parochialism, and indeed question the very principle of a formal separation between Sociology, Economics, History, Anthropology, Political Science, Literary Criticism, Psychology, Geography and International Relations. The examination of social change needs to be a cross-disciplinary, and to that extent a non-disciplinary enterprise. Second, I have advocated a fundamental redefinition of social space, in which the national concept of society gives way to notions of world society, and in which the idea of separate 'levels' of social life is replaced with the postulate of world-systemic relations. This move to integrate the international and the domestic involves among other things a basic reformulation of our conceptions of the state, social structure and developmental trends in world terms. Third, I have urged that we explore the involvement of cross-border activity and international order in the dynamics of social transformation with the same degree of care that has traditionally been devoted to the examination of geographically local and national circumstances. Fourth, I have suggested that studies of social change should steer clear of both materialist and idealist premises, instead examining problems of transformation in terms of interwoven ecological, cultural, political, psychological and economic facets of social life. Fifth, regarding the role of purposeful action in reshaping the social order, I have looked with equal scepticism on the overoptimism of voluntarism and the defeatism of structural and historical determinism. The notion of structuration – that is, the co-determination of agency and order – provides a more adequate, albeit more challenging, conceptualization of causality. Finally, I have highlighted the intimate interrelation of theory and practice, rejecting the objectivism of positivist social enquiry and the nihilism that has developed in some quarters as an overreaction against orthodox scientific method. Thus I have endorsed the view that critical-emancipatory thought offers the optimal way forward in studies and tactics of social transformation.

Of course, these six points only establish broad methodological ground rules rather than a specific explanation of social change. I have not presented a theory of social reconstruction so much as outlined a set of postulates on which such a theory could be based. To my mind the essence of transformation processes can be summarized in the words 'world society', 'system', 'structuration', 'political-economic-cultural-psychological-ecological relations' and 'praxis'. I have reviewed a number of ways that other authors have treated such issues, but I have not in this book consolidated and made explicit my own motivating values, my own characterization of the world social order, and my own more precise conception of the world-systemic dynamics of continuity and change. Although intimations of a more defined position are scattered amongst these pages, the full elaboration of a perspective is a task that goes beyond the scope of the present writing. A long-term programme of extensive empirical research is required in this regard, and even then the resulting specification of the character of social forces in world society would relate only to the particular historical context that had been examined and the particular historical conditions under which the research had been undertaken.

There is in any case plenty of time to write companion volumes to this book. We are surely not, as some commentators would have it, at 'the end of history' (Fukuyama 1989), if by that phrase is meant that the organization of world society has settled into a final pattern. One major twentieth-century challenge to dominant structures and trends in world social relations, communism, has apparently undergone a terminal decline. However, many inhabitants of our planet – and I count myself amongst them – remain dissatisfied with the prevailing social order, and alternative programmes for full-scale social transformation continue to draw substantial followings on a world scale. Communism may be past history, but religious revivalism, feminism, environmentalism and other strivings for fundamental change are not. Indeed, history can hardly stand still when dominant patterns in contemporary world society are so often riven with contradictions: *inter alia* between capitalism and nationality; between militarism and liberalism; between industrial 'mass society' and individualism; between race and gender; between bureaucracy and democracy; between globalization and fragmentation. Even if we were to reach the widely heralded 'post-industrial', 'post-capitalist', 'post-secular' or 'post-modern' condition, it seems unlikely that a veritable 'new world order' of this kind would take us beyond the problem of transformation itself. If this book contains anything approaching a definitive conclusion, it is that change is the ultimate continuity in world social relations.

NOTES

1 INTERNATIONAL RELATIONS AND THE STUDY OF SOCIAL CHANGE

1 A century earlier Richard Zouche, Professor of Civil Law at the University of Oxford, first employed the phrase *inter Gentes* ('between peoples', or 'between nations') (Zouche 1650; see also Suganami 1978).

2 The standard intellectual history of IR divides the field's development into an initial 'utopian' or 'idealist' phase in the 1920s and 1930s and a subsequent 'realist' stage after 1940 (e.g., Holsti 1971). However, a number of major realist writings date from the inter-war period, the supposed heyday of idealism (cf. Meyer 1960; Smith 1986). Moreover, contrasts between idealism and realism are easily exaggerated. Like the self-proclaimed realists, the so-called idealists focused their studies on states, conflict and war. Utopians also usually followed realists in maintaining a dichotomy between the domestic and the international and in generally neglecting questions of international social structure. Differences between the two schools centred on their contrasting assessments of the causes of war and the means for controlling international conflict.

3 Throughout this text I take the term 'state' to refer to the apparatus of government, i.e., a set of public regulatory agencies. In other words, the word 'state' will not be used loosely as a synonym for 'country', a confusion to which many laypersons and even some professional students of IR are prone (cf. Halliday 1987a). By the same token, the terms 'state' and 'nation' will not be interchanged either: the former refers to an institutional apparatus, the latter to a grouping of people.

2 WORLD SOCIETY AND WORLD-SYSTEMIC DYNAMICS OF CHANGE

1 It is important to distinguish between the concepts 'society' and 'system'. As the word is used here, world 'society' refers to the fact that people live in a social condition that extends over large spaces and across national boundaries. Meanwhile, world 'system' is a more specifically explanatory notion which holds that

events and circumstances in world society are produced through the interrelation of its parts.

2 In this example, and throughout this book, I consciously seek to avoid the vocabulary of 'First' and 'Third' worlds, 'North' and 'South', 'core' and 'periphery', 'developed' and 'developing' countries, and so on. These words pervade contemporary discussions of international relations (and they will occasionally creep into the present text, too), but they are fundamentally unsatisfactory. On the one hand, such concepts gloss over the immense diversity that prevails within each of these purported classes of countries (Naipaul 1985). In addition, these notions tend to neglect the major contrasts of wealth and power that prevail inside individual countries, as Ross and Trachte (1983) emphasize in their work on 'peripheralization' within New York City. More particularly in the context of the present discussion, concepts of South–North, etc. tend to reproduce a discourse that views society in territorial rather than world terms.

3 The terminology 'national' is, strictly speaking, incorrect here, since the adjective is being used to refer to a territorial state-unit rather than that particular kind of human population known as a nation, i.e., a people united by language, religion, race, folkways or other shared features and experiences (cf. Chapter 1, note 3). Thus, as we will note at greater length in Chapter 5, a nation is not a type of geographical space. Moreover, territorial distributions of national populations have never corresponded exactly with the boundaries of states. In fact, it could be objected that the use of the word 'national' when referring to a country serves subtly to perpetuate the myth that the world can in practice be divided into ethnically unitary nation-states. However, until an adjectival form of the words 'country' or 'territorial state' becomes available, we are bound to fall back on the misconceived conventional vocabulary.

3 CROSS-BORDER TRANSMISSION OF SOCIAL CHANGE

1 I follow the United Nations in preferring to characterize companies that maintain production facilities in more than one country as 'transnational' (across nations) rather than 'multinational' (many nations). The term 'multinational' suggests activities in multiple countries, when many of these corporations are established in only two national jurisdictions. In addition, 'multinational' can be read to imply involvement by many nationalities, when TNCs generally draw most of their directors from the country of the parent company.

2 This figure is a rough estimate. An exact calculation is not possible because national utility companies measure telephone communications differently, i.e., in terms of numbers of calls, minutes of connections, pulses, etc.

4 INTERNATIONAL ACTIVITY AND SOCIAL CHANGE

1 At constant 1972 US dollars, known FDI in the world totalled $ 72.5 billion in 1914 and $ 91.8 billion in 1960. Thereafter it expanded rapidly to $ 165 billion by 1971 and $ 257.4 billion by 1978 (Teichova et al. 1986: 24, 362; also Dunning 1983).

2 Of course, aggregate sales and GDPs are not strictly comparable figures, but the numbers give a broad indication of just how large TNC operations can be.

3 Marx leaves a somewhat ambiguous heritage in respect of the role of international

trade in the emergence of capitalism. Sometimes, as in the passages quoted, he seems to lean towards an exogenous explanation; yet on other occasions he presents an endogenous argument by locating the origins of capitalism in purported internal contradictions of feudalism (cf. Holton 1985). The importance of international trade in the early development of capitalism is suggested by Ernest Mandel's calculation that the surplus extracted overseas by European mercantile companies between the sixteenth and eighteenth centuries amounted to over one billion pounds sterling, or more than the capital of all steam-operated industries which existed in Europe around the year 1800 (1962: 443–4). Following a world-systemic premise, we would be inclined to take distance from these internecine Marxist squabbles about internal-versus-external causes and to favour the view, elaborated by Perry Anderson (1974) among others, that a combination of domestic and international circumstances were involved in the transformation.

4 Alexandrowicz challenges the received wisdom that modern international law and diplomatic practice developed exclusively in Europe. He notes that European traders and settlers entered into already existing networks of states in Asia in the sixteenth to eighteenth centuries and that the principles of *jus gentium* applied to intercourse between European and Asian states until the onset of formal colonialism in the nineteenth century.

5 This is not to say that war is inherent in human society, as organized group killing has been absent from a number of social contexts, e.g., amongst the Shoshone of the Great Basin, the Lephchas of Sikkim and others (Davie 1929: Ch 4; Russell 1936: Ch 1; Mead 1940; Wright 1942: 546, 561–2, 1216).

6 Again it is important to draw a distinction between a dominant voice and a determining voice (cf. Chapter 2, pp. 38–9). Academic international studies arose between the 1910s and 1930s not only in the USA, but also in Britain, Germany, the Soviet Union, France, Italy, Switzerland, Poland, Bulgaria, Palestine, Canada, Rumania, Australia, New Zealand, India and South Africa (IIC 1929; 1931; King-Hall 1937). Students of IR in the various countries maintained regular contacts with one another at this time through the International Studies Conference (IIC 1937; Zimmern 1939). In addition, IR academics in the USA drew for much of their inspiration upon social and political thought formulated in Europe. Indeed, a number of leading early writers in the field were first-generation immigrants to North America. In short, we cannot explain the emergence of the IR discipline, nor the dominance of realist theory within it, in terms of conditions in the US per se.

5   INTERNATIONAL ORDER AND SOCIAL CHANGE

1 I refer to Islam here not merely as a body of religious doctrine and ritual, but as an all-encompassing framework of social relations. Hamilton Gibb in this sense characterized Islam as 'a complete civilization' and 'a fully-rounded society . . . which comprehends every aspect of human life' (1932: 12, 21).

2 The terms 'nationality' and 'nationhood' are employed interchangeably in this book to denote a particular way of constructing human identity and community (described below). 'Nationality' therefore refers to the social structure, whereas the term 'nationalism' is used to designate a strong consciousness of nationality and political programmes pursued to advance national awareness and solidarity.

3 These authors often use the term 'hegemony' to mean dominance in general, rather

than in the specific Gramscian sense of non-coercive leadership achieved and sustained when a dominant party succeeds in representing its narrow interests as the universal interest. For the latter conception see Cox (1983).

4 The phrase 'balance of power' has multiple and often quite ambiguous meanings (cf. Haas 1953). In the particular sense meant here, i.e., as an equilibrating trend embedded in interstate relations, the balance of power is not a policy that statespersons freely choose from amongst a range of options. Rather, it is an autonomous force of the international order that constrains governments to act, singly and collectively, to prevent the rise of an expansionary state to a position of world empire.

6 FACETS OF WORLD-SYSTEMIC SOCIAL TRANSFORMATION

1 To avoid confusion I use the term 'facet' when speaking of political, economic, cultural, psychological and ecological aspects of social life and the term 'dimension' in reference to international, national and local aspects of social life. As will be seen in the course of this chapter, distinctions between facets, like those between dimensions, entail analytical rather than concrete separations.

2 In principle it is of course possible to expand the range of facets to include, for example, distinct divine forces. However, my agnosticism leads me to exclude this possible (and potentially overriding) aspect of social relations. Instead, I treat notions of the sacred as phenomena whose involvement in the process of social change can be sufficiently accounted for in terms of culture, politics, economics, psychology and ecology.

3 Cf. Ernest Gellner's definition of culture as 'ideas and signs and associations and ways of behaving and communicating' (1983: 7); Raymond Williams' notion of 'culture as the *signifying system* through which necessarily (though among other means) a social order is communicated, reproduced, experienced and explored' (1981: 13); and John Tomlinson's conception of culture as 'the context within which people give *meanings* to their actions and experiences, and make sense of their lives' (1991: 7).

4 The precise weight that Weber himself attached to the Protestant ethic in the rise of capitalism is unclear, insofar as he emphasized the importance of political and economic preconditions (e.g., 'rational' administration and 'free' labour) as well as the development of Protestant values.

5 The terms 'postmodernism' and 'poststructuralism' are often used loosely and interchangeably, so no specific distinction is drawn between them here. On the other hand, a division may be noted between 'radical' postmodernists/poststructuralists like Derrida, who absolutely reduce all social life to a 'text', and others like Foucault, who examine the relations between 'discourses' and social institutions (cf. Callinicos 1985).

6 Many theories of so-called 'political economy' do little more than tag one of these two facets onto the other. For example, mercantilist political economy examines resource allocation as an aspect of interstate competition for power. Meanwhile liberal and Keynesian approaches to political economy focus on the marketplace and conceive of politics as no more than state intervention in the market. Economistic tendencies in much Marxist thought were noted earlier in this chapter.

Indeed, economism is suggested by the very practice of placing 'economy' in the position of noun and 'political' in the role of the adjective in the phrase 'political economy'. On the various approaches to political economy, see Jones (1988) and Murphy and Tooze (1991).

7 Cf. Foucault's description of 'the system of relations' between 'a thoroughly heterogeneous ensemble consisting of discourses, institutions, architectural forms, regulatory decisions, laws, administrative measures, scientific statements, philosophical, moral and philanthropic propositions' (1977b: 194).

7 ORDER AND AGENCY IN WORLD-SYSTEMIC DYNAMICS OF CHANGE

1 In particular I prefer the terminology of 'structures' and 'agents' to the vocabulary of 'wholes' and 'parts'. The equation of 'the whole' with structure seems to belie a structuralist inclination whereby a social system is reduced to its ordering principles. In contrast, as this chapter will make clear, I conceive of a systemic whole as involving the interrelationship and inseparability of action and social order. In this view a social system can no more be reduced to structures than to agents. 'System' and 'structure' are therefore not synonymous, and an important distinction can be made between holism and structural determinism. (Cf. Giddens 1977b: 112*ff.*)

2 In contrast, the view advanced in the present book is that international relations have always involved a plurality of actors. It is not cross-border activity, but Rosenau's approach to IR, that has shifted from state-centrism to 'multi-centrism' during the past thirty years. In fact, the past hundred years have witnessed a substantial increase rather than a decline in the activities, resources and importance of the state in society (cf. Boli 1980; 1987). However, this expansion has gone hand in hand with a growth of formal organizations generally. Hence the more fundamental trend seems to have been one of increasing bureaucratization – in all quarters of world society – not shifts in the relative significance of state and non-state actors. The latter question has all too often become something of a red herring in IR.

3 The general structuration idea is not so new. It might, for example, be read into Karl Marx's well-known dictum that people make history, but not under conditions of their own choosing.

8 THEORY/PRACTICE AND TRANSFORMATION IN WORLD SOCIETY

1 I have admittedly somewhat exaggerated positivist claims for effect in the characterization that follows. Some proponents of positivist epistemology have grappled with questions of conceptualization, evidence, values and the relationship between theory and practice in a much more discerning and self-critical manner than the following discussion might suggest.

BIBLIOGRAPHY

Dates in parentheses refer to the date of first publication. When the edition cited is a later release, its date of issue is noted towards the end of the entry.

Aas, S. and Høivik, T. (1986) 'Demilitarization in Costa Rica: A Farewell to Arms?', in M. Graham *et al.* (eds) *Disarmament and World Development.* Oxford: Pergamon, pp. 173–81 (2nd edn).

Abrams, P. (1968) *The Origins of British Sociology: 1834–1914.* Chicago: University of Chicago Press.

Abu-Lughod, J.L. (1989) *Before European Hegemony: The World System A.D. 1250–1350.* New York: Oxford University Press.

Acton, J.E.E. (1898) Letter of 12 March to the contributors to *The Cambridge Modern History*, reprinted in J.N. Figgis and R.V. Laurence (eds) *Lectures on Modern History.* London: Macmillan, 1906, pp. 315–18.

Alavi, H. *et al.* (1982) *Capitalism and Colonial Production.* London: Croom Helm.

Albertini, R. von (1982a) *Decolonization: The Administration and Future of the Colonies, 1919–1960.* N.p.: Africana.

Albertini, R. von (1982b) *European Colonial Rule, 1880–1940: The Impact of the West on India, Southeast Asia, and Africa.* Westport, CT: Greenwood.

Aldcroft, D.H. (1977) *From Versailles to Wall Street 1919–1929.* London: Allen Lane.

Alexandrowicz, C.H. (1967) *An Introduction to the History of the Law of Nations in the East Indies (16th, 17th and 18th Centuries).* Oxford: Clarendon.

Alger, C.F. (1984–5) 'Bridging the Micro and the Macro in International Relations Research', *Alternatives*, 10 (Winter), pp. 319–44.

Alger, C.F. *et al.* (1988) 'The Local–Global Nexus', *International Social Science Journal*, No. 117 (August), pp. 321–406.

Alisjahbana, S.T. (1976) *Language Planning for Modernization: The Case of Indonesian and Malaysian.* The Hague: Mouton.

Almond, G.A. (1989) 'The International–National Connection', in *A Discipline Divided: Schools and Sects in Political Science.* London: Sage, 1990, pp. 263–89.

Althusser, L. and Balibar, E. (1968) *Reading Capital.* London: New Left Books, 1970.

Ambrose, S.E. (1983) *Rise to Globalism: American Foreign Policy since 1938*. Harmondsworth: Penguin (3rd rev. edn).

Amin, S. (1973) *Unequal Development: An Essay on the Social Formations of Peripheral Capitalism*. Hassocks: Harvester, 1976.

Amin, S. (1984) 'Self-Reliance and the New International Economic Order', in H. Addo (ed.) *Transforming the World Economy?* London: Hodder & Stoughton, pp. 204–19.

Amin, S. *et al*. (eds) (1982) *Dynamics of Global Crisis*. New York: Monthly Review.

Anderson, B. (1991) *Imagined Communities: Reflections on the Origin and Spread of Nationalism*. London: Verso (rev. edn).

Anderson, M. (1989) *Policing the World: Interpol and the Politics of International Police Co-operation*. Oxford: Clarendon.

Anderson, P. (1974) *Lineages of the Absolutist State*. London: New Left Books.

Angell, R.C. (1969) *Peace on the March: Transnational Participation*. New York: Van Nostrand.

Appadurai, A. (1990) 'Disjuncture and Difference in the Global Cultural Economy', *Public Culture*, 2 (Spring), pp. 1–24.

Armstrong, J.D. (1986) 'Non-Governmental Organizations', in R.J. Vincent (ed.) *Foreign Policy and Human Rights: Issues and Responses*. Cambridge: Cambridge University Press, pp. 243–60.

Aron, R. (1954) *The Century of Total War*. New York: Doubleday.

Aron, R. (1962) *Peace and War: A Theory of International Relations*. London: Weidenfeld and Nicolson, 1966.

Aronowitz, S. (1981) 'A Metatheoretical Critique of Immanuel Wallerstein's *The Modern World System*', *Theory and Society*, 10, pp. 503–20.

Arrighi, G. *et al*. (1989) *Antisystemic Movements*. London: Verso.

Arrighi, G. (1990) 'The Three Hegemonies of Historical Capitalism', *Review*, 13 (Summer), pp. 365–408.

Ashworth, G. (ed.) (1985) 'The UN Decade for Women: An International Evaluation', *Women's Studies International Forum*, 8, No. 2.

ATT (1982) *The World's Telephones*. Morris Plains, NJ: AT&T Communications.

Bailey, S.H. (1938) *International Studies in Modern Education*. London: Oxford University Press.

Banks, J.A. (1972) *The Sociology of Social Movements*. London: Macmillan.

Banks, M. and Shaw, M. (eds) (1991) *State and Society in International Relations*. New York: Harvester Wheatsheaf.

Barker, E. (1942) *Reflections on Government*. London: Oxford University Press.

Barnes, H.E. (1930) *World Politics in Modern Civilization: The Contributions of Nationalism, Capitalism, Imperialism and Militarism to Human Culture and International Anarchy*. New York: Knopf.

Barnet, R.J. and Müller, R.E. (1974) *Global Reach: The Power of the Multinational Corporations*. New York: Simon Schuster.

Barr, K. (1979) 'Long Waves: A Selective, Annotated Bibliography', *Review*, 2 (Spring), pp. 675–718.

Barraclough, G. (1964) *An Introduction to Contemporary History*. Harmondsworth: Penguin, 1967.

Barrett Brown, M. (1984) *Models in Political Economy: A Guide to the Arguments*. Harmondsworth: Penguin.

Baster, A.S.J. (1929) *The Imperial Banks*. London: P.S. King.

Baster, A.S.J. (1935) *The International Banks*. London: P.S. King.

Bauman, Z. (1989) 'Hermeneutics and Modern Social Theory', in D. Held and J.B. Thompson (eds) *Social Theory of Modern Societies: Anthony Giddens and His Critics*. Cambridge: Cambridge University Press, pp. 34–55.

BBC (1987a) *BBC Annual Report and Handbook 1987*. London: BBC.

BBC (1987b) 'The World at Your Fingertips'. London: BBC External Services Publicity (July).

Beales, A.C.F. (1931) *The History of Peace: A Short Account of the Organised Movements for International Peace*. London: Bell.

Behrendt, R.F. (1955) 'Der Beitrag der Soziologie zum Verständnis internationaler Probleme', *Schweizerische Zeitschrift für Volkwirtschaft und Statistik*, 91 (June), pp. 145–70.

Bell, D. (1962) *The End of Ideology: On the Exhaustion of Political Ideas in the Fifties*. New York: Free Press (rev. edn).

Bellah, R.N. (ed.) (1965) *Religion and Progress in Modern Asia*. New York: Free Press.

Bentham, J. (1789) *An Introduction to the Principles of Morals and Legislation*. London: Athlone.

Berberoglu, B. (1987) *The Internationalization of Capital: Imperialism and Capitalist Development on a World Scale*. New York: Praeger.

Berger, P.L. (1974) *Pyramids of Sacrifice: Political Ethics and Social Change*. London: Allen Lane, 1976.

Bergesen, A. (1980) 'From Utilitarianism to Globology: The Shift from the Individual to the World as a Whole as the Primordial Unit of Analysis', in A. Bergesen (ed.) *Studies of the Modern World-System*. New York: Academic Press, pp. 1–12.

Bergesen, A. (ed.) (1983) *Crises in the World-System*. Beverly Hills, CA: Sage.

Bergesen, A. and Schoenberg, R. (1980) 'Long Waves of Colonial Expansion and Contraction, 1415–1969', in A. Bergesen (ed.) *Studies of the Modern World-System*. New York: Academic Press, pp. 231–77.

Berlin, I. (1954) *Historical Inevitability*. London: Oxford University Press.

Bernal, M. (1987) *Black Athena: The Afroasiatic Roots of Classical Civilization*. London: Free Association Books.

Bernard, L.L. and Bernard, J. (1934) *Sociology and the Study of International Relations*. St. Louis, MO: Washington University Studies.

Bernstein, H. (1971) 'Modernization Theory and the Sociological Study of Development', *Journal of Development Studies*, 7 (January), pp. 141–60.

Bernstein, R.J. (1976) *The Restructuring of Social and Political Theory*. London: Methuen.

Bernstein, R.J. (1983) *Beyond Objectivism and Relativism: Science, Hermeneutics and Praxis*. Oxford: Blackwell.

Bertalanffy, L. von (1968) *General System Theory: Foundations, Development, Applications*. New York: Braziller.

Besnard, P. (ed.) (1983) *The Sociological Domain: The Durkheimians and the Founding of French Sociology*. Cambridge: Cambridge University Press.

Best, G. (ed.) (1988) *The Permanent Revolution: The French Revolution and Its Legacy 1789–1989*. London: Fontana.

Bhaskar, R. (1975) *A Realist Theory of Science*. Hassocks: Harvester, 1978.

Biersteker, T.J. (1989) 'Critical Reflections on Post-Positivism in International Relations', in Y. Lapid et al., 'The Third Debate', International Studies Quarterly, 33 (September), pp. 263–7.

Binns, P. and Hallas, D. (1976) 'The Soviet Union – State Capitalist or Socialist?', International Socialism, No. 91 (September), pp. 16–27.

BIS (1992) 62nd Annual Report. Basle: Bank for International Settlements.

BIS (1993) 63rd Annual Report. Basle: Bank for International Settlements.

Black, C.E. (1966) The Dynamics of Modernization: A Study in Comparative History. New York: Harper & Row.

Blainey, G. (1988) The Causes of War. New York: Free Press (3rd edn).

Blau, P. (ed.) (1976) Approaches to the Study of Social Structure. London: Open Books.

Blok, A. (1975) The Mafia of a Sicilian Village 1860–1960: A Study of Violent Peasant Entrepreneurs. New York: Harper & Row.

Bloom, W. (1990) Personal Identity, National Identity and International Relations. Cambridge: Cambridge University Press.

Boardman, R. (1981) International Organization and the Conservation of Nature. London: Macmillan.

Boli, J. (1980) 'Global Integration and the Universal Increase of State Dominance, 1910–1970', in A. Bergesen (ed.) Studies of the Modern World-System. New York: Academic Press, pp. 77–107.

Boli, J. (1987) 'World Polity Sources of Expanding State Authority and Organization, 1870–1970', in G.M. Thomas et al., Institutional Structure: Constituting State, Society, and the Individual. Beverly Hills, CA: Sage, pp. 71–91.

Bolt, C. (1969) The Anti-Slavery Movement and Reconstruction: A Study in Anglo-American Co-operation 1833–77. London: Oxford University Press.

Bontemps, A. (ed.) (1972) The Harlem Renaissance Remembered. New York: Dodd, Mead & Co.

Bookchin, M. (1986) The Modern Crisis. Philadelphia: New Society (Institute for Social Ecology).

Born, K.E. (1977) International Banking in the 19th and 20th Centuries. Leamington Spa: Berg.

Bornschier, V. and Lengyel, P. (eds) (1990) World Society Studies. Frankfurt: Campus.

Bottomore, T.B. (1985) Theories of Modern Capitalism. London: Allen & Unwin.

Boudon, R. (1984) Theories of Social Change: A Critical Appraisal. Cambridge: Polity, 1986.

Boulding, E. (1975) 'Female Alternatives to Hierarchical Systems, Past and Present: A Critique of Women's NGOs in the Light of History', International Associations, No. 6–7 (June–July) pp. 340–6.

Boulding, E. (1988) Building a Global Civic Culture: Education for an Interdependent World. Syracuse, NY: Syracuse University Press.

Boulding, K.E. (1968) The Organizational Revolution: A Study in the Ethics of Economic Organization. Chicago: Quadrangle.

Boulding, K.E. (1985) The World as a Total System. Beverly Hills, CA: Sage.

Bourdieu, P. (1972) Outline of a Theory of Practice. Cambridge: Cambridge University Press, 1977.

Bourdieu, P. (1980) 'The Production of Belief: Contribution to an Economy of Symbolic Goods', Media, Culture and Society, 2 (July), pp. 261–93.

Bousquet, N. (1980) 'From Hegemony to Competition: Cycles of the Core?', in T.K. Hopkins and I. Wallerstein (eds) *Processes of the World-System*. Beverly Hills, CA: Sage, pp. 46–83.

Bozeman, A.B. (1971) *The Future of Law in a Multicultural World*. Princeton, NJ: Princeton University Press.

Braudel, F. (1949) *The Mediterranean and the Mediterranean World in the Age of Philip II*. London: Collins, 1972.

Braudel, F. (1958) 'History and the Social Sciences: The *Longue Durée*', in *On History*. London: Weidenfeld and Nicolson, 1980, pp. 25–54.

Braudel, F. (1967) *Capitalism and Material Life 1400–1800*. New York: Harper & Row, 1973.

Braudel, F. (1979a) *Civilization and Capitalism 15th–18th Century. Volume II: The Wheels of Commerce*. London: Collins, 1983.

Braudel, F. (1979b) *Civilization and Capitalism 15th–18th Century. Volume III: The Perspective of the World*. London: Collins, 1984.

Brenner, R. (1977) 'The Origins of Capitalist Development: A Critique of Neo-Smithian Marxism', *New Left Review*, No. 104 (July–August), pp. 25–92.

Brett, E.A. (1983) *International Money and Capitalist Crisis: The Anatomy of Global Disintegration*. London: Heinemann.

Breuilly, J. (1982) *Nationalism and the State*. Manchester: Manchester University Press.

Brewer, A. (1990) *Marxist Theories of Imperialism: A Critical Survey*. London: Routledge (2nd edn).

Brown, C.J. (1988) 'The Globalization of Information Technologies', *Washington Quarterly*, 11 (Winter), pp. 89–101.

Brownlie, I. (1963) *International Law and the Use of Force by States*. Oxford: Clarendon.

Brucan, S. (1971) *The Dissolution of Power: A Sociology of International Relations and Politics*. New York: Knopf.

Brucan, S. (1978a) *The Dialectic of World Politics*. New York: Free Press.

Brucan, S. (1978b) 'The Nation-State: Will It Keep Order or Wither Away?', *International Social Science Journal*, 30, No. 1, pp. 9–30.

Brucan, S. (1980) 'The State and the World System', *International Social Science Journal*, 32, No. 4, pp. 752–69.

Brucan, S. (1984) 'The Global Crisis', *International Studies Quarterly*, 28 (March), pp. 97–109.

Bryant, C.G.A. and Jary, D. (eds) (1991) *Giddens' Theory of Structuration: A Critical Appreciation*. London: Routledge.

Bryce, J. (1919) *World History*. London: British Academy.

Buchanan, J.M. (1966) 'An Individualistic Theory of Political Process', in D. Easton (ed.) *Varieties of Political Theory*. Englewood Cliffs, NJ: Prentice-Hall, pp. 25–37.

Bukharin, N. (1915) *Imperialism and World Economy*. London: Merlin, 1972.

Bulbeck, C. (1988) *One World Women's Movement*. London: Pluto.

Bull, H. (1977) *The Anarchical Society: A Study of Order in World Politics*. London: Macmillan.

Bull, H. and Watson, A. (eds) (1984) *The Expansion of International Society*. Oxford: Clarendon.

Bulmer, M. (1984) *The Chicago School of Sociology: Institutionalization, Diversity, and the Rise of Sociological Research*. Chicago: University of Chicago Press.

Burke, P. (1980) *Sociology and History*. London: Allen & Unwin.

Burnham, J. (1941) *The Managerial Revolution: Or, What Is Happening to the World Now?* London: Putnam, 1942.

Burns, C.D. (1924) *A Short History of International Intercourse*. London: Allen & Unwin.

Burton, D.J. (1981) 'The Political Economy of Environmentalism', *Kapitalistate*, 8, pp. 141–57.

Burton, J.W. (1972) *World Society*. Cambridge: Cambridge University Press.

Bushnell, D. and Macaulay, N. (1988) *The Emergence of Latin America in the Nineteenth Century*. New York: Oxford University Press.

Buzan, B. and Jones, R.J.B. (eds) (1981) *Change and the Study of International Relations: The Evaded Dimension*. London: Pinter.

Cain, M. (1983) 'Introduction: Towards an Understanding of the International State', *International Journal of the Sociology of Law*, 11 (February), pp. 1–10.

Caldwell, L.K. (1984) *International Environmental Policy: Emergence and Dimensions*. Durham, NC: Duke University Press.

Caldwell, L.K. (1991) 'Globalizing Environmentalism: Threshold of a New Phase in International Relations', *Society and Natural Resources*, 4, No. 3, pp. 259–72.

Callinicos, A. (1985) 'Postmodernism, Post-Structuralism, Post-Marxism?', *Theory, Culture & Society*, 2, No. 3, pp. 85–101.

Callinicos, A. (1989) *Against Postmodernism: A Marxist Critique*. Cambridge: Polity.

Calvocoressi, P. (1987) *A Time for Peace: Pacifism, Internationalism and Protest Forces in the Reduction of War*. London: Hutchinson.

Cameron, K.N. (1973) *Humanity and Society: A World History*. Bloomington: Indiana University Press.

Camilleri, J.A. and Falk, J. (1992) *The End of Sovereignty? The Politics of a Shrinking and Fragmenting World*. Aldershot: Elgar.

Caporaso, J.A. (ed.) (1978) 'Dependence and Dependency in the Global System', *International Organization*, 32 (Winter).

Carr, E.H. (1939) *The Twenty Years' Crisis: An Introduction to the Study of International Relations*. London: Macmillan.

Carr, E.H. (1961) *What Is History?* Harmondsworth: Penguin.

Chamberlain, J.P. (1923) *The Regime of the International Rivers: Danube and Rhine*. New York: Longmans.

Chase-Dunn, C. (ed.) (1982) *Socialist States in the World-System*. Beverly Hills, CA: Sage.

Chase-Dunn, C. (1989) *Global Formation: Structures of the World-Economy*. Oxford: Blackwell.

Chetley, A. (1986) *The Politics of Baby Foods: Successful Challenges to an International Marketing Strategy*. London: Pinter.

Chirot, D. (1986) *Social Change in the Modern Era*. San Diego, CA: Harcourt Brace Jovanovich.

Chirot, D. and Hall, T.D. (1982) 'World System Theory', *Annual Review of Sociology*, 8, pp. 81–106.

Cipolla, C.M. (1956) *Money, Prices, and Civilization in the Mediterranean World: Fifth to Seventeenth Century*. Princeton, NJ: Princeton University Press.

Cipolla, C.M. (1967) *Clocks and Culture 1300–1700*. New York: Walker.

Claude, I.L. (1971) *Swords into Plowshares: The Problems and Prospects of International Organization*. New York: Random House (4th edn).

Close, D. (1988) *Nicaragua: Politics, Economics and Society*. London: Pinter.

Clutterbuck, D. *et al.* (1991) *Going Private: Privatisations Around the World*. London: Mercury.

Cohen, B.J. (1977) *Organizing the World's Money: The Political Economy of International Monetary Relations*. London: Macmillan, 1978.

Cohen, I.J. (1989) *Structuration Theory: Anthony Giddens and the Constitution of Social Life*. London: Macmillan.

Cohen, R. (1987) *The New Helots: Migrants in the International Division of Labour*. Aldershot: Avebury.

Collini, S. *et al.* (1983) *That Noble Science of Politics: A Study in Nineteenth-Century Intellectual History*. Cambridge: Cambridge University Press.

Collins, R. (1981) *Sociology since Midcentury: Essays in Theory Cumulation*. New York: Academic Press.

Collins, R. (1985) *Three Sociological Traditions*. New York: Oxford University Press.

Collins, R. (1986) *Weberian Sociological Theory*. Cambridge: Cambridge University Press.

Comte, A. (1830–42) *The Positive Philosophy*. London: Trübner, 1875.

Connell, R.W. (1987) *Gender and Power: Society, the Person and Sexual Politics*. Cambridge: Polity.

Connelly, P. and Perlman, R. (1975) *The Politics of Scarcity: Resource Conflicts in International Relations*. London: Oxford University Press.

Connor, W. (1984) *The National Question in Marxist–Leninist Theory and Strategy*. Princeton, NJ: Princeton University Press.

Cox, R.W. (1981) 'Social Forces, States, and World Orders: Beyond International Relations Theory', *Millennium*, 10 (Summer), pp. 126–55.

Cox, R.W. (1983) 'Gramsci, Hegemony and International Relations: An Essay in Method', *Millennium*, 12 (Summer), pp. 162–75.

Cox, R.W. (1987) *Production, Power, and World Order: Social Forces in the Making of History*. New York: Columbia University Press.

Cox, R.W. and Jacobson, H.K. *et al.* (1973) *The Anatomy of Influence: Decision Making in International Organization*. New Haven, CT: Yale University Press.

Cranston, M. (1973) *What Are Human Rights?* London: Bodley Head.

Crawford, J. (ed.) (1988) *The Rights of Peoples*. Oxford: Clarendon.

Curtin, P.D. (1969) *The Atlantic Slave Trade: A Census*. Madison: University of Wisconsin Press.

Curtin, P.D. (1984) *Cross-Cultural Trade in World History*. Cambridge: Cambridge University Press.

Davie, M.R. (1929) *The Evolution of War: A Study of Its Role in Early Societies*. New Haven, CT: Yale University Press, 1968.

Davies, M. (ed.) (1983) *Third World – Second Sex: Women's Struggles and National Liberation*. London: Zed.

Dawson, F.G. (1990) *The First Latin American Debt Crisis: The City of London and the 1822–25 Loan Bubble*. New Haven, CT: Yale University Press.

Day, A.J. (1986) *Peace Movements of the World*. London: Longman.

Day, C. (1922) *A History of Commerce*. New York: Longmans.

Day, J. (1967) *International Nationalism: The Extra-Territorial Relations of Southern Rhodesian African Nationalists.* London: Routledge.

Day, R.B. (1976) 'The Theory of the Long Cycle: Kondratiev, Trotsky, Mandel', *New Left Review*, No. 99 (September–October), pp. 67–82.

Deakin, F.W. *et al.* (eds) (1975) *A History of World Communism.* London: Weidenfeld and Nicolson.

De Cecco, M. (1974) *Money and Empire: The International Gold Standard, 1890–1914.* Oxford: Blackwell.

DeConde, A. (1988) 'On the Nature of International History', *International History Review*, 10 (May), pp. 282–301.

De Lupis, I.D. (1987) *The Law of War.* Cambridge: Cambridge University Press.

Der Derian, J. and Shapiro, M.J. (eds) (1989) *International/Intertextual Relations: Postmodern Readings of World Politics.* Lexington, MA: Lexington Books.

Deutsch, K.W. (1966) 'External Influences on the Internal Behavior of States', in R.B. Farrell (ed.) *Approaches to Comparative and International Politics.* Evanston, IL: Northwestern University Press, pp. 5–26.

Deutsch, K.W. and Eckstein, A. (1961) 'National Industrialization and the Declining Share of the International Economic Sector 1890–1959', *World Politics*, 13 (January), pp. 267–99.

Devall, B.B. and Sessions, G. (1984) *Deep Ecology.* Layton, UT: Peregrine Smith.

Dizard, W.P. (1966) *Television: A World View.* Syracuse, NY: Syracuse University Press.

Dobb, M. (1963) *Studies in the Development of Capitalism.* London: Routledge.

Dougherty, J.E. and Pfaltzgraff, R.L. (1990) *Contending Theories of International Relations: A Comprehensive Survey.* New York: Harper Collins (3rd edn).

Dover, K.J. (1978) *Greek Homosexuality.* London: Duckworth.

Dower, J.W. (1986) *War without Mercy: Race and Power in the Pacific War.* New York: Pantheon.

Doxey, M.P. (1987) *International Sanctions in Contemporary Perspective.* Basingstoke: Macmillan.

Drachkovitch, M.M. (ed.) (1966) *The Revolutionary Internationals 1864–1943.* Stanford, CA: Stanford University Press.

Drucker, P.F. (1986) 'The Changed World Economy', *Foreign Affairs*, 64 (Spring), pp. 768–91.

Duchacek, I.D. *et al.* (eds) (1988) *Perforated Sovereignties and International Relations: Trans-Sovereign Contacts of Subnational Governments.* Westport, CT: Greenwood.

Duffy, M. (ed.) (1980) *The Military Revolution and the State 1500–1800.* Exeter: University of Exeter Studies in History.

Dunn, D. (1974) 'War and Social Change', in F.S. Northedge (ed.) *The Use of Force in International Relations.* London: Faber, pp. 220–47.

Dunning, J.H. (1983) 'Changes in the Level and Structure of International Production: The Last One Hundred Years', in M. Casson (ed.) *The Growth of International Business.* London: Allen & Unwin, pp. 84–139.

Dunning, J.H. and Cantwell, J. (1987) *IRM Directory of Statistics of International Investment and Production.* London: Macmillan.

Durkheim, E. (1893) *The Division of Labour in Society.* Basingstoke: Macmillan, 1984.

Durkheim, E. (1915) *The Elementary Forms of Religious Life*. London: Allen & Unwin, 1976.

Durkheim, E. and Mauss, M. (1913) 'Note on the Notion of Civilization', *Social Research*, 38 (Winter 1971), pp. 808–13.

Duverger, M. (1964) *The Idea of Politics: The Uses of Power in Society*. London: Methuen, 1967.

Eggan, F. (1968) 'One Hundred Years of Ethnology and Social Anthropology', in J.O. Brew (ed.) *One Hundred Years of Anthropology*. Cambridge, MA: Harvard University Press, pp. 119–49.

Ehteshani, A. and Varasteh, M. (eds) (1991) *Iran and the International Community*. London: Routledge.

Eisenstadt, S.N. (ed.) (1968) *The Protestant Ethic and Modernization: A Comparative View*. New York: Basic Books.

Eisenstadt, S.N. (ed.) (1970) *Readings in Social Evolution and Development*. Oxford: Pergamon.

Ekholm, K. and Friedman, J. (1980) 'Towards a Global Anthropology', in L. Blussé *et al.* (eds) *History and Underdevelopment: Essays on Underdevelopment and European Expansion in Asia and Africa*. Leiden: Centre for the History of European Expansion, pp. 61–76.

Ekins, P. (1992) *A New World Order: Grassroots Movements for Global Change*. London: Routledge.

El-Hinnawi, E. and Hashmi, M.H. (eds) (1982) *Global Environmental Issues: United Nations Environment Programme*. Dublin: Tycooly.

Elias, N. (1939) *The Civilizing Process. Volume 2: State Formation and Civilization*. Oxford: Blackwell, 1982.

Elsbree, W.H. (1953) *Japan's Role in South-East Asian Nationalist Movements*. Cambridge, MA: Harvard University Press.

Elshtain, J.B. (1987) *Women and War*. New York: Basic Books.

Elson, D. (ed.) (1991) *Male Bias in the Development Process*. Manchester: Manchester University Press.

Elster, J. (1982) 'Marxism, Functionalism, and Game Theory: The Case for Methodological Individualism', *Theory and Society*, 11 (July), pp. 453–82.

Emerson, R. (1960) *From Empire to Nation: The Rise to Self-Assertion of Asian and African Peoples*. Cambridge, MA: Harvard University Press.

Engels, F. (1890) Letter to Joseph Bloch of 21 September, reprinted in *Karl Marx, Selected Works: Volume I*. London: Lawrence and Wishart, 1942.

Engels, F. (1892) *Socialism: Utopian and Scientific*. London: Allen & Unwin.

Enloe, C. (1989) *Bananas, Beaches and Bases: Making Feminist Sense of International Relations*. London: Pandora.

Esposito, J.L. (ed.) (1990) *The Iranian Revolution: Its Global Impact*. Miami: University Presses of Florida.

Etzioni, A. (1963) 'The Epigenesis of Political Communities at the International Level', *American Journal of Sociology*, 68 (January), pp. 407–21.

Evans, P.B. *et al.* (eds) (1985) *Bringing the State Back In*. Cambridge: Cambridge University Press.

Falk, R. and Kim, S.S. (1983) 'World Order Studies and the World System', in W.R. Thompson (ed.) *Contending Approaches to World System Analysis*. Beverly Hills, CA: Sage, pp. 203–37.

Fawcett, J.E.S. (1984) *Outer Space: New Challenges to Law and Policy.* Oxford: Clarendon.

Feather, F. (ed.) (1980) *Through the '80s: Thinking Globally, Acting Locally.* Washington, DC: World Future Society.

Featherstone, M. (ed.) (1990) *Global Culture: Nationalism, Globalization and Modernity.* London: Sage.

Featherstone, M. (1991) *Consumer Culture and Postmodernism.* London: Sage.

Febvre, L. and Martin, L.J. (1958) *The Coming of the Book: The Impact of Printing 1450–1800.* London: Verso, 1984.

Ferrier, R.W. and Fursenko, A. (eds) (1989) *Oil in the World Economy.* London: Routledge.

Finlayson, J. and Zacher, M. (1981) 'The GATT and the Regulation of Trade Barriers: Regime Dynamics and Functions', *International Organization*, 35 (Autumn), pp. 561–602.

Fliess, P.J. (1966) *Thucydides and the Politics of Bipolarity.* Baton Rouge: Louisiana State University Press.

Foster-Carter, A. (1985) 'The Sociology of Development', in M. Haralambos (ed.) *Sociology: New Directions.* Ormskirk: Causeway, pp. 89–213.

Foucault, M. (1966) *The Order of Things.* London: Tavistock, 1970.

Foucault, M. (1969) *The Archaeology of Knowledge.* London: Tavistock, 1972.

Foucault, M. (1977a) 'Truth and Power', in *Power/Knowledge.* Brighton: Harvester, pp. 109–33.

Foucault, M. (1977b) 'The Confession of the Flesh', in *Power/Knowledge.* Brighton: Harvester, pp. 194–228.

Foucault, M. (1980) *Power/Knowledge: Selected Interviews and Other Writings 1972–1977.* Brighton: Harvester.

Francome, C. (1984) *Abortion Freedom: A Worldwide Movement.* London: Allen & Unwin.

Frank, A.G. (1976) 'Long Live Transideological Enterprise! The Socialist Economies in the Capitalist International Division of Labor and West-East-South Relations', in *Crisis: In the World Economy.* London: Heinemann, 1980, pp. 178–262.

Frank, A.G. (1978) *Dependent Accumulation and Underdevelopment.* London: Macmillan.

Freeman, A. (1991) 'The Economic Background and Consequences of the Gulf War', in H. Bresheeth and N. Yuval-Davis (eds) *The Gulf War and the New World Order.* London: Zed, pp. 153–65.

Freeman, C. (ed.) (1983) *Long Waves in the World Economy.* London: Butterworths.

Freese, J. (1979) *International Data Flow.* Lund (Sweden): Studentlitteratur.

Freud, S. (1929) *Civilization and Its Discontents.* New York: Norton, 1961.

Friedman, M. and Friedman, R. (1980) *Free to Choose: A Personal Statement.* New York: Harcourt Brace.

Friedmann, J. (1986) 'The World City Hypothesis', *Development and Change*, 17 (January), pp. 69–83.

Fröbel, F. *et al.* (1977) *The New International Division of Labour: Structural Unemployment in the Industrialized Countries and Industrialization in the Developing Countries.* Cambridge: Cambridge University Press, 1980.

Fukuyama, F. (1989) 'The End of History?', *The National Interest*, 16 (Summer), pp. 3–18.

Fukuyama, F. (1992) *The End of History and the Last Man*. London: Hamish Hamilton.

Galli, R.E. (ed.) (1981) *The Political Economy of Rural Development: Peasants, International Capital, and the State*. Albany: State University of New York Press.

Galtung, J. (1980) 'The Non-Territorial System', in *The True Worlds: A Transnational Perspective*. New York: Free Press, pp. 305–40.

Gandhi, M.K. (1909) Letter to H.S.L. Polak of 14 October, printed in R. Iyer (ed.) *The Moral and Political Writings of Mahatma Gandhi. Volume I: Civilization, Politics, and Religion*. Oxford: Clarendon.

Garnett, J.C. (1984) *Commonsense and the Theory of International Politics*. London: Macmillan.

Gay, P. (1966) *The Enlightenment: An Interpretation. The Rise of Modern Paganism*. New York: Norton, 1977.

Gellner, E. (1983) *Nations and Nationalism*. Oxford: Blackwell.

George, S. (1989) *A Fate Worse Than Debt*. London: Penguin (rev. edn).

Gettas, G.J. (1990) 'The Globalization of Sesame Street: A Producer's Perspective', *Educational Technology Research and Development*, 38, No. 4, pp. 55–63.

Gibb, H.A.R. (ed.) (1932) *Whither Islam? A Survey of Modern Movements in the Moslem World*. London: Gollancz.

Giddens, A. (1976) *New Rules of Sociological Method*. London: Hutchinson.

Giddens, A. (1977a) *Central Problems in Social Theory: Action, Structure and Contradiction in Social Analysis*. London: Hutchinson.

Giddens, A. (1977b) *Studies in Social and Political Theory*. London: Hutchinson.

Giddens, A. (1981) *A Contemporary Critique of Historical Materialism. Volume 1: Power, Property and the State*. London: Macmillan.

Giddens, A. (1984) *The Constitution of Society: Outline of the Theory of Structuration*. Cambridge: Polity.

Giddens, A. (1985) *The Nation-State and Violence. Volume Two of A Contemporary Critique of Historical Materialism*. Cambridge: Polity.

Giddens, A. (1987) *Social Theory and Modern Sociology*. Cambridge: Polity.

Giddens, A. (1989) 'A Reply to My Critics', in D. Held and J.B. Thompson (eds) *Social Theory of Modern Societies: Anthony Giddens and His Critics*. Cambridge: Cambridge University Press, pp. 249–301.

Giddens, A. (1990) *The Consequences of Modernity*. Cambridge: Polity.

Giddens, A. (1991) 'Structuration Theory: Past, Present and Future', in C.G.A. Bryant and D. Jary (eds) *Giddens' Theory of Structuration: A Critical Appreciation*. London: Routledge, pp. 201–21.

Gill, S. and Law, D. (1988) *The Global Political Economy: Perspectives, Problems, and Policies*. Hemel Hempstead: Harvester-Wheatsheaf.

Gilpin, R. (1981) *War and Change in World Politics*. London: Cambridge University Press.

Glossop, R.J. (1988) 'Language Policy and a Just World Order', *Alternatives*, 13 (July), pp. 395–409.

Goldblat, J. (1982) *Arms Control Agreements: A Handbook*. London: Taylor & Francis.

Goldstein, J.S. (1985) 'Kondratieff Waves as War Cycles', *International Studies Quarterly*, 29 (December), pp. 411–44.

Goldstein, J.S. (1988) *Long Cycles: Prosperity and War in the Modern Age*. New Haven, CT: Yale University Press.

Goodman, S.E. (1991) 'The Globalization of Computing: Perspectives on a Changing World', *Communications of the ACM*, 34 (January), pp. 19–21.

Goodwin-Gill, G.S. (1978) *International Law and the Movement of Persons between States*. Oxford: Clarendon.

Gordon-Ashworth, F. (1984) *International Commodity Control: A Contemporary History and Appraisal*. London: Croom Helm.

Gorz, A. (1975) *Ecology as Politics*. London: Pluto, 1983.

Gourevitch, P. (1978) 'The Second Image Reversed: The International Sources of Domestic Politics', *International Organization*, 32 (Autumn), pp. 881–911.

Grant, R. and Newland, K. (eds) (1991) *Gender and International Relations*. Milton Keynes: Open University Press.

Gray, C.S. (1977) *The Geopolitics of the Nuclear Era: Heartland, Rimlands, and the Technological Revolution*. New York: Crane Rusak.

Gregory, D. (1989) 'Foreword', in J. Der Derian and M.J. Shapiro (eds) *International/ Intertextual Relations*. Lexington, MA: Lexington Books.

Groom, A.J.R. and Guilhaudis, J.F. (1989) 'UNSSODS: The Quest for Structure and Norms', in P. Taylor and A.J.R. Groom (eds) *Global Issues in the United Nations' Framework*. Basingstoke: Macmillan, pp. 116–47.

Groom, A.J.R. and Heraclides, A. (1985) 'Integration and Disintegration', in M. Light and A.J.R. Groom (eds) *International Relations: A Handbook of Current Theory*. London: Pinter, pp. 174–93.

Grosser, A. (1956) 'L'étude des relations internationales, specialité américaine?', *Revue française de science politique*, 6 (July–September), pp. 634–51.

Grunwald, J. and Flamm, K. (1985) *The Global Factory: Foreign Assembly in International Trade*. Washington, DC: Brookings Institution.

Guest, I. (1988) 'Magna Carta for Unkind Mankind', *The Guardian*, 10 December, p. 21.

Guha, R. (1989) *The Unquiet Woods: Ecological Change and Peasant Resistance in the Himalaya*. Delhi: Oxford University Press.

Haar, B. ter (1939) *Adat Law in Indonesia*. New York: Institute of Pacific Relations, 1948.

Haas, E.B. (1953) 'The Balance of Power: Prescription, Concept, or Propaganda?', *World Politics*, 5 (July), pp. 442–77.

Habermas, J. (1973) *Legitimation Crisis*. London: Heinemann, 1976.

Habermas, J. (1976) *Communication and the Evolution of Society*. London: Heinemann, 1979.

Habermas, J. (1981) *The Theory of Communicative Action*. Boston, MA: Beacon, 1984 and 1987 (2 volumes).

Hagen, E.E. (1962) *On the Theory of Social Change*. Homewood, IL: Dorsey.

Haggard, S. and Simmons, B.A. (1987) 'Theories of International Regimes', *International Organization*, 41 (Summer), pp. 491–517.

Hall, J.A. (1985) *Powers and Liberties: The Causes and Consequences of the Rise of the West*. Oxford: Blackwell.

Hall, J.A. (1986a) 'Theory', in M. Haralambos (ed.) *Developments in Sociology. Volume 2*. Ormskirk: Causeway, pp. 149–74.

Hall, J.A. (ed.) (1986b) *States in History*. Oxford: Blackwell.

Hall, J.A. (1987) 'War and the Rise of the West', in C. Creighton and M. Shaw (eds) *The Sociology of War and Peace*. Basingstoke: Macmillan, pp. 37–53.

Hall, J.A. and Ikenberry, G.J. (1989) *The State*. Milton Keynes: Open University Press.

Halliday, F. (1985) 'A "Crisis" of International Relations?', *International Relations*, 8 (November), pp. 407–12.

Halliday, F. (1987a) 'State and Society in International Relations: A Second Agenda', *Millennium*, 16 (Summer), pp. 215–29.

Halliday, F. (1987b) 'Alan Sked and International Relations: A Note', *Millennium*, 16 (Summer), pp. 263–4.

Halliday, F. (1990) ' "The Sixth Great Power": On the Study of Revolution and International Relations', *Review of International Studies*, 16 (July), pp. 207–21.

Halpern, M. (1966) 'The Revolution of Modernization in National and International Society', in C.J. Friedrich (ed.) *Revolution*. New York: Atherton, pp. 178–214.

Hamelink, C.J. (1983) *Cultural Autonomy in Global Communications: Planning National Information Policy*. London: Centre for the Study of Communication and Culture, 1988.

Hamilton, A. (1986) *The Financial Revolution: The Big Bang Worldwide*. Harmondsworth: Viking.

Hannerz, U. (1990) 'Cosmopolitans and Locals in World Culture', in M. Featherstone (ed.) *Global Culture: Nationalism, Globalization and Modernity*. London: Sage, pp. 237–51.

Harari, J.V. (ed.) (1979) *Textual Strategies: Perspectives in Post-Structuralist Criticism*. London: Methuen, 1980.

Hardin, G. (1977) *The Limits of Altruism: An Ecologist's View of Survival*. Bloomington: Indiana University Press.

Harff, B. (1984) *Genocide and Human Rights: International Legal and Political Issues*. Denver, CO: Graduate School of International Studies, University of Denver.

Harris, N. (1983) *Of Bread and Guns: The World Economy in Crisis*. Harmondsworth: Penguin.

Harrison, D.H. (1988) *The Sociology of Modernization and Development*. London: Unwin Hyman.

Harvey, D. (1989) *The Condition of Postmodernity: An Enquiry into the Origins of Cultural Change*. Oxford: Blackwell.

Hayes, C.J.H. (1926) *Essays on Nationalism*. New York: Russell, 1966.

Hayter, T. and Watson, C. (1985) *Aid: Rhetoric and Reality*. London: Pluto.

Heckscher, E.F. (1955) *Mercantilism*. London: Allen & Unwin (2nd edn).

Hegedus, A. (1976) *Socialism and Bureaucracy*. London: Allen & Busby.

Henderson, J. (1989) *The Globalisation of High Technology Production: Society, Space and Semiconductors in the Restructuring of the Modern World*. London: Routledge.

Henry, C.E. (1985) *The Carriage of Dangerous Goods by Sea: The Role of the International Maritime Organisation in International Legislation*. London: Pinter.

Herder, J.G. von (1784–91) *Reflections on the Philosophy of the History of Mankind*. Chicago: University of Chicago Press, 1968.

Hermann, M. (1980) 'Explaining Foreign Policy Behavior Using the Personal Characteristics of Political Leaders', *International Studies Quarterly*, 24 (March), pp. 7–46.

Hexter, J.H. (1972) 'Fernand Braudel and the Monde Braudellien', in *On Historians*. London: Collins, 1979, pp. 61–145.

Higgonet, M.R. *et al.* (eds) (1987) *Behind the Lines: Gender and the Two World Wars*. New Haven, CT: Yale University Press.

Hilferding, R. (1910) *Finance Capital: A Study of the Latest Phase of Capitalist Development*. London: Routledge, 1981.

Hill, C. (1985) 'History and International Relations', in S. Smith (ed.) *International Relations: British and American Perspectives*. Oxford: Blackwell, pp. 126–45.

Hilton, R. (ed.) (1978) *The Transition from Feudalism to Capitalism*. London: Verso.

Hinsley, F.H. (1986) *Sovereignty*. Cambridge: Cambridge University Press (2nd edn).

Hintze, O. (1906) 'Military Organization and the Organization of the State', in F. Gilbert (ed.) *The Historical Essays of Otto Hintze*. New York: Oxford University Press, 1975, pp. 180–215.

Hintze, O. (1929) 'Economics and Politics in the Age of Modern Capitalism', in F. Gilbert (ed.) *The Historical Essays of Otto Hintze*. New York: Oxford University Press, 1975, pp. 424–52.

Hobhouse, L.T. (1906) *Morals in Evolution: A Study in Comparative Ethics*. London: Chapman & Hall, 1915.

Hoffmann, S. (1960) *Contemporary Theory in International Relations*. Englewood Cliffs, NJ: Prentice-Hall.

Hoffmann, S. (1977) 'An American Social Science: International Relations', *Daedalus*, 106 (Summer), pp. 41–60.

Hofstadter, R. (1944) *Social Darwinism in American Thought 1860–1915*. Philadelphia: University of Pennsylvania Press.

Hogan, M.J. (1987) *The Marshall Plan: America, Britain and the Reconstruction of Western Europe 1947–52*. London: Cambridge University Press.

Holland, R.F. (1985) *European Decolonization, 1918–1981: An Introductory Survey*. London: Macmillan.

Hollis, M. and Smith, S. (1991) 'Beware of Gurus: Structure and Action in International Relations', *Review of International Studies*, 17 (October), pp. 393–410.

Hollist, W.L. and Rosenau, J.N. (eds) (1981) *World System Structure: Continuity and Change*. Beverly Hills, CA: Sage.

Holsti, K.J. (1971) 'Retreat from Utopia: International Relations Theory, 1945–70', *Canadian Journal of Political Science*, 4 (June), pp. 165–77.

Holsti, K.J. (1992) *International Politics: A Framework for Analysis*. Englewood Cliffs, NJ: Prentice-Hall (6th edn).

Holsti, O.R. *et al.* (eds) (1980) *Change in the International System*. Boulder, CO: Westview.

Holton, R.J. (1985) *The Transition from Feudalism to Capitalism*. Basingstoke: Macmillan.

Hopkins, R.F. (1976) 'The International Role of "Domestic" Bureaucracy', *International Organization*, 30 (Summer), pp. 405–32.

Hopkins, T.K. *et al.* (1979) 'Cyclical Rhythms and Secular Trends of the Capitalist World-Economy: Some Premises, Hypotheses, and Questions', *Review*, 2 (Spring), pp. 483–500.

Howard, M. (1976) *War in European History*. Oxford: Oxford University Press.

Howard, M. (1978) *War and the Liberal Conscience*. Oxford: Oxford University Press.

Hughes, B.B. (1991) *Continuity and Change in World Politics: The Clash of Perspectives*. Englewood Cliffs, NJ: Prentice-Hall.

Huntington, S.P. (1968) *Political Order in Changing Societies*. New Haven, CT: Yale University Press.

Huth, A. (1937) *La radiodiffusion. Puissance mondiale*. Paris: Gallimard.

Hymer, S. (1979) *The Multinational Corporation: A Radical Approach*. Cambridge: Cambridge University Press.

IBRD (1992) *World Development Report: Development and the Environment*. New York: Oxford University Press (for the World Bank).

ICAO (1991) *Civil Aviation Statistics of the World 1990*. Montreal: International Civil Aviation Organization (Doc. 9180/16).

IIC (1929) *Handbook of Institutions for the Scientific Study of International Relations*. Paris: Institute of Intellectual Co-operation.

IIC (1931) *Handbook of Reference Centres for International Affairs*. Paris: International Institute of Intellectual Co-operation (Conference of Institutions for the Scientific Study of International Relations).

IIC (1937) *The International Studies Conference: Origins, Functions, Organisation*. Paris: International Institute of Intellectual Co-operation.

ILO (1982) *International Labour Conventions and Recommendations 1919–1981*. Geneva: International Labour Office.

Immerman, R.H. (1982) *The CIA in Guatemala: The Foreign Policy of Intervention*. Austin: University of Texas Press.

Inkeles, A. and Smith, D.H. (1974) *Becoming Modern: Individual Change in Six Developing Countries*. London: Heinemann.

ISA (1966) *Transactions of the Sixth World Congress of Sociology. Evian, 4–11 September 1966*. Geneva: International Sociological Association.

ISO (1982) *Units of Measurement*. Geneva: International Organization for Standardization (ISO Standards Handbook).

ITU (1990) *Yearbook of Public Telecommunication Statistics*. Geneva: International Telecommunication Union (17th edn).

Jacobson, H.K. (1984) *Networks of Interdependence: International Organizations and the Global Political System*. New York: Knopf (2nd edn).

James, A. (1976) 'International Institutions: Independent Actors?', in A. Shlaim (ed.) *International Organisations in World Politics: Yearbook 1975*. London: Croom Helm, pp. 72–92.

James, A. (1978) 'International Society', *British Journal of International Studies*, 4 (July), pp. 91–106.

James, A. (1986) *Sovereign Statehood: The Basis of International Society*. London: Allen & Unwin.

James, A. (1989) 'The Realism of Realism: The State and the Study of International Relations', *Review of International Studies*, 15 (July), pp. 215–29.

James, S. (1984) *The Content of Social Explanation*. Cambridge: Cambridge University Press.

Jarvis, A. (1989) 'Societies, States and Geopolitics: Challenges from Historical Sociology', *Review of International Studies*, 15 (July), pp. 281–93.

Jary, D. (1991) ' "Society as Time-Traveller": Giddens on Historical Change, Historical Materialism and the Nation-State in World Society', in C.G.A. Bryant and D. Jary (eds) *Giddens' Theory of Structuration: A Critical Appreciation*. London: Routledge, pp. 116–59.

Jayawardena, K. (1986) *Feminism and Nationalism in the Third World*. London: Zed.

Jeffords, S. (1989) *The Remasculinization of America: Gender and the Vietnam War*. Bloomington: Indiana University Press.

Jenkins, R. (1985) 'Internationalization of Capital and the Semi-Industrialized Countries: The Case of the Motor Industry', *Review of Radical Political Economics*, 17 (Spring/Summer), pp. 59–81.

Jenkins, R. (1987) *Transnational Corporations and Uneven Development: The Internationalization of Capital and the Third World*. London: Methuen.

Johnston, R.B. (1983) *The Economics of the Euro-Market: History, Theory and Policy*. London: Macmillan.

Jones, G. (1980) *Social Darwinism and English Thought: The Interaction between Biology and Social Theory*. Brighton: Harvester.

Jones, R.E. (1981) 'The English School of International Relations: A Case for Closure', *Review of International Studies*, 7 (January), pp. 1–12.

Jones, R.J.B. (ed.) (1988) *The Worlds of Political Economy: Alternative Approaches to the Study of Contemporary Political Economy*. London: Pinter.

Jönsson, C. (1987) *International Aviation and the Politics of Regime Change*. London: Pinter.

Joyner, C.C. and Chopra, S.K. (eds) (1988) *The Antarctic Legal Regime*. Dordrecht: Nijhoff.

Julius, D. (1990) *Global Companies and Public Policy: The Growing Challenge of Foreign Direct Investment*. London: Pinter.

Kaldor, M. (1982a) *The Baroque Arsenal*. London: Deutsch.

Kaldor, M. (1982b) 'Warfare and Capitalism', in E.P. Thompson *et al.*, *Exterminism and Cold War*. London: NLB/Verso, pp. 261–87.

Kaldor, M. and Eide, A. (eds) (1979) *The World Military Order: The Impact of Military Technology on the Third World*. London: Macmillan.

Kamenka, E. (1973) 'Political Nationalism – The Evolution of the Idea', in E. Kamenka (ed.) *Nationalism: The Nature and Evolution of an Idea*. London: Arnold, 1976, pp. 2–20.

Kautsky, K. (1914) 'Ultra-Imperialism', *New Left Review*, No. 59 (January–February 1970), pp. 41–6 (translated excerpt from original).

Katzenstein, P.J. (1989) 'International Relations Theory and the Analysis of Change', in E.O. Czempiel and J.N. Rosenau (eds) *Global Changes and Theoretical Challenges: Approaches to World Politics for the 1990s*. Lexington, MA: Lexington Books, pp. 291–304.

Kazancigil, A. (ed.) (1986) *The State in Global Perspective*. Aldershot: Gower.

Kemp, D.D. (1990) *Global Environmental Issues: A Climatological Approach*. London: Routledge.

Kennedy, P.M. (1987) *The Rise and Fall of the Great Powers: Economic Change and Military Conflict from 1500 to 2000*. New York: Random House.

Kenwood, A.G. and Lougheed, A.L. (1983) *The Growth of the International Economy 1820–1980: An Introductory Text*. London: Allen & Unwin.

Keohane, R.O. (ed.) (1986) *Neorealism and Its Critics*. New York: Columbia University Press.

Keohane, R.O. and Nye, J.S. (eds) (1971) *Transnational Relations and World Politics*. Cambridge, MA: Harvard University Press.

Khadduri, M. (1955) *War and Peace in the Law of Islam*. Baltimore, MD: Johns Hopkins University Press.

Khan, K.M. (ed.) (1986) *Multinationals of the South: New Actors in the International Economy*. London: Pinter.

Killick, T. (ed.) (1984) *The Quest for Economic Stabilisation: The IMF and the Third World*. Aldershot: Gower.

Kim, K.W. (1970) *Revolution and International System*. New York: New York University Press.

King, A.D. (1984) *The Bungalow: The Production of a Global Culture*. London: Routledge.

King, A.D. (1990a) *Global Cities: Post-Imperialism and the Internationalization of London*. London: Routledge.

King, A.D. (1990b) *Urbanism, Colonialism, and the World-Economy: Cultural and Spatial Foundations of the World Urban System*. London: Routledge.

King, A.D. (ed.) (1991) *Culture, Globalization and the World-System: Contemporary Conditions for the Representation of Identity*. Basingstoke: Macmillan.

King-Hall, W.S.R. (1937) *Chatham House: A Brief Account of the Origins, Purposes and Methods of the Royal Institute of International Affairs*. Oxford: Oxford University Press.

Kissinger, H.A. (1957) *A World Restored*. Boston, MA: Houghton Mifflin.

Knieper, R. (1983) 'The Conditioning of National Policy-making by International Law: The Stand-By Arrangements of the International Monetary Fund', *International Journal of the Sociology of Law*, 11 (February), pp. 41–64.

Knight, R.V. and Gappert, G. (eds) (1989) *Cities in a Global Society*. Newbury Park, CA: Sage.

Knorr, K. (1973) *Power and Wealth: The Political Economy of International Power*. New York: Basic Books.

Knorr, K. and Verba, S. (eds) (1961) *The International System: Theoretical Essays*. Princeton, NJ: Princeton University Press.

Kohn, H. (1944) *Nationalism: A Study in Its Origins and Background*. Toronto: Collier-Macmillan, 1967.

Kohn, H. (1965) *Nationalism: Its Meaning and History*. New York: Van Nostrand (rev. edn).

Koht, H. (1947) 'The Dawn of Nationalism in Europe', *American Historical Review*, 52 (January), pp. 265–80.

Kolko, G. (1985) *Vietnam: Anatomy of a War, 1940–1975*. London: Allen & Unwin, 1986.

Kondratieff, N.D. (1926) 'The Long Waves in Economic Life', *Review*, 2 (Spring 1979), pp. 519–62.

Kostakos, G. *et al.* (1991) 'Britain and the New UN Agenda: Towards Global Riot Control?', *Review of International Studies*, 17 (January), pp. 95–105.

Krasner, S.D. (ed.) (1983) *International Regimes*. Ithaca, NY: Cornell University Press.

Krippendorff, E. (1975a) *International Relations as a Social Science*. Brighton: Harvester, 1982.

Krippendorff, E. (1975b) *Internationales System als Geschichte. Einführung in die internationale Beziehungen*. Frankfurt: Campus.

Krippendorff, E. (1975c) 'Towards a Class Analysis of the International System', *Acta Politica*, 10 (January), pp. 3–13.

Krippendorff, E. (1987) 'The Dominance of American Approaches to International Relations', *Millennium*, 16 (Summer), pp. 207–14.

Kristof, L.K.D. (1960) 'The Origins and Evolution of Geopolitics', *Journal of Conflict Resolution*, 4, pp. 15–51.

Kurian, G.T. (ed.) (1982) *World Press Encyclopedia*. London: Mansell.

Kurzweil, E. (1980) *The Age of Structuralism: Lévi-Strauss to Foucault*. New York: Columbia University Press.

LaFeber, W. (1983) *Inevitable Revolutions: The United States in Central America*. New York: Norton.

Landecker, W. (1938) 'The Scope of a Sociology of International Relations', *Social Forces*, 17 (December), pp. 175–83.

Landheer, B. *et al.* (eds) (1971) *Worldsociety: How Is an Effective and Desirable World Order Possible?* The Hague: Nijhoff.

Langhorne, R. (1981–2) 'The Development of International Conferences, 1648–1830', *Studies in History and Politics* (Québec: Bishops University), 2, No. 2, pp. 61–91.

Langhorne, R. (1992) 'Regulation of Diplomatic Practice: The Beginnings to the Vienna Convention on Diplomatic Relations, 1961', *Review of International Studies*, 18 (January), pp. 3–17.

Lapid, Y. *et al.* (1989) 'The Third Debate: On the Prospects of International Theory in a Post-Positivist Era', *International Studies Quarterly*, 33 (September), pp. 235–79.

Laqueur, W. (ed.) (1976) *Fascism: A Reader's Guide*. London: Wildwood.

Larus, J. (ed.) (1964) *Comparative World Politics: Readings in Western and Premodern Non-Western International Relations*. Belmont, CA: Wadsworth.

Lash, S. and Urry, J. (1987) *The End of Organized Capitalism*. Cambridge: Polity.

Laue, T.H. von (1969) *The Global City: Freedom, Power, and Necessity in the Age of World Revolutions*. Philadelphia: Lippincott.

Laue, T.H. von (1987) *The World Revolution of Westernization: The Twentieth Century in Global Perspective*. New York: Oxford University Press.

Lauterpacht, E. (ed.) (1970) *International Law: Being the Collected Papers of Hersch Lauterpacht. Volume I*. Cambridge: Cambridge University Press.

Lee, C.C. (1979) *Media Imperialism Reconsidered: The Homogenizing of Television Culture*. Beverly Hills, CA: Sage.

Leiss, W. (1972) *The Domination of Nature*. New York: Braziller.

Leive, D.M. (1976) *International Regulatory Regimes: Case Studies in Health, Meteorology, and Food*. Lexington, MA: D.C. Heath.

Lenin, V.I. (1917) *Imperialism, The Highest Stage of Capitalism*. New York: International Publishers, 1939.

Lerner, N. (1980) *The U.N. Convention on the Elimination of All Forms of Racial Discrimination*. Alphen a/d Rijn (Netherlands): Sijthoff.

Levtzion, N. (1979) *International Islamic Solidarity and its Limitations*. Jerusalem: Magnes.

Levy, M.J. (1972) *Modernization: Latecomers and Survivors*. New York: Basic Books.

Lewis, W.A. (1978) *The Evolution of the International Economic Order*. Princeton, NJ: Princeton University Press.

Lilley, C.R. and Hunt, M.H. (1987) 'On Social History, the State, and Foreign

Relations: Commentary on "The Cosmopolitan Connection"', *Diplomatic History*, 11 (Summer), pp. 243–50.

Linklater, A. (1990) *Beyond Realism and Marxism: Critical Theory and International Relations*. Basingstoke: Macmillan.

Little, R. (1985) 'Structuralism and Neo-Realism', in M. Light and A.J.R. Groom (eds) *International Relations: A Handbook of Current Theory*. London: Pinter, pp. 74–89.

Loescher, G. and Monahan, L. (eds) (1989) *Refugees and International Relations*. Oxford: Oxford University Press.

Lorwin, L.L. (1953) *The International Labor Movement: History, Policies, Outlook*. New York: Harper.

Lovelock, J.E. (1979) *Gaia: A New Look at Life on Earth*. Oxford: Oxford University Press.

Luard, E. (1976) *Types of International Society*. New York: Free Press.

Luard, E. (1977) *International Agencies: The Emerging Framework of Interdependence*. London: Macmillan.

Luard, E. (1989) *A History of the United Nations. Volume 2: The Age of Decolonization*. Basingstoke: Macmillan.

Luhmann, N. (1982) 'The World Society as a Social System', *International Journal of General Systems*, 8 (July), pp. 131–8.

Lukács, G. (1919) 'The Changing Function of Historical Materialism', in *History and Class Consciousness: Studies in Marxist Dialectics*. London: Merlin, 1971, pp. 223–55.

Lukes, S. (1968) 'Methodological Individualism Reconsidered', *British Journal of Sociology*, 19, pp. 119–29.

Lukes, S. (1977) 'Power and Structure', in *Essays in Social Theory*. London: Macmillan, pp. 3–29.

Luxemburg, R. (1913) *The Accumulation of Capital*. New Haven, CT: Yale University Press, 1951.

Lyotard, J.-F. (1979) *The Postmodern Condition: A Report on Knowledge*. Manchester: Manchester University Press, 1984.

MAF (1948) Ministry of Food file number 83/3132, Public Record Office, Kew.

MacBride, S. *et al.* (1980) *Many Voices, One World: Towards a New, More Just and More Efficient World Information and Communication Order*. Paris: United Nations Educational, Scientific and Cultural Organization.

McClelland, D.C. (1961) *The Achieving Society*. New York: Van Nostrand.

McCormick, J. (1989) *Reclaiming Paradise: The Global Environmental Movement*. Bloomington: Indiana University Press.

McCormick, T.J. (1970) 'The State of American Diplomatic History', in H.J. Bass (ed.) *The State of American History*. Chicago: Quadrangle, pp. 119–41.

McCrum, R. *et al.* (1986) *The Story of English*. London: Faber and Faber.

Mackinder, H.J. (1919) *Democratic Ideals and Reality: A Study in the Politics of Reconstruction*. Harmondsworth: Penguin, 1944.

Maclean, J.S. (1981) 'Marxist Epistemology, Explanations of "Change" and the Study of International Relations', in B. Buzan and R.J.B. Jones (eds) *Change and the Study of International Relations. The Evaded Dimension*. London: Pinter, pp. 46–67.

Maclean, J.S. (1988) 'Marxism and International Relations: A Strange Case of Mutual Neglect', *Millennium*, 17 (Summer), pp. 295–319.

McLuhan, M. and Fiore, Q. (1968) *War and Peace in the Global Village*. New York: McGraw-Hill.

McMahon, R.J. *et al.* (1990) 'Writing the History of U.S. Foreign Relations: A Symposium', *Diplomatic History*, 14 (Fall) pp. 553–605.

McMillan, C.H. (1987) *Multinationals from the Second World: Growth of Foreign Investment by Soviet and East European Enterprises*. Basingstoke: Macmillan.

McNeill, W.H. (1963) *The Rise of the West: A History of the Human Community*. Chicago: University of Chicago Press.

McNeill, W.H. (1964) *Europe's Steppe Frontier 1500–1800*. Chicago: University of Chicago Press.

McNeill, W.H. (1967) *A World History*. Oxford: Oxford University Press, 1979.

McNeill, W.H. (1974) *The Shape of European History*. New York: Oxford University Press.

McNeill, W.H. (1976) *Plagues and Peoples*. Oxford: Blackwell.

McNeill, W.H. (1982) *The Pursuit of Power: Technology, Armed Force, and Society since A.D. 1000*. Oxford: Blackwell, 1983.

McNeill, W.H. (1985) *Polyethnicity and National Unity in World History*. Toronto: University of Toronto Press, 1986.

McNeill, W.H. (1986) 'Organizing Concepts for World History', *Review*, 10 (Fall), pp. 211–29.

Maizels, A. (1992) *Commodities in Crisis: The Commodity Crisis of the 1980s and the International Political Economy of International Commodity Policies*. Oxford: Clarendon.

Mandel, E. (1962) *Marxist Economic Theory*. London: Merlin, 1968.

Mandel, E. (1972) *Late Capitalism*. London: Verso, 1975.

Mann, M. (1986) *The Sources of Social Power. Volume I: A History of Power from the Beginning to A.D. 1760*. Cambridge: Cambridge University Press.

Mann, M. (1988) *States, War and Capitalism: Studies in Political Sociology*. Oxford: Blackwell.

Mann, M. (ed.) (1990) *The Rise and Decline of the Nation State*. Oxford: Blackwell.

Manning, C.A.W. (1962) *The Nature of International Society*. London: Bell.

Mansbach, R.W. *et al.* (1976) *The Web of World Politics: Nonstate Actors in the Global System*. Englewood Cliffs, NJ: Prentice-Hall.

Mansfield, P. (1976) *The Arabs*. Harmondsworth: Penguin, 1980.

Marwick, A. (1974) *War and Social Change in the Twentieth Century: A Comparative Study of Britain, France, Germany, Russia, and the United States*. London: Macmillan.

Marwick, A. (ed.) (1988) *Total War and Social Change*. Basingstoke: Macmillan.

Marwick, A. (1989) *The Nature of History*. London: Macmillan (3rd edn).

Marx, K. (1847) *The Poverty of Philosophy*. Moscow: Foreign Languages Publishing House, n.d.

Marx, K. (1859) *A Contribution to the Critique of Political Economy*. London: Lawrence and Wishart, 1971.

Marx, K. (1867) *Capital, Volume I*. London: Lawrence and Wishart, 1970.

Marx, K. (1894) *Capital, Volume III*. London: Lawrence and Wishart, 1959.

Marx, K. and Engels, F. (1846) *The German Ideology*. London: Lawrence and Wishart, 1974.

Marx, K. and Engels, F. (1848) *The Communist Manifesto*. New York: Washington Square Press, 1965.

Mathisen, T. (1959) *Methodology in the Study of International Relations*. New York: Macmillan.

Mattelart, A. (1976) *Multinational Corporations and the Control of Culture: The Ideological Apparatuses of Imperialism*. Brighton: Harvester, 1979.

Mattingly, G. (1955) *Renaissance Diplomacy*. London: Cape, 1962.

May, E.R. (1973) *'Lessons' of the Past: The Use and Misuse of History in American Foreign Policy*. London: Oxford University Press.

Mead, M. (1940) 'Warfare: An Invention – Not a Biological Necessity', in *Anthropology: A Human Science. Selected Papers, 1939–1960*. Princeton, NJ: Van Nostrand, 1964, pp. 126–33.

Mendershausen, H. (1969) 'Transnational Society vs. State Sovereignty', *Kyklos*, 22, No. 2, pp. 251–75.

Mendes, C. (1989) *Fight for the Forest: Chico Mendes in His Own Words*. London: Latin America Bureau.

Mendlovitz, S.H. and Walker, R.B.J. (eds) (1987) *Towards a Just World Peace: Perspectives from Social Movements*. London: Butterworths.

Merchant, C. (1980) *The Death of Nature: Women, Ecology, and the Scientific Revolution*. London: Wildwood, 1982.

Merle, M. (1974) *The Sociology of International Relations*. Leamington Spa: Berg, 1987.

Meron, T. (ed.) (1984) *Human Rights in International Law: Legal and Policy Issues*. Oxford: Clarendon.

Merton, R.K. (1968) *Social Theory and Social Structure*. New York: Free Press (2nd edn).

Mészáros, I. (1989) *The Power of Ideology*. Hemel Hempstead: Harvester Wheatsheaf.

Meyer, D.B. (1960) *The Protestant Search for Political Realism, 1919–1941*. Berkeley, CA: University of California Press.

Meyrowitz, J. (1985) *No Sense of Place: The Impact of Electronic Media on Social Behavior*. New York: Oxford University Press.

Mies, M. (1986) *Patriarchy and Accumulation on a World Scale: Women in the International Division of Labour*. London: Zed.

Miliband, R. (1970) 'The Capitalist State: Reply to Nicos Poulantzas', *New Left Review*, No. 59 (January–February), pp. 53–60.

Miliband, R. (1987) 'Class Analysis', in A. Giddens and J.H. Turner (eds) *Social Theory Today*. Cambridge: Polity, pp. 325–46.

Miliband, R. and Panitch, L. (eds) (1992) *Socialist Register 1992: The New World Order*. London: Merlin.

Miller, J.D.B. (1981) *The World of States: Connected Essays*. London: Croom Helm.

Milward, A.S. (1977) *War, Economy and Society 1939–1945*. London: Allen Lane.

Mintz, S.W. (1977) 'The So-Called World System: Local Initiative and Local Response', *Dialectical Anthropology*, 2 (November), pp. 253–70.

Mitter, S. (1986) *Common Fate, Common Bond: Women in the Global Economy*. London: Pluto.

Modelski, G. (1972) *Principles of World Politics*. New York: Free Press.

Modelski, G. (1987) *Long Cycles in World Politics*. Basingstoke: Macmillan.

Moon, P.M. (1925) *Syllabus on International Relations*. New York: Macmillan.
Moore, W.E. (1966) 'Global Sociology: The World as a Singular System', *American Journal of Sociology*, 71 (March), pp. 475–82.
Moore, W.E. (1974) *Social Change*. Englewood Cliffs, NJ: Prentice-Hall (2nd edn).
Moore, W.E. (1979) *World Modernization: The Limits of Convergence*. New York: Elsevier.
Morgan, L.H. (1877) *Ancient Society, or Researches in the Lines of Human Progress from Savagery through Barbarism to Civilization*. Chicago: Kerr.
Morgenthau, H.J. (1948) *Politics among Nations: The Struggle for Power and Peace*. New York: Knopf.
Morgenthau, H.J. (1967) 'Common Sense and Theories of International Relations', *Journal of International Affairs*, 21, No. 2, pp. 207–14.
Morgenthau, H.J. and Thompson, K.W. (eds) (1950) *Principles and Problems of International Politics*. New York: Knopf.
Mortimer, R.A. (1984) *The Third World Coalition in International Politics*. Boulder, CO: Westview.
Mowlana, H. (1986) *Global Information and World Communication: New Frontiers in International Relations*. New York: Longman.
Mrázek, R. (1972) 'Tan Malaka: A Political Personality's Structure of Experience', *Indonesia*, No. 14 (October), pp. 1–48.
Munck, R. (1986) *The Difficult Dialogue: Marxism and Nationalism*. London: Zed.
Murphy, C. and Tooze, R. (eds) (1991) *The New International Political Economy*. Boulder, CO: Rienner.
Murray, R. (ed.) (1981) *Multinationals Beyond the Market: Intra-Firm Trade and the Control of Transfer Pricing*. Brighton: Harvester.
Naess, A. (1977) 'Spinoza and Ecology', *Philosophia: Philosophical Quarterly of Israel*, 7 (March), pp. 45–54.
Naipaul, S. (1985) 'A Thousand Invisible Men', *The Spectator*, 254 (18 May), pp. 9–11.
Nardin, T. (1983) *Law, Morality, and the Relations of States*. Princeton, NJ: Princeton University Press.
Nef, J.U. (1950) *War and Human Progress: An Essay on the Rise of Industrial Civilization*. Cambridge, MA: Harvard University Press.
Nelson, D. (1983) 'Why World Systems Theory? Accepting a New Paradigm', *International Interactions*, 9, No. 4, pp. 353–68.
Nettl, J.P. and Robertson, R. (1968) *International Systems and the Modernization of Societies: The Formation of National Goals and Attitudes*. London: Faber.
Newell, W.H. (ed.) (1981) *Japan in Asia 1942–1945*. Singapore: Singapore University Press.
Niebuhr, R. (1932) *Moral Man and Immoral Society: A Study in Ethics and Politics*. New York: Scribner.
Niebuhr, R. (1940) *Christianity and Power Politics*. New York: Scribner.
Nisbet, R. (ed.) (1972) *Social Change*. Oxford: Blackwell.
Nordenstreng, K. and Varis, T. (1974) *Television Traffic – A One-Way Street? A Survey and Analysis of the International Flow of Television Programme Material*. Paris: UNESCO Reports and Papers on Mass Communication No. 70.
Norris, C. (1992) *Uncritical Theory: Postmodernism, Intellectuals and the Gulf War*. London: Lawrence and Wishart.

North, D. (1691) *Discourses upon Trade*, reprinted in J.R. McCulloch (ed.) *Early English Tracts on Commerce*. Cambridge: Cambridge University Press, pp. 505–40.

Northedge, F.S. (1976a) *The International Political System*. London: Faber.

Northedge, F.S. (1976b) 'Transnationalism: The American Illusion', *Millennium*, 5 (Spring), pp. 21–7.

Northedge, F.S. (1986) *The League of Nations: Its Life and Times 1920–1946*. Leicester: Leicester University Press.

Nye, J.S. (1975) 'Transnational and Transgovernmental Relations', in G.L. Goodwin and A. Linklater (eds) *New Dimensions of World Politics*. London: Croom Helm, pp. 36–53.

Nyerere, J. (1968) *Ujamaa: Essays on Socialism*. London: Oxford University Press.

O'Brien, D.C. (1979) 'Modernization, Order, and the Erosion of a Democratic Ideal: American Political Science 1960–70', in D. Lehmann (ed.) *Development Theory: Four Critical Studies*. London: Cass, pp. 49–76.

O'Brien, R. (1992) *Global Financial Integration: The End of Geography*. London: Pinter.

O'Connell, D.P. (1982/1984) *The Law of the Sea* (edited by I.A. Shearer). Oxford: Clarendon (2 volumes).

O'Neill, J. (ed.) (1973) *Modes of Individualism and Collectivism*. London: Heinemann.

Onimode, B. (ed.) (1989) *The IMF, the World Bank and the African Debt*. London: Zed (2 volumes).

Onuf, N.G. (1989) *World of Our Making: Rules and Rule in Social Theory and International Relations*. Columbia: University of South Carolina Press.

Outhwaite, W. (1989) 'Theory', in M. Haralambos (ed.) *Developments in Sociology*. Ormskirk: Causeway, pp. 165–86.

Ovenden, K. and Cole, T. (1989) *Apartheid and International Finance: A Program for Change*. Harmondsworth: Penguin.

Palloix, C. (1977) 'The Self-Expansion of Capital on a World Scale', *Review of Radical Political Economics*, 9 (Summer), pp. 1–28.

Panikkar, K.M. (1953) *Asia and Western Dominance: A Survey of the Vasco da Gama Epoch in Asian History 1498–1945*. London: Allen & Unwin.

Parker, G. (1988) *The Military Revolution: Military Innovation and the Rise of the West, 1500–1800*. Cambridge: Cambridge University Press.

Parsons, T. (1961) 'Order and Community in the International Social System', in J.N. Rosenau (ed.) *International Politics and Foreign Policy: A Reader in Research and Theory*. New York: Free Press, pp. 120–9.

Parsons, T. (1966) *Societies: Evolutionary and Comparative Perspectives*. Englewood Cliffs, NJ: Prentice-Hall.

Parsons, T. (1971) *The System of Modern Societies*. Englewood Cliffs, NJ: Prentice Hall.

Paterson, T.G. *et al.* (1990) 'A Round Table: Explaining the History of American Foreign Relations', *Journal of American History*, 77 (June), pp. 93–180.

Peet, R. (1991) *Global Capitalism: Theories of Societal Development*. London: Routledge.

Percy, C.H. (1975) *Report to the Committee on Government Operations, U.S. Senate, on the World Conference of the International Women's Year*. Washington, DC: United States Government Printing Office.

Peters, R. (1979) *Islam and Colonialism: The Doctrine of Jihad in Modern History.* The Hague: Mouton.

Petras, J.F. and Brill, H. (1985) 'The Tyranny of Globalism', in J.F. Petras *et al., Latin America: Bankers, Generals, and the Struggle for Social Justice.* Totowa, NJ: Rowman and Littlefield, 1986, pp. 3–20.

Pettman, R. (1979) *State and Class: A Sociology of International Affairs.* London: Croom Helm.

Picciotto, S. (1988) 'The Control of Transnational Capital and the Democratisation of the International State', *Journal of Law and Society,* 15 (Spring), pp. 58–76.

Picciotto, S. (1991) 'The Internationalisation of the State', *Capital & Class,* No. 43 (Spring), pp. 43–63.

Pieterse, J.N. (1988) 'A Critique of World System Theory', *International Sociology,* 3 (September), pp. 251–66.

Pieterse, J.N. (1990) *Empire and Emancipation: Power and Liberation on a World Scale.* London: Pluto.

Pietilä, H. and Vickers, J. (1990) *Making Women Matter: The Role of the United Nations.* London: Zed.

Pijl, K. van der (1984) *The Making of an Atlantic Ruling Class.* London: Verso.

Pirenne, J. (1943–56) *Les grands courants de l'histoire universelle.* Neuchâtel (Switzerland): Baconnière (7 volumes).

Piscatori, J.P. (1986) *Islam in a World of Nation-States.* Cambridge: Cambridge University Press.

Pischel, E.C. and Robertazzi, C. (eds) (1968) *L'Internationale Communiste et les problèmes coloniaux 1919–1935.* Paris: Mouton.

Plant, S. (1992) *The Most Radical Gesture: The Situationist International in a Postmodern Age.* London: Routledge.

Polanyi, K. (1944) *The Great Transformation.* Boston, MA: Beacon.

Pollis, A. and Schwab, P. (eds) (1980) *Human Rights: Cultural and Ideological Perspectives.* New York: Praeger.

Pool, I. de Sola (1990) *Technologies without Boundaries: On Telecommunications in a Global Age* (edited by E.M. Noam). Cambridge, MA: Harvard University Press.

Popper, K.R. (1957) *The Poverty of Historicism.* London: Routledge.

Porter, R. (1990) *The Enlightenment.* Basingstoke: Macmillan.

Poulantzas, N. (1969) 'The Problem of the Capitalist State', *New Left Review,* No. 58 (November–December), pp. 67–78.

Poulantzas, N. (1974) 'Internationalisation of Capitalist Relations and the Nation-State', *Economy and Society,* 3, pp. 145–79.

Pufendorf, S. von (1688) *De Jure Naturae et Gentium Libri Octo [The Law of Nature and Nations. Eight Books].* New York: Oceana, 1964.

Purnell, R. (1973) *The Society of States: An Introduction to International Politics.* London: Weidenfeld and Nicolson.

Queuille, P. (1965) *Histoire de l'Afro-Asiatisme jusqu'à Bandoung. La naissance du tiers-monde.* Paris: Payot.

Rahman, F. (1982) *Islam & Modernity: Transformation of an Intellectual Tradition.* London: University of Chicago Press.

Ramaswamy, T.N. (ed.) (1962) *Essentials of Indian Statecraft: Kautilya's Arthasastra for Contemporary Readers.* London: Asia.

Rasler, K.A. and Thompson, W.R. (1989) *War and Statemaking: The Shaping of the Global Powers*. Boston, MA: Unwin Hyman.

Redclift, M. (1987) *Sustainable Development: Exploring the Contradictions*. London: Methuen.

Reich, W. (1933) *The Mass Psychology of Fascism*. London: Souvenir, 1972.

Reich, W. (1949) *Character Analysis*. New York: Noonday.

Rey, P.P. (1973) *Les alliances des classes*. Paris: Maspero.

Rikhye, I.J. (1984) *The Theory and Practice of Peacekeeping*. London: Hurst.

Rizzi, B. (1939) *The Bureaucratization of the World*. London: Tavistock, 1985.

Robbins, L. (1935) *An Essay on the Nature and Significance of Economic Science*. London: Macmillan (2nd edn).

Roberts, J.M. (1976) *The Hutchinson History of the World*. London: Hutchinson.

Robertson, R. (1985) 'The Sacred and the World System', in P.E. Hammond (ed.) *The Sacred in a Secular Age: Toward Revision in the Scientific Study of Religion*. Berkeley, CA: University of California Press, pp. 347–58.

Robertson, R. (1990) 'Mapping the Global Condition: Globalization as the Central Concept', in M. Featherstone (ed.) *Global Culture: Nationalism, Globalization and Modernity*. London: Sage, pp. 15–30.

Robertson, R. and Chirico, J. (1985) 'Humanity, Globalization and Worldwide Religious Resurgence: A Theoretical Exploration', *Sociological Analysis*, 46, No. 3, pp. 219–42.

Robertson, R. and Lechner, F. (1985) 'Modernization, Globalization and the Problem of Culture in World-Systems Theory', *Theory, Culture & Society*, 2, No. 3, pp. 103–17.

Robertson, R. (1992) *Globalization: Social Theory and Global Culture*. London: Sage.

Robinson, J. (1983) *Multinationals and Political Control*. Aldershot: Gower.

Rogers, B. (1980) *The Domestication of Women: Discrimination in Developing Societies*. London: Kogan Page.

Rosecrance, R. (1986) *The Rise of the Trading State: Commerce and Conquest in the Modern World*. New York: Basic Books.

Rosenau, J.N. (ed.) (1967) *Domestic Sources of Foreign Policy*. New York: Free Press.

Rosenau, J.N. (ed.) (1969) *Linkage Politics: Essays on the Convergence of National and International Systems*. New York: Free Press.

Rosenau, J.N. (1990) *Turbulence in World Politics: A Theory of Change and Continuity*. Princeton, NJ: Princeton University Press.

Rosenau, P. (1990) 'Once Again into the Fray: International Relations Confronts the Humanities', *Millennium*, 19 (Spring), pp. 83–110.

Rosenberg, J. (1992) 'Secret Origins of the State: The Structural Basis of *Raison d'Etat*', *Review of International Studies*, 18 (April), pp. 131–59.

Ross, R. and Trachte, K. (1983) 'Global Cities and Global Classes: The Peripheralization of Labor in New York City', *Review*, 6 (Winter), pp. 393–431.

Rosting, H. (1923) 'Protection of Minorities by the League of Nations', *American Journal of International Law*, 17 (October), pp. 641–60.

Rostow, W.W. (1960) *The Stages of Economic Growth: A Non-Communist Manifesto*. London: Cambridge University Press.

ROW (1983) *Women's Rights & the EEC*. N.p: Rights of Women Europe.

Rubenstein, C. (1991) 'The Flying Silver Message Stick: Update 1985–86 on Long

Songs Collected 1971–74', *Sarawak Museum Journal*, 42, No. 63 (new series), pp. 61–157.

Rudolf, G.R. (1926) *The York-Antwerp Rules: Their History and Development, With Comments on the Rules of 1924*. London: Stevens.

Russell, F.M. (1936) *Theories of International Relations*. New York: Appleton-Century.

Sadli, M. (1971) 'Reflections on Boeke's Theory of Dualistic Economies', in B. Glassburner (ed.) *The Economy of Indonesia: Selected Readings*. Ithaca, NY: Cornell University Press, pp. 99–123.

Said, E.W. (1978) *Orientalism*. New York: Vintage.

Saint-Simon, C.H. (1821) 'Du système industriel', reprinted in *Oeuvres de Saint-Simon, tome VI*. Paris: Dentu, 1869.

Sampson, A. (1973) *Sovereign State: The Secret History of I.T.T.* London: Hodder.

Sampson, A. (1975) *The Seven Sisters: The Great Oil Companies and the World They Shaped*. New York: Bantam, 1976.

Sampson, E.E. (1989) 'The Challenge of Social Change for Psychology: Globalization and Psychology's Theory of the Person', *American Psychologist*, 44 (June), pp. 914–21.

Sampson, M. (1987) 'Cultural Influences on Foreign Policy', in C.F. Hermann *et al.* (eds) *New Directions in the Study of Foreign Policy*. Boston, MA: Allen & Unwin, pp. 384–405.

Sanderson, S.K. (1988) 'The Neo-Weberian Revolution: A Theoretical Balance Sheet', *Sociological Forum*, 3 (Spring), pp. 307–14.

Sauvant, K. (1986) *International Transactions in Services: The Politics of Transborder Data Flows*. Boulder, CO: Westview.

Sawyer, R. (1986) *Slavery in the Twentieth Century*. London: Routledge.

Schneider, J. (1977) 'Was There a Pre-Capitalist World-System?', *Peasant Studies*, 6 (January), pp. 20–9.

Scholte, J.A. (1990) 'A World-Historical-Sociological Perspective on the Course of Decolonisation in Indonesia 1945–1949.' Doctoral thesis, University of Sussex.

Scholte, J.A. (1993) 'From Power Politics to Social Change: An Alternative Focus for International Studies', *Review of International Studies*, 19 (January), pp. 3–21.

Schonberger, H.B. (1989) *Aftermath of War: Americans and the Remaking of Japan, 1945–1952*. Kent, OH: Kent State University Press.

Schwarzenberger, G. (1941) *Power Politics: An Introduction to the Study of International Relations and Post-War Planning*. London: Cape.

Seeley, J.R. (1885) *Introduction to Political Science: Two Series of Lectures*. London: Macmillan, 1896.

Shannon, T.R. (1989) *An Introduction to the World-System Perspective*. Boulder, CO: Westview.

Shapiro, F.C. (1989) 'Letter from Beijing', *New Yorker*, 65 (5 June), pp. 73–82.

Shaw, M. (ed.) (1984) *War, State and Society*. London: Macmillan.

Shaw, M. (1988) *The Dialectics of War: An Essay in the Social Theory of Total War and Peace*. London: Pluto.

Shaw, M. (1989) 'War and the Nation-State in Social Theory', in D. Held and J.B. Thompson (eds) *Social Theory of Modern Societies: Anthony Giddens and His Critics*. Cambridge: Cambridge University Press, pp. 129–46.

Sieghart, P. (1983) *The International Law of Human Rights*. Oxford: Clarendon.

Sims, N.A. (1979) *Approaches to Disarmament: An Introductory Analysis*. London: Quaker Peace & Service (rev. edn).

Sinclair, A. (1970) *Guevara*. London: Fontana.

Singer, J.D. (1961) 'The Level-of-Analysis Problem in International Relations', *World Politics*, 14 (October), pp. 72–92.

Sivard, R.L. (1986) *World Military and Social Expenditures 1986*. Washington, DC: World Priorities.

Sked, A. (1987) 'The Study of International Relations: A Historian's View', *Millennium*, 16 (Summer), pp. 251–62.

Skjelsbaek, K. (1971) 'The Growth of International Nongovernmental Organization in the Twentieth Century', *International Organization*, 25 (Summer), pp. 420–42.

Sklair, L. (1991) *Sociology of the Global System*. Hemel Hempstead: Harvester Wheatsheaf.

Skocpol, T. (1976) 'France, Russia, China: A Structural Analysis of Social Revolutions', *Comparative Studies in Society and History*, 18 (April), pp. 175–210.

Skocpol, T. (1977) 'Wallerstein's World Capitalist System: A Theoretical and Historical Critique', *American Journal of Sociology*, 82 (March), pp. 1075–90.

Skocpol, T. (1979) *States and Social Revolutions: A Comparative Analysis of France, Russia, and China*. Cambridge: Cambridge University Press.

Skocpol, T. (ed.) (1984) *Vision and Method in Historical Sociology*. Cambridge: Cambridge University Press.

Skocpol, T. (1985) 'Bringing the State Back In: Strategies of Analysis in Current Research', in P. B. Evans *et al.* (eds) *Bringing the State Back In*. Cambridge: Cambridge University Press, pp. 3–37.

Smith, A.D. (1973) *The Concept of Social Change: A Critique of the Functionalist Theory of Social Change*. London: Routledge.

Smith, A.D. (1976) *Social Change: Social Theory and Historical Processes*. London: Longman.

Smith, A.D. (1979) *Nationalism in the Twentieth Century*. Oxford: Martin Robertson.

Smith, A.D. (1983) *Theories of Nationalism*. New York: Holmes & Meier (2nd edn).

Smith, C.A. (1984) 'Local History in Global Context: Social and Economic Transitions in Western Guatemala', *Comparative Studies in Society and History*, 26, pp. 193–228.

Smith, J. *et al.* (eds) (1984) *Households and the World-Economy*. Beverly Hills, CA: Sage.

Smith, J. *et al.* (eds) (1988) *Racism, Sexism, and the World-System*. New York: Greenwood.

Smith, M.J. (1986) *Realist Thought from Weber to Kissinger*. Baton Rouge: Louisiana State University Press.

Sombart, W. (1913) *Krieg und Kapitalismus*. Munich/Leipzig: Von Duncker and Humblot.

Sorokin, P.A. (1937) *Social and Cultural Dynamics. Volume Three: Fluctuation of Social Relationships, War, and Revolution*. New York: American Book Company.

Sorokin, P.A. (1942) *Man and Society in Calamity: The Effects of War, Revolution, Famine, Pestilence upon Human Mind, Behavior, Social Organization and Cultural Life*. Westport, CT: Greenwood, 1968.

Spencer, H. (1862) *First Principles*. London: Williams & Norgate, 1910.

Spengler. O. (1918/1922) *The Decline of the West*. New York: Random House, 1962 (2 volumes).

Spero, J.E. (1990) *The Politics of International Economic Relations*. London: Unwin Hyman (4th edn).

Spykman, N. (1933) 'Methods of Approach to the Study of International Relations', in *Proceedings of the Fifth Conference of Teachers of International Law and Related Subjects, Held at Washington, D.C., 26–27 April, 1933*. Washington, DC: Carnegie Endowment.

Staniland, M. (1985) *What Is Political Economy? A Study of Social Theory and Underdevelopment*. New Haven, CT: Yale University Press.

Stavrianos, L.S. (1981) *Global Rift: The Third World Comes of Age*. New York: Morrow.

Sterling, R.W. (1974) *Macropolitics: International Relations in a Global Society*. New York: Knopf.

Stopford, J.M. and Strange, S. (1991) *Rival States, Rival Firms: Competition for World Market Shares*. Cambridge: Cambridge University Press.

Strange, S. (1986) *Casino Capitalism*. Oxford: Blackwell.

Strasser, H. and Rundall, S.C. (1981) *An Introduction to Theories of Social Change*. London: Routledge.

Suganami, H. (1978) 'A Note on the Origin of the Word "International"', *British Journal of International Studies*, 4 (October), pp. 226–32.

Survey (1987) 'New Lines for Old: A Survey of Telecommunications', *The Economist* (Supplement), 305, No. 7520 (17 October).

Szymanski, A. (1981) *The Logic of Imperialism*. New York: Praeger.

Tacke, E.F. *et al.* (1963) *The World Sugar Economy: Structure and Policies*. London: International Sugar Council.

Taylor, P.J. (1989) *Political Geography: World-Economy, Nation-State and Locality*. London: Longman (2nd edn).

Taylor, T. (1978) 'Power Politics', in T. Taylor (ed.) *Approaches and Theory in International Relations*. London: Longman, pp. 122–40.

Tehranian, M. (1990) *Technologies of Power: Information Machines and Democratic Prospects*. Norwood, NJ: Ablex.

Teichova, A. *et al.* (eds) (1986) *Multinational Enterprise in Historical Perspective*. Cambridge: Cambridge University Press.

Tew, B. (1985) *The Evolution of the International Monetary System 1945–85*. London: Hutchinson (3rd edn).

Thompson, J.B. (1989) 'The Theory of Structuration', in D. Held and J.B. Thompson (eds) *Social Theory of Modern Societies: Anthony Giddens and His Critics*. Cambridge: Cambridge University Press, pp. 56–76.

Thompson, J.B. (1990) *Ideology and Modern Culture: Critical Social Theory in the Era of Mass Communication*. Cambridge: Polity.

Thompson, K. (1985) *Exporting Entertainment: America in the World Film Market 1907–1934*. London: British Film Institute.

Thompson, K.W. (1985) *Toynbee's Philosophy of World History and Politics*. Baton Rouge: Louisiana State University Press.

Thompson, W.R. (1982) 'Phases of the Business Cycle and the Outbreak of War', *International Studies Quarterly*, 26 (June), pp. 301–11.

Thompson, W.R. (ed.) (1983) *Contending Approaches to World System Analysis*. Beverly Hills, CA: Sage.

Thompson, W.R. (1988) *On Global War: Historical-Structural Approaches to World Politics*. Columbia: University of South Carolina Press.

Thorne, C. (1982) *Racial Aspects of the Far Eastern War of 1941–1945*. London: British Academy.

Thorne, C. (1985) *The Issue of War: States, Societies, and the Far Eastern Conflict of 1941–1945*. London: Hamish Hamilton.

Thorne, C. (1987) 'Societies, Sociology and the International: Some Contributions and Reflections, with Particular Reference to Total War', in W. Outhwaite and M. Mulkay (eds) *Social Structure and Social Criticism: Essays for Tom Bottomore*. Oxford: Blackwell, pp. 124–53.

Thorne, C. (1988) *Border Crossings: Studies in International History*. Oxford: Blackwell.

Tilly, C. (ed.) (1975) *The Formation of National States in Western Europe*. Princeton, NJ: Princeton University Press.

Tilly, C. (1981) *As Sociology Meets History*. New York: Academic Press.

Tilly, C. (1985) 'War Making and State Making as Organized Crime', in P.B. Evans *et al.* (eds). *Bringing the State Back In*. Cambridge: Cambridge University Press, pp. 169–91.

Tilly, C. (1990) *Coercion, Capital, and European States, AD 990–1990*. Oxford: Blackwell.

Timberlake, M. (ed.) (1985) *Urbanization in the World-Economy*. London: Academic Press.

Tinker, H. (1977) *Race, Conflict and the International Order: From Empire to United Nations*. London: Macmillan.

Tiryakian, E.A. (1986) 'Sociology's Great Leap Forward: The Challenge of Internationalisation', *International Sociology*, 1 (June), pp. 155–71.

Tomlinson, J. (1991) *Cultural Imperialism: A Critical Introduction*. London: Pinter.

Touraine, A. (1978) *The Voice and the Eye: An Analysis of Social Movements*. Cambridge: Cambridge University Press, 1981.

Touraine, A. (1984) *Return of the Actor: Social Theory in Postindustrial Society*. Minneapolis: University of Minnesota Press, 1988.

Toynbee, A.J. (1934–61) *A Study of History*. London: Oxford University Press.

Trotsky, L. (1930) *The Permanent Revolution and Results and Prospects*. New York: Merit, 1969.

Tucker, W. (1980) 'Environmentalism: The Newest Toryism', *Policy Review*, 14 (Fall), pp. 141–52.

Turack, D.C. (1972) *The Passport in International Law*. Lexington, MA: Lexington Books.

Turner, B.S. (1981) *For Weber: Essays on the Sociology of Fate*. London: Routledge.

Turner, B.S. (ed.) (1991) *Theories of Modernity and Postmodernity*. London: Sage.

Tylor, E.B. (1871) *Primitive Culture*. London: Murray, 1873.

UIA (1987) *Yearbook of International Organizations 1987/88*. Munich: Saur (Union of International Associations).

UNCTC (1992) *World Investment Report 1992: Transnational Corporations as*

Engines of Growth. New York: United Nations Department of Economic and Social Development (Doc. ST/CTC/130).

UNEP (1985) *Register of International Treaties and Other Agreements in the Field of the Environment.* Nairobi: United Nations Environment Programme (Doc. UNEP/GC/INFORMATION/11/Rev.1).

UNESCO (1982) *Statistics of Students Abroad 1974–1978.* Paris: United Nations Educational, Scientific and Cultural Organization (Statistical Studies No. 27).

UNESCO (1991) *Statistical Yearbook.* Paris: United Nations Educational, Scientific and Cultural Organization.

Ushiba, N. *et al.* (1983) *Sharing International Responsibilities among the Trilateral Countries.* New York: Trilateral Commission (Task Force Report No. 25).

Varis, T. (1985) *International Flow of Television Programmes.* Paris: UNESCO Reports and Papers on Mass Communication No. 100.

Vasquez, J.A. (1983) *The Power of Power Politics: A Critique.* London: Pinter.

Vernon, R. (1977) *Storm over the Multinationals: The Real Issues.* Cambridge, MA: Harvard University Press.

Villamil, J.J. (ed.) (1979) *Transnational Capitalism and National Development: New Perspectives on Dependence.* Hassocks: Harvester.

Vincent, R.J. (1983) 'Change in International Relations', *Review of International Studies,* 9 (January), pp. 63–70.

Vogler, C.M. (1985) *The Nation State: The Neglected Dimension of Class.* Aldershot: Gower.

Wal, S.L. van der (1968) 'De Nationaal-Socialistische Beweging in Nederlands-Indië', *Bijdragen en Mededelingen van het Historisch Genootschap,* 82, pp. 35–58.

Wallace, M. and Singer, J.D. (1970) 'Intergovernmental Organization in the Global System, 1815–1964: A Quantitative Description', *International Organization,* 24 (Spring), pp. 237–87.

Wallensteen, P. *et al.* (1985) *Global Militarization.* Boulder, CO: Westview.

Wallerstein, I. (1974a) *The Modern World-System, 1: Capitalist Agriculture and the Origins of the European World-Economy in the Sixteenth Century.* New York: Academic Press.

Wallerstein, I. (1974b) 'The Rise and Future Demise of the World Capitalist System: Concepts for Comparative Analysis', reprinted in *The Capitalist World-Economy.* Cambridge: Cambridge University Press, 1979, pp. 1–36.

Wallerstein, I. (1983) 'The Three Instances of Hegemony in the History of the Capitalist World-Economy', reprinted in *The Politics of the World-Economy: The States, the Movements, and the Civilizations.* Cambridge: Cambridge University Press, 1984, pp. 37–46.

Wallerstein, I. (1986a) 'Societal Development, or Development of the World-System?', *International Sociology,* 1 (March), pp. 3–17.

Wallerstein, I. (1986b) 'Walter Rodney: The Historian as Spokesman for Historical Forces', *American Ethnologist,* 13 (May), pp. 330–7.

Wallerstein, I. (1991a) *Geopolitics and Geoculture: Essays on the Changing World-System.* Cambridge: Cambridge University Press.

Wallerstein, I. (1991b) *Unthinking Social Science.* Cambridge: Polity.

Waltz, K.N. (1959) *Man, the State and War: A Theoretical Analysis.* New York: Columbia University Press.

Waltz, K.N. (1979) *Theory of International Politics.* Reading, MA: Addison-Wesley.

Waltz, K.N. (1986) 'Reflections on *Theory of International Politics*: A Response to My Critics', in R.O. Keohane (ed.) *Neorealism and Its Critics*. New York: Columbia University Press, pp. 322–45.

Ward, K.B. (1984) *Women in the World-System: Its Impact on Status and Fertility*. New York: Praeger.

Watt, D.C. (1983) *What about the People? Abstraction and Reality in History and the Social Sciences*. London: London School of Economics and Political Science.

Watt, D.C. *et al.* (1985) 'What Is Diplomatic History?', *History Today*, 35 (July), pp. 33–41.

Webb, M.C. and Krasner, S.D. (1989) 'Hegemonic Stability Theory: An Empirical Assessment', 15 (April), pp. 183–98.

Weber, M. (1904–5) *The Protestant Ethic and the Spirit of Capitalism*. London: Allen & Unwin, 1930.

Weber, M. (1922a) *Economy and Society: An Outline of Interpretive Sociology*. New York: Bedminster Press, 1968 (3 volumes).

Weber, M. (1922b) *The Sociology of Religion*. London: Methuen, 1963.

Webster, C.K. (1923) *The Study of International Politics: An Inaugural Lecture Delivered before the University College of Wales Aberystwyth*. Cardiff: University of Wales Press Board.

Weissbrodt, D. (1984) 'The Contribution of International Nongovernmental Organizations to the Protection of Human Rights', in T. Meron (ed.) *Human Rights in International Law: Legal and Policy Issues*. Oxford: Clarendon, pp. 403–38.

Wells, C. (1987) *The UN, UNESCO and the Politics of Knowledge*. Basingstoke: Macmillan.

Wells, H.G. (1920) *The Outline of History: Being a Plain History of Life and Mankind*. London: Cassell, 1934.

Wendt, A. (1987) 'The Agent-Structure Problem in International Relations Theory', *International Organization*, 41 (Summer), pp. 335–70.

Wertheim, W.F. (1974) *Evolution and Revolution: The Rising Waves of Emancipation*. Harmondsworth: Penguin.

White, L.C. (1951) *International Non-Governmental Organizations: Their Purposes, Methods, and Accomplishments*. New Brunswick, NJ: Rutgers University Press.

Whitrow, G.J. (1988) *Time in History: The Evolution of Our General Awareness of Time and Temporal Perspective*. Oxford: Oxford University Press.

Wight, M. (1946) *Power Politics*. London: Royal Institute of International Affairs.

Wight, M. (1977) *Systems of States*. Leicester: Leicester University Press.

Wilhelm, D. (1990) *Global Communications and Political Power*. New Brunswick, NJ: Transaction.

Willett, R. (1989) *The Americanization of Germany 1945–1949*. London: Routledge.

Willetts, P. (ed.) (1982) *Pressure Groups in the Global System: The Transnational Politics of Issue-Orientated Non-Governmental Organizations*. London: Pinter.

Williams, M. (1991) *Third World Cooperation: The Group of 77 in UNCTAD*. London: Pinter.

Williams, R. (1961) *The Long Revolution*. London: Chatto & Windus.

Williams, R. (1981) *Culture*. London: Fontana.

Wilson, P. (1989) 'The English School of International Relations: A Reply to Sheila Grader', *Review of International Studies*, 15 (January), pp. 49–58.

Wolf, E.R. (1969) *Peasant Wars of the Twentieth Century*. New York: Harper & Row.

Wolf, E.R. (1982) *Europe and the People without History*. Berkeley, CA: University of California Press.

Wolfe, T.W. (1970) *Soviet Power and Europe 1945–1970*. Baltimore, MD: Johns Hopkins University Press.

Wolpe, H. (ed.) (1980) *The Articulation of Modes of Production*. London: Routledge.

Woodcock, G. (1963) *Anarchism: A History of Libertarian Ideas and Movements*. Harmondsworth: Penguin.

Worsley, P. (1984) *The Three Worlds: Culture and World Development*. London: Weidenfeld and Nicolson.

Wright, Q. (1942) *A Study of War*. Chicago: University of Chicago Press.

WTO (1991) *Current Travel and Tourism Indicators*. Madrid: World Tourism Organization (Document CTI 4–1990).

Zimmern, A. (1935) 'Introductory Report to the Discussions in 1935 on University Teaching of International Relations', in *University Teaching of International Relations*. Paris: International Institute of Intellectual Co-operation, 1939.

Zimmern, A. (1939) *University Teaching of International Relations: A Record of the Eleventh Session of the International Studies Conference, Prague, 1938*. Paris: International Institute of Intellectual Co-operation.

Zolberg, A.R. (1986) 'Strategic Interactions and the Formation of Modern States: France and England', in A. Kazancigil (ed.) *The State in Global Perspective*. Aldershot: Gower, pp. 72–106.

Zouche, R. (1650) *An Exposition of Fecial Law and Procedure, Or of Law between Nations, and Questions Concerning the Same*. Washington, DC: Carnegie Institution.

INDEX

RESOURCE POLITICS
FRESHWATER AND REGIONAL RELATIONS

Caroline Thomas and Darryl Howlett (eds)

A systematic study of the international politics of freshwater resources is long overdue. This is a serious omission, for life, agriculture and industry depend on an assured supply of a certain quality of freshwater. Demand for this resource is constantly growing but its quantity and quality is threatened by various human activities. Moreover, with over two hundred river and lake basins shared by two or more states – and the number is increasing with the disintegration of the Soviet Union – the potential for inter-state hostilities over water is increasing.

This book furthers our understanding of the international political dimensions of the freshwater issue. It takes a regional approach since it is at the regional level that conflict between states over the resource is most likely to occur and where cooperation must be expediated. It explores the implications of freshwater availability in the interlinking contexts of environmental, developmental and security needs. *Resource Politics* argues that a holistic analysis is integral to the formulation of politically viable, environmentally sensitive and developmentally sustainable water management strategies.

Contents
The freshwater issue in international relations – The Great Lakes: exploring the ecosystem – Water politics in Latin America – The issue of water in the Middle East and North Africa – South-east Asia: the Mekong river – South Asia: the Ganges and the Brahmaputra – Sub-Saharan Africa – Eurasia – The European Community and freshwater – Anthropogenic causes of freshwater pollution – Geomorphological alteration by water – Index.

Contributors
Chris Brady, Peter Calvert, Frank Gregory, Anne Guest, Darryl Howlett, Adrian Hyde-Price, C. Ian Jackson, George Joffé, Paikiasothy Saravanamuttu, Caroline Thomas, Peter Wilkin, Sandra Wilkins.

224pp   0 335 15775 0 (Hardback)

HUMAN RIGHTS

Scott Davidson

This book is an introduction to the international law of human rights. It provides the reader with a systemic and concise treatment of the major UN and regional instruments in the field, and discusses and analyses the institutions and mechanisms established to fulfil the objectives of human rights promotion and protection. The book also places human rights in context by describing their historical development and some of the theories which have been put forward in an attempt to determine their nature. Since human rights law is a specialist branch of public international law, a short chapter on the nature and creation of international law is included for those who do not have any previous knowledge in this area.

This book will be an invaluable resource for students in the fields of law, politics and international relations. It will also appeal to the general reader who wishes to acquire an understanding of one of the dominant issues of the post-1945 era.

Contents
Historical development of human rights – Theories of human rights – Human rights and international law – The United Nations and international law – The European system for protecting human rights – The inter-American system for protecting human rights – The African system for protecting human and people's rights – Concluding observations – Notes – Appendices – Index.

224pp   0 335 15768 8 (Paperback)   0 335 15769 6 (Hardback)

THE CONDITION OF STATES

Cornelia Navari (ed.)

How is the state doing? Is it growing stronger, is it becoming increasingly integrated, or is it withering away? Rejecting the view that states may be studied in isolation from one another, and proceeding from the assumption that political theory and international theory are part of a single continuum, this important collection of essays employs both comparative method and an international perspective to assess what is happening to the chief political form of our time.

In doing so, it questions recent major approaches to European and American scholarship which have tended to view the state as a formation serving capital, interests or classes. The approach of these essays is legal and constitutional, highlighting the changing nature of political communities and changing patterns of government. The authors argue that attention to the nature and scope of governmental powers and how they are impinged upon, by foreigners as well as citizens, is vital to any understanding of the modern state.

Contents
Preface – Introduction: The state as a contested concept in international relations – Reality and illusion in the acquisition of statehood – The variety of states – Foreign policy and the domestic factor – Diplomacy and the modern state – The state and integration – The state and war – On the withering away of the state – Hegel, civil society and the state – What ought to be done about the condition of states? – The duties of liberal states – States, food and the world common interest – Index.

Contributors
John Baker, Christopher Brewin, John Charvet, Michael Donelan, Mervyn Frost, Willie Henderson, Christopher Hill, Martin Kolinsky, James Mayall, Cornelia Navari, Brian Porter, Philip Windsor.

256pp   0 335 09667 0 (Paperback)   0 335 09668 9 (Hardback)